PRESSING FORWARD

*Alfred, Lord Tennyson
and the Victorian Age*

PRESSING FORWARD

Alfred, Lord Tennyson and the Victorian Age

Louis A. Markos

Sapientia Press
of Ave Maria University

Sapientia Press
of Ave Maria University
1025 Commons Circle
Naples, FL 34119
888-343-8607

Cover Design: Eloise Anagnost

Printed in the United States of America.

Library of Congress Control Number: 2006939257

ISBN-10: 1-932589-36-8

ISBN-13: 978-1-932589-36-8

DEDICATION

I HAVE BEEN fortunate at Houston Baptist University
to have served under four Deans (Calvin Huckabay, Harold
Raley, James Taylor, Brian Runnels) and two Chairs (Elysee Peavy,
Phyllis Thompson) who have been supportive of both me and my
work. I would like to acknowledge all six of these fine adminis-
trators and friends, and to dedicate this book in particular to
Phyllis B. Thompson.

TABLE OF CONTENTS

PREFACE

It is almost a commonplace for humanities professors to claim that the age they are teaching is very much like our own. This is not surprising since all professors hope to make what they teach relevant to the contemporary world that they and their students inhabit. Add to this the fact that human nature is more or less a constant and that the *really* big questions (Who am I? Why am I here? What is my purpose?) never change (though they may be temporarily eclipsed), and it becomes almost a fait accompli that they will find at least some parallels between the past age under study and that ever fluctuating, hard-to-define present age that we call our own.

Still, despite this ubiquitous practice, I feel no hesitation in asserting firmly that it is the Victorian Age, above all others, that is most like our own. The ancient Athenians, the Florentines of the Renaissance, and the eighteenth-century Parisians may all stake their claims, but it is finally a group of nineteenth-century middle-class Londoners who were the first to face directly the challenges, confusions, and upheavals of the modern world. It is *their* struggles that are most like our own, and it is therefore their solutions (partial and tentative though they may be) that most demand our attention. The Victorians were the heirs of 2,000 years of Judeo-Christian,

Greco-Roman culture, 200 years of skepticism and liberalism that rose up out of the Enlightenment and French Revolution, and a generation of swift developments in science, technology, and commerce that made all that came before seem stagnant and outdated. Their Romantic forbears could partly hold at bay the struggles and contradictions inherent in this triple heritage by looking both backward and inward, but such introspection and nostalgia could not last forever. Sooner or later Europe (and, through her, the world) would have to press forward to find a new integration that could usher us into the modern world without sacrificing all that makes us uniquely human. It will be the goal of this study to enter, alongside the Victorians, into these struggles, into their individual and collective crises of faith and into that vital spirit of progress that animated the age and helped to pull its inhabitants out of their crises into a fuller vision.

In seeking to fulfill that goal, this book will survey and analyze the life and writings of Alfred, Lord Tennyson in the context of the Victorian Age. Thus, though our focus will be on Tennyson's poetry (about two-thirds of the chapters), we shall compare and contrast that poetry with the prose works of six Victorian essayists (or sages) whose lives and writings both embodied the vast range of Victorian values and ideals and represented a powerful (and influential) critique of those very values and ideals. In the first part of the book ("Tennyson and the Victorian Crisis of Faith"), chapters 1 to 12, our focus will be on how Tennyson (along with three of the sages) was challenged (intellectually, emotionally, and spiritually) by the new developments in science (particularly evolution and the age of the earth), by the growing Enlightenment focus on rationalism, materialism, and skepticism, and by a new pragmatic, utilitarian ethos that was sweeping the country. In the second part ("Tennyson and the Victorian Spirit of Progress"), chapters 13 to 24, we shall shift our focus to how Tennyson (in company with the other three sages) reacted to the optimistic, positivistic Victorian faith that, through technology, social planning, the free-market economy, and universal education, England could build a utopia of peace and plenty.

Part I begins with an introduction to the Victorian Age in chapter 1 that considers closely four key characteristics of the Victorian Age by contrasting it to the Romantic Age that preceded it, and a survey of the new developments in science discussed in chapter 2 as they were popularized by Darwin's unofficial spokesman and "bulldog," T. H. Huxley. In chapters 3 to 6, we study the autobiographies of two Victorian sages—Cardinal Newman and John Stuart Mill—who suffered intense crises of faith but who dealt with those crises in very different ways. In chapter 4, we set the conservative, Catholic Newman against the liberal, skeptical Huxley, and see how they advocated very different views on authority and education. Then, in chapters 7 through 12, we turn our focus fully to Tennyson and consider his major work, *In Memoriam*, an epic poem that, more than any other work of the nineteenth century, embodied all of its age's struggles, griefs, and resolutions. We see here how Tennyson suffered his own crisis of faith (sparked by the sudden death of his closest friend and soon-to-be brother-in-law, Arthur Hallam) and how, through that crisis, he not only was able to mature from a Romantic to a Victorian but was able to fashion a new relationship to religion and science that both reflected and shaped the new ethos of his age.

Part II will begin by stepping back slightly and taking a deeper look at the early years of Tennyson in chapter 13. As in the chapters on *In Memoriam*, we again take up Tennyson's vital shift from Romantic to Victorian, but shall examine that shift from a new perspective. Thus, in chapters 14 and 15, we first analyze closely four poems that demonstrate the young Tennyson's obsession with melancholy poet-figures who are tempted to reject the world in favor of a self-absorbed, solipsistic isolation ("The Lady of Shalott," "Tithonus," "The Lotos-Eaters," and "The Palace of Art"); in chapters 16 and 17 we consider three slightly later poems in which Tennyson leaves behind his melancholy to embrace in full the Victorian spirit of progress (*In Memoriam* #106, "Ulysses," and "Locksley Hall"). Having established the full nature and dimensions of this spirit of progress, in chapters 18 and 19 we consider two more sages, Thomas Carlyle and John Ruskin, who in two of their greatest works (*Sartor Resartus* and "The Nature of the Gothic," respectively) leveled a strong critique against this spirit from both a spiritual (Carlyle) and an aesthetic (Ruskin) vantage point. In the three chapters that follow, we return to Tennyson to consider some of his later works that themselves offer a critique of Tennyson's own earlier faith in progress. Chapter 20 takes up his extended dramatic monologue, *Maud,* a work in which Tennyson delves deep into the mind of a disturbed, unbalanced young man who becomes isolated from his age; chapters 21 and 22 will then offer close readings of the first and eighth Idylls ("The Coming of Arthur," and "The Holy Grail") of Tennyson's epic-scale treatment of the legends of King Arthur and the Round Table, *Idylls of the King.* Finally, in the concluding two chapters, we consider, as a contrast to Tennyson, Matthew Arnold, a poet who, unable to make the shift from Romantic to Victorian, eventually abandoned poetry to become one of the great essayists and prose prophets of his age. These two chapters will be constructed around one poem and one essay that are representative of the two stages of Arnold's career ("Stanzas from the Grand Chartreuse" and "The Function of Criticism at the Present Time").

As I hope this brief overview makes clear, this is a book written for the non-specialist who wishes to engage directly with the major poetry and prose of the Victorian Age. Indeed, it is written in the very style and spirit of those great Victorian "men of letters" who conceived of their essays not as technical, specialized monographs meant only for an insular academy, but as literary pieces meant to provoke and entertain (that is to say, teach and please) the wider reading public. The book demands no previous

knowledge of literary theory or aesthetic history, only a willing-
ness to be challenged (and perhaps changed) by the creative works
of poets and essayists who lived and died before our grandfathers
were born. Those who have picked up this book in order to feel
smugly superior to a group of "repressed" Victorians who are woe-
fully unenlightened by modern, liberal standards will most likely
be disappointed. But those who come with minds and hearts
ready to learn, those who possess the sympathetic imagination to
enter into the struggles of people not so much unlike ourselves,
those who truly believe that poetry can be a vehicle for truth—to
such this book should prove a bracing and, I trust, fulfilling read.

    Each of the chapters is short and condensed enough to read and
digest in a single sitting. As such, they are ideal in length and cov-
erage for an hour-long class or discussion group. As a supplement
to the chapters themselves, I have included not only a timeline, a
glossary, and a "who's who" list, but an annotated bibliography to
help guide both the college student and the interested amateur
toward further reading. As I note in the bibliography, I have so
selected the poems and essays covered in this book that readers who
wish to accompany their study of the chapters with a study of the
original texts may do so by purchasing only two further books: the
Oxford edition of *Victorian Prose and Poetry* edited by Lionel
Trilling and Harold Bloom and the Norton Critical Edition of *Tennyson's Poetry* edited by Robert Hill. Finally, for film buffs who
would like to "see" as well as read about the Victorian Age, I have
put together an annotated list of some of the best British and
American attempts to capture Victorianism on film.

    With that, I turn you over to the Victorians themselves. May
their internal and external wrestlings provoke and inspire you to
join them as they grapple valiantly with faith, with science, and
with that indomitable human spirit that we all share as our
mutual heritage.

I

TENNYSON AND THE VICTORIAN CRISIS OF FAITH

I

INTRODUCTION
From Romantic to Victorian

THE VICTORIAN AGE in England was a period and a movement that knowingly and quite deliberately broke from the concerns and ideals of the Romantic Age. Just as one generation (or one individual within that generation) will often (for good or ill) rebel against the preceding generation, so did the great fashioners of the Victorian "project" forge a vision of man, nature, and society that consciously parted company with the vision of those very writers and thinkers on whom they had been raised. Call it (with Freud) the Oedipal overthrow of the father; call it (with Harold Bloom) an "anxiety of influence" caused in part by a "sense of belatedness," of having lived too late to be a member of the generation of the fathers.[1] In either case, there appears to be something within human nature that drives it to define itself in opposition to what came before. So it is with people; so it is with aesthetic movements. Indeed, there are at least four areas in which Victorianism not only broke from, but marked the polar opposite of, Romanticism.

---

[1] See Harold Bloom, *The Anxiety of Influence: A Theory of Poetry* (Oxford: Oxford University Press, 1973).

INDIVIDUAL TO SOCIETY

The first and most obvious area in which the Victorian Age stands in stark contrast to the Romantic is in its tendency to shift the central focus of society from the single, unique individual to the collective group. Of course, in one sense, this shift from the individual to the group, from the solitary to the social, is part of an ongoing pendulum swing that has rocked Europe since the Classical Age. Classical Greece (the birthplace of humanism) put an emphasis on the individual that the ancient world had not seen before, an emphasis that swung back to the group during that long millennium we refer to collectively as the Middle Ages. The Medieval Period gave way, in turn, to the Renaissance (Individual), the Enlightenment (Group), Romanticism (Individual), and Victorianism (Group). To continue this simplistic but helpful paradigm, we might say that the lost generation of the 1920s marked a return to the Individual, and that the post-World War II years (at least in America) reestablished the rule of the Group. With the Hippie culture of the 1960s and '70s, America (and Europe) returned once again to the Individual, leaving us to wonder if a resurgence of the group looms ahead. Regardless of how we interpret our own day, it is clear that the Victorians saw it as one of their prime callings to lead England away from the individualistic excesses of Romanticism toward a more communal ethos of social engagement.

Whereas Romantic writers such as Wordsworth, Shelley, and Keats could feel justified in withdrawing from society to pursue, in solitude, a poetry that was radically inward, Victorian writers felt a need (nay, a duty) to be involved in society, to address in their writings the issues and struggles of their day. No longer could poetry justify itself merely as a form of self-expression or as a journal of the emotional life of the poet; the Victorian artist needed to serve a more outward, public function. Thus, Alfred, Lord Tennyson, though he began his career writing Keatsian self-reflective studies of the isolated artist, slowly evolved into a spokesman for his age. Robert Browning, though his poetry does not embody the Victo-

rian ethos in the way that Tennyson's does, also rejected the Romantic religion of the self (his early model was Shelley) to fashion and
perfect a new genre of poetry (the dramatic monologue) in which
the poet's personality is effaced. Matthew Arnold, perhaps the most
interesting Victorian "case study," began life as a poet, but when he
discovered that he was unable (in his poetry) to escape from the
personal angst and intense self-consciousness of the Romantics (his
first love was Wordsworth), he turned to prose essays.

Indeed, whereas the dominant voice of the Romantic Age is
poetic, the Victorian Age is often most fully captured in the prose
writings of its great essayists: T. H. Huxley, Cardinal Newman,
John Stuart Mill, John Ruskin, Thomas Carlyle, and Matthew
Arnold (all of whom bore the title of "Victorian sage"). In their
essays on art, religion, politics, and science these men of letters
directly engaged the values, prejudices, and struggles of their society; though each composed in a personal and even idiosyncratic
style, what they had to say presupposed an active (and interactive)
public readership. I might add here that another dominant (and
very social) voice of the Victorian Age is that of its great novelists—
the Brontës, Thackeray, Eliot, Meredith, and, above all, Dickens—
however, for the sake of brevity and focus, I will confine myself in
this book solely to the poetry and non-fiction prose of the period.

COUNTRY TO CITY

The Victorian shift from individual to group was accompanied by a
second, more geographical, shift from the country to the city, from
a focus on things natural to a concern with all things urban. If the
capital of eighteenth-century Europe was Paris, then the capital of
the nineteenth was London. When Queen Victoria began her long
reign in 1837, the population of London was roughly 2 million;
when she died in 1901, it had risen to nearly 6 1/2 million. The
numerical growth is impressive, but more vital than the shift in
numbers was the shift in values. To the Romantic, the city was a
barren, unnatural place whose inhabitants were atomized, cut off

from their true inner selves; to the Victorian, it was a thriving center of life, energy, and growth. When William Blake in his poem, "London" reflects on the city, he sees only horror, slavery, and decay, and hears only the cries of wounded soldiers, exploited workers, and disease-scarred infants. All those who dwell in this hellish prison are inextricably bound by what Blake calls "mind-forged manacles," invisible chains that shackle spirit and mind alike. When Tennyson (in "Locksley Hall") turns his own Victorian gaze upon the city he discerns far different sights and sounds: namely, those of science and technology stretching out their arms to bring progress and prosperity, first to London, and later to the world.

By mid-century, the Romantic love for the rootedness and stability of the land had given way to a volatile, liquid, mercantile economy: the fastest growing and most profitable in the world. The Industrial Revolution both initiated this growth and was fed by it, and Victorian London soon swelled into a capitalist factory where each worker served as a cog in the machine. Of course, the great Victorian writers listed above did not accept this transformation as an absolute good. All of them attacked, in their own way, the exploitation of labor, the alienation of the laborer from his product (see Karl Marx, who published his *Communist Manifesto* in 1848 and who composed his *Das Capital* in London), and the smallness of mind generated by repetitive work and unchecked avarice. However, in their critiques, they are less like Thoreau, who abandoned the city for the country, and more like Woody Allen, who, though he never tires of exposing the shallowness and skewed values of New Yorkers, loves Manhattan and would never think of abandoning it to live in a log cabin. All the Victorians (whatever their criticisms) felt that they were part of a vast social movement and that they needed to contribute their own skills and labor to the realization of that movement. If the loss of man's link to nature was a problem for society, then the solution was not to abandon the city for the farm, but to build another park where urban children could play on the Sabbath.

EDEN TO UTOPIA

And this leads us to our third shift: the abandonment of the nostalgic, Romantic backward glance toward Eden in favor of a forward-looking, progressivist reaching for utopia. If the Romantic ideal is a pastoral one, a reestablishment of a garden-world that privileges the innocence and naive wonder of the child, the Victorian ideal is decidedly adult: It seeks to build a complex yet efficiently run state with the will and resources to eliminate poverty and ignorance.

That is to say, whereas the Romantic is an heir of Rousseau (with his celebration of the noble savage and his belief that only in nature is man free), the Victorians are heirs of the Enlightenment (with its privileging of the rational over the emotional/intuitive and its innate faith in the power of science, logic, and social planning to create a "brave new world"). By the middle of the nineteenth century, Wordsworth's interiorized, quietistic religion of the human heart gives way to a new, more aggressive faith in positivism: the belief that, through science, technology, and universal education, man can propel himself into utopia. For the Victorians, as for Adam and Eve at the end of *Paradise Lost*, the world lay all before them (not behind), and therefore the only possible movement could be forward. For Auguste Comte, the French founder of positivism, and his Victorian disciples, the traditional values of Europe, based as they were on religion, on revelation, on emotion, were outdated and antiprogressive (nothing but relics of medieval superstition). The social and natural sciences, not the humanities, were to be the beacons leading humanity onward to ever greater heights of knowledge and of power.

Perhaps the crowning symbol of Victorian positivism was London's Great Exhibition of 1851, a sort of World's Fair housed in the giant manmade Crystal Palace: a visual hymn to the scientific ingenuity of its builders and to their ability to blend artistic imagination with social utility. Indeed, at the core of positivism and its goals lay utilitarianism: a new, uniquely Victorian ethic that held that the final goal of all social planning is (1) to bring the greatest good to the greatest number, and (2) to produce happiness by increasing pleasure and decreasing pain. Again, the Victorian poets and sages often attacked the amoral nature of utilitarianism, with its seeming privileging of creature comforts over deeper spiritual growth, yet they all, in their work, felt compelled to defend their own ideas in terms of social utility!

The builders of this Victorian utopia called themselves liberals; however, their creed lies midway between what modern Americans view as liberal and conservative ideals and policies. Like the modern liberal Democrat, the Victorian had a firm faith in the perfectibility of man and believed in the necessity of social programs and free, universal education to effect this goal; like the modern conservative Republican, he believed that to accomplish this goal, the market must be left free of government regulation—free, that is, to be controlled by Adam Smith's invisible hand (laissez-faire). In the nineteenth century those who held the above opinions tended to congregate in the Whig party, while those who resisted these changes and clung to more traditional policies made up the Tories. The Whigs saw little of value in the old traditions and institutions (not to mention the old prejudices) of England; the old was valuable only inasmuch as it had prepared the way for the coming of the new. In fact, Thomas Babington Macaulay, the great Whig statesman and historian, interpreted all of history as but a prelude to the foreordained, unstoppable rise of the Whig party and its noble vision to pave the way for the coming utopia.[2]

ARISTOCRACY TO MIDDLE CLASS

But who was to build this "brave new world?" Surely not the leisure-loving, land-based, reactionary aristocrats who congregated in the Tory party and resisted any changes that might compromise their age-old rights and prerogatives. To build utopia a new slate of leaders would have to be found (our fourth shift), and this group

---

2 See Thomas Babington Macaulay, *The History of England* (London: Penguin Classics, 1979).

would be culled not from the barons and earls, but from the hard-working, volatile, upwardly mobile middle class. It is during the nineteenth century that the middle class comes into its own, not only seizing the political reins of power but eventually becoming the standard-setters of their day. Indeed, though many would posit 1837 (the beginning of Victoria's rule) as the birth year of the Victorian Age, most would place it five years earlier (1832) when the First Reform Bill was passed. This historic piece of legislation, by widening the suffrage to the middle class and eliminating British-style gerrymandering, effectively ended the aristocracy's monopolistic control. It was followed by the Second Reform Bill (1867), which extended the vote to the working class and was accompanied by the repeal of the Corn Laws (1846), a tariff-busting, free-trade-enhancing act that helped solidify the dominance of the mercantile class and the middle-class-favoring economy they fostered.

But the shift from the aristocracy to the bourgeoisie did not stop here; as middle-class economic ideals seized control so did that package of virtues and values that Alfred Doolittle (of *Pygmalion* and *My Fair Lady* fame) dubs "middle-class morality." The Protestant work ethic, the stable, nuclear family with father as breadwinner and mother as domestic goddess, the non-aristocratic noblesse oblige that manifests itself in charitable work, the well-behaved children who must learn honesty, frugality, and chastity: all that we in America identify (rightly or no) with the 1950s found its fullest expression in Victorian London. In fact, so central were these new values to the Victorian ethos that the queen herself, along with her beloved consort, Albert, and their numerous progeny, conducted themselves not as the royals of old but as a respectable, somewhat stuffy bourgeois family: replete with numerous paintings of their family at play and the resuscitation (after an extended Puritan winter) of Christmas celebrations round the proverbial family hearth and tree.

And with these middle-class values came the British equivalent of what in America was known as "manifest destiny": the belief that it was the clear will of God that we (British or American) export our ideals, values, and institutions (in particular, democratic capitalism) to the farthest corners of the globe. And the Victorians did just that with a fervor and an earnestness that is dizzying. They fulfilled their call (the "white man's burden"), and they did so in part through dedicated missionaries who brought to Asia and Africa not only the Gospel but Western medicine, communication, and transportation. It is easy to make fun of them (Oscar Wilde made fun of their earnestness, as George Bernard Shaw did of their middle-class morality), but they did change their world, mostly for the better!

2

T. H. Huxley and
the New Science

Perhaps no single issue rocked the hearts and minds of Victorian England more than evolution. At first glance, the theory that all life on this planet—including man—arose through a long, slow process of gradual change and adaptation may seem of concern only to traditional Christians who advocate a literal six-day creation. Nothing could be further from the truth. To a great many Victorians, evolution represented a challenge not only to the authority of Scripture, but to the very nature and status of God himself.

The Challenge of Evolution

By positing that the final origin of all things is physical rather than spiritual, evolution, if it did not eliminate God outright, rendered him unnecessary, a theological proposition to be taken or left. For even if God does exist, he is to be seen either as himself a product of evolution or as a removed, deistic God who is finally equivalent to, or at least bound by, the laws of nature. As a moral and ethical system initiated by a proto-Victorian sage (Jesus), Christianity would continue to exert much force in society; as a sacred history of creation, fall, and redemption guided by a history-invading, miracle-working Triune God, it would slowly lose its grip on both the upper and lower classes of London.

But the direct influence of evolution, and the materialist/naturalist worldview that accompanied it, impacted far more than the reigning view of God. Just as vitally for the Victorian psyche, evolution stripped man of his special status as the crown of creation and left him adrift (existentially) with no set purpose or essence. Medieval and Renaissance writers alike viewed man as a microcosm: as summing up in himself all the various virtues that God spread so liberally throughout the natural and animal kingdoms. Evolution, driven as it was by unconscious forces ignorant of any final goal, aim, or design, divested man of his preordained role as the culmination and telos (purposeful end) of the creative process. Man could no longer take for granted that he was "very good" (Genesis 1:31); he simply was.

Of course, by challenging the authority of man, the newly minted theory of evolution also challenged, by extension, the authority of all institutions built by man, especially religious ones. People's faith in Christ, Bible, and Church, if not destroyed, was disrupted: "If only the Geologists would let me alone," wrote Ruskin, "I could do very well, but those dreadful hammers! I hear the clink of them at the end of every cadence of the Bible verses!"[1] Nothing seemed certain or stable any more; the Rock of Ages was shaken. Worse yet, the process by which evolution worked carried its own disturbing message. Along with evolution came the necessary corollary that we live not on a "young earth" (created in 4004 B.C. according to Bishop Ussher) but on a world billions of years old. "Not for six thousand, nor for sixty thousand, nor for six thousand thousand, but for aeons embracing untold millions of years, this earth has been the theater of life and death" (John Tyndall).[2] From a young-earth point of view, a lifespan of seventy years would cover about 1 percent of the entire history of the planet (a significant number); faced with a history of billions of

---

[1] Quoted in *The Norton Anthology of English Literature*, 7th ed., vol. 2 (New York: W. W. Norton, 2000), 1051.

[2] Ibid.

years, our individual lives shrink into insignificance, even as our planet is reduced to an infinitesimal dot in the cosmos.

But we *still* have not reached the worst; the greatest horror of all is the process of natural selection (survival of the fittest) that propels evolution and allows it to "work." Not only does God have no regard for the individual, natural selection suggests; nature herself views all life as fodder. Such a vision could not help but impact the way people interact with each other in society. If natural selection is the process that birthed us, then should we not imitate that process in our business practices? If growth and progress are all that matter, is not the worker ultimately dispensable? Given such questions, which flow quite naturally out of Darwin's theories, it should come as no surprise that the process of natural selection was soon adapted by philosopher and sociologist Herbert Spencer (1820–1903) to the pragmatic, "dog-eat-dog" realities of the workplace. Spencer's adaptation came to be known as social Darwinism, a theory that suggested that unregulated, unchecked individual force and enterprise was the best method for propelling society forward (or, stripped of all euphemism: "Greed is good").

Working in the same vein as Spencer, utilitarian economists such as Thomas Malthus (1766–1834) and David Ricardo (1772–1823) fashioned mathematical laws and ratios to describe the growth and decline of the labor force, of wages, and of the population itself. Once the surplus population grew too large, starvation, famine, war, or some other "natural" calamity would, in due course, set in to right the balance of workers, jobs, and wages. To the modern reader (one hopes!) such theories sound harsh and antihuman, but to many Victorians they simply described inescapable laws that were bound in iron. Unemployment, disease, war, and starvation could all be calculated along the same lines as the fluctuating ratio of supply and demand. Indeed, it is just such utilitarian theories as these that Dickens critiques when he has Scrooge tell the two men who come to his office seeking charitable funds for the poor that if the poor are slated to die, they might as well do so quickly and thus decrease the surplus population.

But I, of course, am putting the worst face possible on the Victorian reaction to evolution; though many held to (and strongly felt) the reservations listed above, not all Victorians reacted negatively.

DARWIN'S BULLDOG

Although Charles Darwin (1809–92) is the man most responsible for formulating the theory of evolution through natural selection, it was T. H. Huxley (1825–95) who disseminated that theory to the public. Though himself a competent and respected scientist, Huxley, after reading Darwin's *Origin of Species* (1859), made it his main goal in life to propagate and popularize Darwin's theories. Darwin was a shy and reclusive man, not given to public speaking and defense of his theories; to remedy this, Huxley agreed to be his spokesman and public defender: in a word, his "bulldog." Throughout a long and successful career as speaker and essayist (that is, as Victorian sage), Huxley defended evolution not only as a scientific theory but as a sort of humanistic philosophy that pointed the way toward a right and proper view of man, of ethics, of government, and of education. In chapter 4, I return to Huxley and consider some key elements of this humanistic philosophy; in what remains of this chapter, I confine myself to his defense of evolution. And nowhere does he do so more forcefully and eloquently than in a lecture he gave in 1868 with the bold title "On the Physical Basis of Life."

From the very outset of his lecture, Huxley asserts, unapologetically and enthusiastically, that the final origin of all life on earth is a physical (rather than a spiritual) substance. Human life is not the end-product of a creation *ex nihilo* (out of nothing) descending from an eternal spirit; it is, rather, the product of an upward movement out of a primordial, material base. Huxley dubs that material base *protoplasm* (Greek for "first form"), and then takes his audience on a thrilling journey in search of it. Like a detective on the trail of an elusive suspect, "Sherlock" Huxley gathers all the clues one by one till he can trace a straight line back to this universal, material substance that lies at the core of all life. His ultimate goal is to reduce all living organisms to a physical base (and to physical processes) that can account for all the complexity that we see in both nature and ourselves.

Ironically, in pursuing this goal, Huxley drew the attention of England backward to the teachings of a set of ancient Greek philosophers (Thales, Anaximander, Anaximenes, Anaxagoras, Empedocles, and so on) who, in the decades before Socrates, sought to isolate a single physical "arche" (or first principle) out of which all matter rose (Thales thought it was water; Anaximenes thought it was air). These proto-evolutionists were soon overthrown by the non-materialistic Plato, but their legacy never quite died. Indeed, though Huxley rejects their notion that the four essential elements of the material universe are earth, air, fire, and water, he *does* assert in his speech that there *are*, in fact, four elements that form the building blocks of nature: carbon, hydrogen, oxygen, and nitrogen. Further, like the Pre-Socratics, Huxley not only substituted the traditional questions of why and who for the more "critical" questions of how and what, but depicted human life as a thing that did not exist apart from the physical, material world. By so doing, Huxley betrayed himself as being at one with the projects of two other great (non-English) Victorians, Marx and Freud. Just as Huxley sought to reduce all of life to a physical basis that could be explained by natural laws, so Marx and Freud sought to reduce economics and human psychology to the material processes of class conflict and the unconscious mind.

Nevertheless, though Huxley shares this reductive orientation with the founders of socialism and psychoanalysis, his rhetoric is, I would argue, finally more persuasive. Unlike his fellow Victorians, Huxley (who refused to be labeled as a materialist) humanizes his discourse and his method by cloaking it in a shroud of wonder and mystery that is wholly lacking in Marx and that attaches to Freud only because of the centrality of the dream to his theories. For example, Huxley casts his search for the "physical basis of life" in the guise of a quest for an almost mystical hidden bond that shimmers just beneath the surface. Even when he speaks of the mechanistic nature of the cell, he enlivens and softens what would otherwise come across as crass materialism by ascribing to the cell the same division of labor, the same assembly-line efficiency that had made London the industrialized leader of the world. Huxley finds on the microscopic level the same force and progress that had made England great. Early in his lecture, Huxley alludes to the "spectacle afforded by the wonderful energies prisoned within the compass of the microscopic hair of a plant," a spectacle he describes in language that one would expect to encounter in the journals of a Renaissance explorer.

CO-OPTING SPIRITUAL LANGUAGE

New avenues in science opened by the theories of evolution will not, it seems, so much close the doors of religion as they will open the door to a new and hidden world of discovery. Indeed, Huxley not only subtly presents the work of the evolutionist as a substitute for that of the theologian, he actually co-opts biblical images, metaphors, and themes. Thus, after musing on the "wonderful energies" locked up in every cell of every plant, he concludes (like a biblical prophet; nay, like Christ himself) that it is only "the dullness of our hearing" that prevents us from catching the murmurings of life that roar around us in a seemingly "silent" forest. It is the theologians, not the scientists, who have ears but do not hear, eyes but do not see.

Other biblical borrowings surface when Huxley compares protoplasm to the clay on a potter's wheel and when he asserts that he and his fellow scientists "live in the hope and in the faith" that further research will uncover all the physical processes by which complex life arose on earth. He even recounts a parable by Balzac and then extracts from it a "physiological truth."

However, perhaps his boldest co-opting of spiritual language comes in his discussion of what occurs when a man eats a leg of mutton: that is, the man breaks down the protoplasm of the dead animal and then recombines it in such a way as to add to (and rejuvenate) his own protoplasm.

By such digestive mechanisms, Huxley exclaims, will he "convert the dead protoplasm into living protoplasm and transubstantiate sheep into man." Boldly (and perhaps shamelessly) Huxley here takes the greatest miracle of the Bible (the Resurrection of Christ) and the central miracle of the Catholic Church (the transubstantiation of the bread and wine into the body and blood of Christ) and recasts them as wholly physical, material processes.

Huxley is, of course, having fun, but it is a very serious, very earnest kind of fun. As Victorian sage, Huxley is attempting not merely to sway the opinions of his audience but to change their very mindset (to effect what Thomas Kuhn calls a paradigm shift). And let us not be fooled: When we alter someone's paradigm—when we change the types of questions he asks, the terminology that he uses, and the kinds of answers he will accept—we alter as well his beliefs, his values, and his actions. It is enough for a Romantic to change himself; a true Victorian must change his world. And so Huxley draws us in with the power of his rhetoric, helps us feel "cozy and warm" in a blanket of comforting metaphors, let's us know that scientific inquiry will still speak to our hearts. Yet all the while he is altering our key assumptions about ourselves and our origins.

In the conclusion of his essay, he reveals the sting in the adder's tail: Though we may cling to our spiritual metaphors (as Huxley himself does) to illustrate and elucidate, the true progress of science demands that we must adopt "materialistic terminology" for all serious discourse. With great aplomb, he dismisses "spiritualistic terminology" as "utterly barren" and as leading only to "obscurity and confusion of ideas." From now on clear thinking will mean materialistic thinking; indeed, as Victorians dedicated to subjecting nature to our control, it is our *duty* to adopt such language. And "control" here is a vital word, for another way in which Huxley's vision is finally more appealing and humanistic than that of Marx or Freud is that Huxley totally rejects determinism. That is to say, though Huxley posits a material base for all life, he believes that we can, through our own volition not only ascertain the order of nature but shape that order as well. He thus achieves what might at first seem impossible: to convince us simultaneously that we are the products of material forces outside of our control and that we are free agents imbued with the power to shape our lives, our ideals, and our world.

As a British Victorian, Huxley is ever practical, ever committed to common sense. Despite the theoretical focus of his essay, he is also concerned with action, with change, with progress. The negative implications of evolution discussed above never frightened Huxley, never caused him to suffer a "dark night of the soul." Quite to the contrary, to his mind evolution helped clear out the cobwebs of medieval superstitions and the obscurantist practices of reactionary clerics. For Huxley, no theory that rested on supernatural assumptions could anymore be thought useful or even tenable; the only way to go was forward: and forward he pressed, like the true Victorian he was. "Onward naturalist soldier!"

3

CARDINAL NEWMAN
The Bumpy Road to Faith

WHEREAS HUXLEY IDENTIFIED fully with the growing skepticism of his day toward the relevance of Christian beliefs, doctrines, institutions, and terminology in a modern, scientific, rational world, John Henry Newman (1801–90; later Cardinal Newman) refused, at great personal cost, to embrace this new mindset. Newman consciously (both emotionally and intellectually) accepted Christianity at the age of fifteen, and, aside from some shaky college years when he fell in with a somewhat heterodox group known as the "Noetics," remained a firm believer in the creeds and doctrines of the Christian Church. That is to say, while many of his fellow Englishmen, particularly the intellectual "set," were slowly gravitating toward a non-credal Christianity, Newman remained firmly orthodox.

CREDAL VS. LIBERAL CHRISTIANITY

C. S. Lewis argues in his preface to *Mere Christianity* that in our modern day the word "Christian" has come to be an essentially meaningless word. In the past, "Christian" was an objective noun with a set, unambiguous meaning. It denoted a person who believed a certain creed, in the same way that the word "gentleman" once denoted a person of a certain pedigree in possession of a certain title or amount of property. Today, however, "Christian" (like "gentleman") has evolved into a hazy, finally subjective adjective used to describe a person who behaves in a way that the user of the word thinks (or feels) a true Christian or gentleman *should* behave. It is a fine thing, Lewis concedes, to encourage Christians to act like Christians and gentlemen to behave like gentlemen, but it is sad that we had to sacrifice a perfectly good word in order to do so. Indeed, to be frank, if by "Christian" we merely mean someone who does good deeds, lives a moral life, gives to charitable causes, and attends religious services, then most of the Hindus, Muslims, and Buddhists in the world are, in fact, Christians. To rectify this subjectivizing of the word "Christian," one is often forced to modify the word: to distinguish, say, between a believing, or credal, Christian on the one hand and a cultural, or noncredal, Christian on the other. Indeed, the proliferation of phrases such as "evangelical Christian" or "born-again Christian" or "Bible-believing Christian" pays testimony to the fact that the word "Christian" (rather like the image of the Cross worn round the neck) no longer suffices as a clear marker that the one who bears it (or wears it) shares the historic faith of Paul, Augustine, Aquinas, and Luther.

I stated above that the growing majority of intellectuals in Victorian London were, unlike Newman, non-credal Christians. By noncredal, I mean, simply, that their faith (as opposed to their behavior) was not grounded in the main tenets of the Nicene Creed—the Trinity, the Incarnation, the Atonement, the Resurrection, and so on. A non-credal Christian is one who is likely to downplay the person of Christ as God-Man in favor of his teachings and his example, to promote a social gospel of good works and public service over a gospel of salvation through grace, and to substitute natural explanations for the supernatural elements of the faith. Whereas the credal ("believing") Christian considers Christ's death on the Cross to be salvific (a supernatural act that ushered in our salvation and restored the relationship between God and man), the non-credal Christian considers it merely exemplary (by following Christ's supreme example of self-sacrifice and unselfish devotion to a higher cause, we achieve enlightenment and spiritual power). Whereas the credal Christian considers the Bible to be the uniquely inspired Word of God and to hold authority in the life of the believer, the non-credal Christian considers it to be a cultural product of a certain time and place that can teach us good things but that is in constant need of modification and modernization.

The adjective that Victorians generally used to designate such non-credal believers was "liberal." According to Newman himself, the following phrases (all taken from a "Note on Liberalism" that he appended to his *Apologia Pro Vita Sua*) are characteristics of the liberal Christian:

> No religious tenet is important, unless reason shows it to be . . .
> no theological doctrine is any thing more than an opinion which happens to be held by bodies of men.

For the liberal, the ultimate test of truth is not revelation (the Bible and the Creeds of the Church) but reason; or, to put it another way, doctrines are not God-revealed, eternal truths that the Church has preserved, but manmade theories put forth by theologians whose cultural baggage and moral tastes are not our own.

> It is immoral in a man to believe more than he can spontaneously receive as being congenial to his moral and mental nature.

The final test of spiritual truth is our own conscience and sense of ethics. As an example of this, Newman highlights the modern dislike for the doctrine of hell. In our own day, perhaps the best example of this liberal tendency to measure doctrine against our own contemporary likes and dislikes rather than against the Bible and Sacred Tradition is the growing acceptance of actively gay clergy and even of Church-ordained gay marriage.

> No revealed doctrines or precepts may reasonably stand in the way of scientific conclusions

This phrase, of course, brings us back to Huxley and the New Science. No longer is the Bible (and Church tradition) to be the touchstone of intellectual inquiry; henceforth, it is the Bible that must adapt itself to any and all new discoveries. Christianity is necessarily modified by the growth of civilization. Caught up in the general Victorian spirit of progress, liberals argued that the Church must move with the times, in both its doctrines and its institutional arrangement.

Indeed, this liberal ethos toward the Anglican Church of England grew so strong that (the Whig) Parliament felt confident enough to start interfering in the affairs of the Church. The effect of this government intervention (with its threat of an eventual disestablishment of the Church itself) sparked a response that changed the course of Newman's life.

THE OXFORD MOVEMENT

The response alluded to above was set in motion by a sermon preached by John Keble in 1833 and soon became known as the Oxford Movement. The goal of this movement, simply put, was to stem the tide of liberalism in the Anglican Church (and in English society in general) and promote a return to tradition. The most famous names associated with the movement are Newman, Keble, Hurrell Froude, and Edward Pusey, all of whom attended Oxford together and were, politically, Tories. Their objectives, expressed in a series of tracts (the leaders of the Oxford Movement were also knows as Tractarians), was to restore the doctrines of the Anglican Church to their original purity, to revive the traditional "high-church" aspects of the faith (such as liturgical rituals, the sacraments, and monasticism), and to counteract the rationalism and scientism of the liberals with mysticism and piety.

In seeking to get back to the roots of Anglicanism, the Tractarians inevitably emphasized elements that the Church of England shared with the Roman Catholic Church (from which it had separated during the reign of Henry VIII); nevertheless, they insisted that they were not Catholics "in disguise." Indeed, Newman, who soon became the leader of the movement, as well as its most eloquent spokesman, was vocal in his condemnation of several aspects of Catholicism (most notably, Mariolatry, transubstantiation, and papal authority) that he felt the Anglicans had correctly altered. In fact, Newman was shocked and dismayed when some of his disciples (who were legion) converted to the Church of Rome. At first, Newman, along with his fellow Tractarians, pressed for a middle way (or *via media*) between Anglicanism and Catholicism; however, deep in Newman's heart was a greater desire for unity between the two churches—a desire predicated in part on a growing belief that both could not be true.

Slowly, through intense study and prayer, he came to believe that the Catholic position was stronger and the Anglican weaker than he had originally thought (and been taught by his Church!). Newman, being a conscientious Victorian with a strong sense of the duty he owed his followers and disciples, chose, in 1843, to remove himself from active clerical duties. He felt he could no longer be an official member of the Anglican clergy when his own beliefs were so uncertain. Finally, in 1845, he converted formally to Catholicism, a decision that outraged his fellow countrymen. The years surrounding his conversion were difficult ones for Newman, and yet he never regretted his decision. Quite to the contrary, Newman saw himself not as a traitor to his Church or his country but as a weary prodigal who had finally come home. Despite the jeers that greeted him, the undaunted Newman resumed his writing and speaking.

Ironically, though Newman's decision separated him from the Victorian ethos of his home country, the decision itself, which showed that Newman had the courage to question accepted beliefs and to follow his convictions no matter where they led, was a very Victorian one! Of course, as is the nature of such ironies, it would take Victorian society many years (two decades, in fact) to realize this, but once they did, it would, for a second time, completely change Newman's life and vocation. The tide began to turn in 1863 when, in an article in *Macmillan's Magazine*, Charles Kingsley, a staunch anti-Catholic, accused both the Catholic Church and Newman of corruption, insincerity, and a misuse of the truth. Newman quickly answered the charge, igniting a war of words between the two men. Kingsley eventually published an apology, but it was far from sincere or conciliatory.[1] In response, Newman dashed off (in the space of a mere three months) a full-length autobiographical account of his long, difficult road from the Church of England to the Church of Rome. It was his chance to speak directly to the British public, to explain why he, after convincing his followers of the purity of the original Church of England, had abandoned that very Church. He, appropriately, gave his work a Latin title, *Apologia Pro Vita Sua* ("an apology, or defense, of his life"), and, to everyone's surprise, it became hugely popular with the British reading public. Even more surprisingly, it caused the British to embrace the wayward son that they had twenty years earlier repudiated. Kingsley had wanted to slur Newman as anti-British, a sort of traitor and spy in one, but the *Apologia*, to Kingsley's consternation, recast Newman into a true Victorian sage.

A BULWARK AGAINST SKEPTICISM

In his *Apologia*, Newman does far more than defend his decision to join Rome and trace the personal milestones leading up to that decision. In true Victorian fashion, he uses his private autobiography as a public forum for addressing the key issues of his day and offering his own personal solutions and resolutions. This aspect of the work comes out most strongly in the final chapter of the book, where Newman recounts the "position of my mind since 1845" (the year of his conversion to Catholicism). In startling contrast to his fellow Victorian sages, most of whom struggled with almost

---

[1] The war of words between Kingsley and Newman has been anthologized in the Norton Critical Edition of Newman's *Apologia Pro Vita Sua* (New York: W. W. Norton, 1968), 297–369.

endless anxiety and doubt, Newman claims at the outset of this chapter that, ever since his decision, he has known "perfect peace and contentment." Still, though personally assured of the rightness of his decision, Newman, again in true Victorian style, agrees "to accept the responsibility" for defending his new mother Church. Indeed, lest we forget this vital (and very Victorian) connection between Newman himself and the system of which he is a part, Newman, after mounting his powerful defense of Catholic doctrine and polity, reminds us that in defending Rome, he is still defending himself. As I noted at the end of chapter 2, whereas it is enough for the Romantic to change himself, the Victorian must change as well the world (and institutions) around him. It is simply impossible for Newman to defend himself without also defending the Church of Rome.

And defend it he does, by presenting the Catholic Church as an institution that, far from being rendered obsolete by advances in science, is even more vital in an age of intellectual ferment and change. Our world, Newman asserts, is "out of joint," a fallen, anarchic world in which the "all-corroding, all-dissolving skepticism of the intellect" threatens to silence God's voice in the world. To combat this skepticism, God has given (as a gift) the Catholic Church, a concrete, in-the-world institution with the force, authority, and tradition to stem the liberal tide. The Church is God's "provision for retaining in the world a knowledge of Himself, so definite and distinct as to be proof against the energy of human skepticism." It is the great bulwark against every false teaching, every pride-based heresy, every intellectual rebellion, whether it rear its head in fourth-century Nicea or nineteenth-century London.

Now, the Protestant will most likely disagree with Newman on this point, claiming instead that God's *true* provision for retaining the Christian faith in its original purity is not the Church but the Bible. Newman counters that though the Bible is indeed the Word of God and carries full authority, it is still only a book and, by itself alone, lacks the power to restrain the rebellious, skeptical mind:

Experience proves surely that the Bible does not answer a purpose for which it was never intended. It may be accidentally the
means of the conversion of individuals; but a book, after all,
cannot make a stand against the wild living intellect of man.

Newman proved prophetic here as to the inability of the Bible
alone to resist the encroachments of liberalism. By the end of the
century, a German school of biblical scholarship—founded in the
late eighteenth century and known collectively as "higher criticism"—successfully used "scientific" methods of textual analysis to
chip away at the traditional authority of the Bible. Applying a distinctly evolutionary schema to biblical texts and to Christian theology in general, they cast into doubt the Mosaic authorship of the
Pentateuch and the Pauline authorship of roughly half of the epis-
tles that bear his name.

Though, as a Victorian and an Englishman, Newman supported
freedom of thought and speech, he also knew that such freedom
needed a watchdog to "rescue it from its own suicidal excesses."
The Roman Catholic Church is God's chosen instrument for that
purpose, his lion-tamer to subdue the rebellious sons of Adam.
More than that, it has become (in the modern world) the last bas-
tion of defense against "the immense energy of the aggressive,
capricious, untrustworthy intellect." This is its true calling and
purpose in the world, but to fulfill it, it must be empowered with
that very papal authority that is perhaps at the root of most anti-
Catholic sentiment.

Yes, as shocking as it may sound, the free-minded, argumenta-
tive Newman accepted fully that most controversial, seemingly
"anti-modern" of Catholic doctrines: papal infallibility. Or perhaps not so shocking. Newman viewed the Church not as an
institution that crushed and held man back, but as one that, in
actuality, allowed him to develop and progress. As a Catholic,
Newman was not a Calvinist. Though he believed firmly that
man was fallen ("original sin"), he did not believe that man was
totally depraved: Man's nature could be purified, restored, and

channeled for good. That is to say, Newman, who for all his Tory conservatism was (dare I say it again) a full-blooded Victorian, shared his era's optimism: its faith in progress and its desire for utopia. In contrast to the medieval view of our earth as a "vale of tears," the Victorian Newman saw it (or at least that portion of it that lay under the auspices of the Catholic Church) as a "moral factory for the melting, refining, and moulding . . . of the raw material of human nature."

The Church (not in spite of, but *because of* its authority) is there to aid and guide us in the long struggle upward.

4

NEWMAN VS. HUXLEY
On Authority and Education

As ONE MIGHT GUESS from the previous two chapters, Newman and Huxley disagreed on every key issue of their day. Indeed, one can hardly conceive of two men whose worldviews were more at odds with one another. Viewed from the naturalistic, non-credal mindset of Huxley, Newman's faith was founded on outdated superstitions, unproven assumptions, and antiprogressive prejudices; viewed from the supernatural, credal mindset of Newman, Huxley's faith was a flimsy thing built on shifting sand: volatile, unstable, and finally self-destructive. Neither could accept either the presuppositions or the conclusions of the other. Theirs was a complex and all-encompassing disagreement, and at its core lay two opposing conceptions of the role and nature of authority.

THE ORIGINS OF TRUTH

For Newman, final authority rested in the Catholic Church, not merely because of its age and traditions, but because it both contained and propagated on earth the revelation of God. Nevertheless, Newman did not discount the power and necessity of private judgment. The Protestants are wrong, argues Newman in the last chapter of his *Apologia*, when they claim that the Catholics have all the authority (or infallibility) and the Protestants all the private judgment (or reason). Truth, writes Newman, comes out of a struggle, a synergy between the two: Infallibility without reason leads to stagnation and tyranny; judgment without authority leads to rebellion and error. We must have both, but only a divinely ordained institution such as the Catholic Church can provide an "arena for both combatants in that awful, never-dying duel."

The history of the Church is the history of this duel, a duel that has made her more supple and elastic, not more authoritarian and absolutist. Indeed, because of this history, she is most fit to referee the modern struggle between the claims of religion and the claims of science, and, by so doing, effect a reconciliation between the two. The Church, however, accomplishes this goal not by declaring that "anything goes," but by laying down a strict set of guidelines, or first principles, which neither combatant may question. These first principles constitute those elements of the Christian faith that have come down through direct revelation by God: elements that form the core of the apostolic creeds.

In that same note on liberalism quoted in chapter 3, Newman identifies the chief error of liberalism as

> the mistake of subjecting to human judgment those revealed
> doctrines which are in their nature beyond and independent of
> it, and of claiming to determine on intrinsic grounds the truth
> and value of propositions which rest for their reception simply
> on the external authority of the Divine Word.

First principles, by their very nature, cannot be questioned or "reasoned away." They are the groundless grounds, the a priori assumptions, the major premises on which all human logic rests. (So it is that Richard John Neuhaus, a modern convert to Catholicism who shares a public and private vision similar to that of Newman, calls the journal that he edits *First Things*.) We argue not *for* but *from* first principles. In their absence, logical (deductive) thought cannot even begin. Apart from them, we are left adrift in a world without verities, without signposts, without boundaries. If we are ignorant of (or simply reject) these first principles, then we will be ignorant as well of the ultimate origin not only of Truth and Authority, but of theology, philosophy, ethics, and aesthetics as well.

It is not too much to say that Huxley's greatest mission as speaker and essayist lay in contradicting and defeating all that is implied in the preceding paragraph. For Huxley, true knowledge cannot even begin until Newman's first principles are dethroned and replaced by a new standard of scientific verification via direct observation and experimentation. If Newman's ethic stems finally from a medieval scholastic view that enthroned authority and revelation as the final touchstone of truth, Huxley's is a direct outgrowth of what scholars have come to call the Enlightenment Project: that is, the desire to refound all truth claims on a rational, scientific basis. Beginning with Kant's (late-eighteenth-century) attempt to ground ethics and morality on principles derived from logical reasoning rather than from divine law codes received via revelation, and culminating in the logical positivism of the twentieth century (with its insistence that all statements be empirically verified), the modern world has increasingly pushed metaphysical thought to the periphery of serious inquiry.

Despite the fact that a significant percentage of Europeans (and perhaps a majority of Americans) still subscribe to Newman's first principles, the media, the scientific establishment, and nearly all of academia have allied themselves with Huxley in the battle for truth. Darwin's bulldog proved to be far more than a popularizer of Darwinian theory; he was one of a group of Victorian thinkers and educators who helped to alter radically the methods of inquiry. For Huxley and his heirs, first principles are no longer the givens that guide us toward asking the right questions; they are the very things we *must* question. They are the decayed relics of old unscientific notions that must be swept away so the real work of science can begin. Though he respected the Bible as a great work of literature, and even heralded it, in a late essay, as a democratizing force and as "the *Magna Charta* of the poor and of the oppressed," Huxley rejected completely (on the grounds, he claimed, of scientific analysis) its supernatural elements and its miracles.[1] Indeed, in an essay called "Agnosticism and Christianity" Huxley, after quoting a sentence from one of Newman's writings, comments that, whereas for Newman the "attainment of faith . . . is the highest aim of the mental life," for Huxley it is the "ascertainment of truth" that is the true goal. He then quotes Tertullian's definition of faith as "the power of saying you believe things which are incredible" and comments that as far as he is concerned "faith, in this sense, is an abomination."[2]

Hardly can there be two more categorically opposed views than those of Newman and of Huxley, yet both (as Victorians) rested much of the passion of their convictions on their sincere belief that their opposing systems were best suited for furthering the well-being of the human race. For Newman, as we have seen, this system begins with first principles; for Huxley it begins with what he variously termed agnosticism or skepticism. Though he tended to downplay the word "agnosticism" (and his role as the unofficial leader of the school of thought associated with it), Huxley was responsible for making it a household word, as were his two famous grandsons, Julian Huxley (a biologist and popularizer of science) and Aldous Huxley (a prolific essayist and novelist, best known as the author of *Brave New World*). Etymologically speaking, an agnostic is one who "doesn't know." Though he does not, like the theist, acknowledge the existence of God as a given and absolute reality, the agnostic does not, like the atheist, claim to know that God does not exist. Rather he rejects both theism and atheism as insupportable suppositions that cannot be backed up by scientific observation or verification. The agnostic, that is to say, leaves all first principles alone (whether they be supernatural or natural, metaphysical or materialistic) and trusts to his reason and senses alone.

---

[1] "Prologue to 'Controverted Questions,'" Selection from the *Essays of Huxley* (Croft Classics, 1948), 104.

[2] "Anosticism and Christianity," in ibid., 94.

Related to the agnostic is the skeptic, a word that Huxley, at the conclusion of "On the Physical Basis of Life," vigorously defends from those who would dismiss it as a synonym for cynicism. The true skeptic, argues Huxley, is one who, like David Hume, does not waste time on matters of thought that cannot be backed up by facts and numbers. The skeptic ignores completely questions about the political practices of the inhabitants of the moon, not because he does not care or is cynical, but because the subject of "lunar politics" is one about which nothing scientific (rational, empirical) can be known. Such is the case, argues Huxley here and throughout his career, with all questions of the supernatural, including the existence of God; we can never know for sure, so why bother, why waste time. And with this exhortation not to waste time, the Victorian side of Huxley surfaces. We have so much to do on this planet of ours, he exhorts, so much misery and ignorance to combat; it is "the plain duty of each and all of us to try to make the little corner he can influence somewhat less miserable and somewhat less ignorant than it was before he entered it."

For Newman, of course, this goal can be accomplished only through the guidance of the Church; for Huxley, the Church (with its groundless first principles and its finally useless doctrines) is itself one of the main obstacles!

RAISING THE NEXT GENERATION

Given their competing views of the nature of authority and of truth, it is no wonder that Huxley and Newman were just as strongly opposed as to the kind of educational system their age most needed. For Huxley, England needed to educate its citizens in the rigors and methods of science, a form of pedagogy that necessitated both a negative and a positive phase. The negative phase is best expressed in a sentence from his 1866 essay, "On the Advisableness of Improving Natural Knowledge": "every great advance in natural knowledge has involved the absolute rejection of authority." The modern pupil must learn to question, to subject all forms of thought to logical analysis, no matter how hallowed that source may be.

Huxley's education, however, is not all debunking; the negative phase must in turn give way to the positive. Once the ground has been cleared, the pupil is ready to learn the real "rules of the game," rules far different from Newman's first principles. For these rules are none other than the laws of nature, precepts that only a scientific education based on observation can uncover and discern. Though not hostile to the classics, Huxley felt that an education that placed all its focus on the Greco-Roman writers robbed its pupils of far truer and more reliable sources of wisdom and truth. In *Science and Culture* (1880), Huxley "bids the learner seek for truth not among words but among things." The answers lie not in old dusty books but in the physical matter that surrounds us, not in the supernatural Word of God (as for Newman) but in the natural things, the "stuff" of our world. Although Huxley was himself a very cultured and well-read man, his theories of education are closer to the modern conception of the vocational school than they are to the traditional liberal-arts university: This is not surprising, since Huxley shared his age's pragmatic, positivistic, utilitarian views.

Newman, on the other hand, favored a liberal-arts paradigm that centered on the humanities and the study of the classics: *both* the pagan classics of Greece and Rome and the *Christian* classics of Europe. Like Huxley, Newman was a humanist, but he was a Christian (rather than a secular) humanist. Though he believed that man is a free and rational creature who possesses innate dignity and value and whose life and achievements on this earth are of intrinsic and lasting worth, he believed these achievements could be fully measured/appreciated only against the touchstones of Christ, Church, and Scripture. Or to put it another way, though complete truth is found only in Christ, fragments of truth are to be found scattered throughout all cultures at all times (all truth is God's truth). "All that is good," writes Newman in a paraphrase of Philippians 4:8, "all that is true, all that is beautiful, all that is beneficent, be it great or small, be it perfect or fragmentary, natural as well as supernatural, moral as well as material, comes from [God]."[3]

The ideal university would fuse together the streams of knowledge that issued from Athens and Jerusalem, streams that, Newman believed, met and combined in the Catholic Church of Rome. Indeed, so committed was he to this vision that in Dublin in 1852, he delivered a series of nine discourses that were intended to break ground for just such a Catholic university in Ireland. The project failed, but the discourses were later published as *The Idea of a University*. These discourses, I firmly believe, should be required reading for any administrator or educator who works at a liberal arts university. In the discourses (especially the seventh, from which I will be quoting below), Newman distinguishes clearly between the kind of narrow, vocational education advocated by thinkers like Huxley and the more wide-ranging, well-rounded education offered at a liberal arts university. At the former, students are equipped only to perform a certain trade; at the latter, they are taught to think critically about a number of different topics, not just those in their "major."

Indeed, I believe it is Newman who has given to the English-speaking world what is surely the best and most noble definition of the true purpose of a liberal arts university:

A University training is the great ordinary means to a great but ordinary end. . . . It is the education which gives a man a clear conscious view of his own opinions and judgments, a truth in developing them, an eloquence in expressing them and a force in urging them. It teaches him to see things as they are, to go right to the point, to disentangle a skein of thought, to detect what is sophistical, and to discard what is irrelevant. It prepares him to fill any post with credit, and to master any subject with facility.

---

[3] From Discourse III.7 of *The Idea of a University* (New York: Confucian Press, 1981), 59.

It shows him how to accommodate himself to others, how to throw himself into their state of mind, how to bring before them his own, how to influence them, how to come to an understanding with them, how to bear with them. He is at home in any society, he has common ground with every class; he knows when to speak and when to be silent; he is able to converse, he is able to listen; he can ask a question pertinently, and gain a lesson seasonably, when he has nothing to impart himself.

The point of a liberal arts education is to prepare its charges not just to *do* something, but to *be* someone: someone who is unafraid to think, to explore, and to grow. Yes, the education offered at such a university will be grounded in first principles, but that does not mean that it will encourage simple conformity and obedience in its students. Secure in the foundation of these principles, students will be able truly to question and interpret the key issues of the day and to mingle and interact with people from all classes and walks of life. Trained in rigorous thinking and equipped with the kind of critical skills and methods needed to analyze and synthesize new knowledge and experience, they will be empowered to think for themselves and to survive (and thrive) in any situation. The word "liberal" comes from the Latin *liber* (free), and it is freedom, Newman knew, that is the final goal of *both* credal Christianity and the liberal-arts university.

Were Newman as truly medieval at heart as he was in his religious and educational vision, I could end the chapter here, but Newman (need I repeat it) was a Victorian, not a medieval. As such, it was not enough for him merely to lay out his vision for a Catholic university in Ireland; he had, as well, to defend his pedagogical vision along practical lines. And so, as if answering the unstated critique of Huxley and his disciples, Newman assures his audience (in Discourse VII) that a liberal arts, Christian-humanist university will neither hold back the scientific and material progress of society nor produce non-technical, unskilled thinkers unable to survive in and contribute to a modern society. Rather it will provide society with a refined yet pragmatic core of well-rounded gentlemen who can adapt to any situation, converse on any subject, and see from a number of different perspectives. "The man," asserts Newman,

> who has learned to think and to reason . . . who has refined his taste, and formed his judgment . . . will not indeed at once be a lawyer, or a pleader, or an orator, . . . but he will be placed in that state of intellect in which he can take up any one of the sciences . . . with an ease, a grace, a versatility, and a success, to which another is a stranger.

More than that, he will learn to be good, and, Newman proclaims boldly, the good is both useful and prolific: "not useful in any low, mechanical, mercantile sense, but as diffusing good . . . first to the owner, then through him to the world." In a clever move that is characteristic of his genius, Newman here accepts the utilitarian criterion of usefulness and then redefines (or, better, enlarges) it to encompass not the simple, vulgar creature-comfort sense the word had come to carry in his day but a higher, more spiritual sense that raises it almost to the status of divine love.

5

JOHN STUART MILL
The Autobiography of a Steam Engine

MORE PERHAPS THAN ANY man who ever lived, John Stuart Mill (1806–73) was, literally, a product of his age. Not only did he embody in his writings and his political career all the goals, ideals, and struggles of Victorianism; those very goals, ideals, and struggles formed both the mold out of which the young Mill was fashioned and the crucible in which he was tried. Indeed, as to the truth of the latter half of the previous sentence, we need not trust to idle speculation: We have it all in Mill's own words. In his late forties, Mill, famous for his precisely analyzed works, turned the analytical razor back against himself and subjected his own formative years to an almost scientific scrutiny. The result was a remarkable record of a remarkable education that, for all its success, should probably never be tried again.

HOMESCHOOLING WITH A VENGEANCE

As Mill recounts in his *Autobiography* (begun, and mostly completed, in 1853–54 but not published until after his death in 1873), his education was an experiment in rigid utilitarian thought, an experiment carried out by his father, James Mill (1773–1836), a respected philosopher and author in his own right. Like Huxley, James was a complete agnostic/skeptic in the matter of religion who believed that all ideas and systems must be built on (and justified by) rational, empirical principles. There was to be no hazy, emotional thinking in his household; if ideas were to be held and supported, they would have to be founded not on faith but on reason, not on first principles but on logic, observation, and experimentation.

According to his son, James Mill was, at once, a Stoic, an Epicurean, and a Cynic. In his personality he was a Stoic; though basically just and kind, he avoided in his actions and interactions with people (including his family), any display of feeling, sentiment, or tenderness.

Morally speaking, he was an Epicurean, believing, along with the utilitarians, that the final test of right and wrong is whether the action performed will increase pleasure and decrease pain. However, though he believed in the abstract that happiness and pleasure were the final goals of life, he (like the Cynics of Greece and Rome) distrusted pleasure and thought it not worth the price. This somewhat conflicted philosophy left James Mill to live a paradoxical (though not wholly uncommon) life: the life, that is, of a man who seeks continually and with great resolve to procure happiness for himself, his family, and his society, while never seeming to experience any of that happiness in himself or with others.

Chief among James's influences was the spokesman of utilitarianism, Jeremy Bentham (1748–1832). According to John Stuart Mill's account, Bentham's final goal, which he pursued with great energy, was to take all elements of British society (from its institutions to its policies to its laws), break them down into their constituent parts, and then reformulate them along strict lines of utility. Sloppy thinking was forbidden: Nothing was to be justified by appeals to the moral sense, the laws of nature, or right reason, since such appeals are merely cover-ups for dogmatism and sentiment. The only true standard was to be utility, the only true motivation the fear of punishment and the desire for reward (whether the source of that punishment/reward be the law, God, or the public). Armed with these basic doctrines, Bentham and James Mill felt they had the method and the means to reform their society and usher in a utopic state. Little John would be their first pupil.

One of the reasons John Stuart Mill wrote his *Autobiography* was to prove "how much more than is commonly supposed may be taught, and well taught, in those early years which, in the common modes of what is called instruction, are little better than wasted." Mill here does not exaggerate. Through a strict, systematic regimen of learning, conducted solely by his father, John Stuart Mill gained, by the age of fourteen, an education superior to that of most four-year-college graduates. At age three, he began to study Greek under his father's tutelage; by eight, he had read Herodotus and six of Plato's dialogues; between eight and twelve, he read (in their original Greek and Latin) Homer, Sophocles, Thucydides and Aristotle, Virgil, Horace, Livy and Ovid; at twelve, he studied logic and political economy. However, just as vital as his voluminous reading was the strict honing of his mental powers. His father demanded precision from the boy: All ideas were to be tested, their assumptions rooted out. Intellectually speaking, Mill's education was a great success. While still in his teens, Mill was both editing his father's and Bentham's works and writing his own articles for respected journals. In his late thirties, he wrote treatises on logic and political economy that are still read today. There was, of course, one subject that was left out of the curriculum altogether; Mill's education totally ignored religion (he was, he wrote, one of the few people of his age who "has, not thrown off religious belief, but never had it"). For most people, this omission would have been disastrous; for Mill, it ultimately did not matter, for he soon adopted his own substitute religion: the realization of Bentham's utilitarian dream. With a passion as great as (if not greater than) that of James Mill and Jeremy Bentham, Mill set out to reform the world.

Still, there was one element in his education that was lacking: warmth. Though not cruel or harsh in the conventional sense (part of Mill's education consisted in long walks during which John would recite to his father the stories he had read in his history lessons), the stoic James was a cold and unsentimental taskmaster who spent no time cultivating his son's imagination or feelings. Indeed, because of the emotionless, assembly-line nature of Mill's education, Thomas Carlyle dubbed Mill's *Autobiography* "the autobiography of a steam engine." As might be expected, Mill's education led him to suffer a nervous breakdown at the age of twenty-one (see next chapter). Nevertheless, after Mill recovered, he went on to become one of the truly great thinkers of the nineteenth century: one who helped develop a kinder, gentler form of utilitarianism.

MILL'S PLATFORM

John Stuart Mill possessed a powerfully synthetic mind that allowed him to draw together all that was best in the utilitarian, progressivist, utopian ideals of the Victorian Age. We have seen already how he absorbed Bentham's ideals like mother's milk; he did the same with the population and wage studies of Malthus and Ricardo. Without ever falling into the Marxist abyss of determinism, Mill studied scientifically the social and economic factors that cause poverty and set out to find practical ways to combat these factors. He was a planner, yet, unlike so many planners of his age, he had the highest possible respect and regard for human freedom and self-determination (not to mention private property).

That is to say, Mill was strongly influenced by, but never became a full advocate of, one of the more colorful movements of the Victorian Age: utopian socialism. Spurred on by the writings of Robert Owen, Charles Fourier, and the Saint-Simonians, the utopian socialists of the nineteenth century sought to establish planned societies where labor would be divided evenly and equality would be the rule. Many even put their ideals into practice and set up large-scale communes both in England and in the New World. Of the latter, the most famous and best known is surely Brook Farm. Established in 1841 in West Roxbury, Massachusetts, Brook Farm featured amongst its sometime members such famous personages as Margaret Fuller, Charles Dana, and Nathaniel

Hawthorne; in fact, Hawthorne's novel *The Blithedale Romance* includes a strong critique of Brook Farm and its inhabitants. Mill hailed the goals of the utopian socialists, but was put off by their subjugating of personal liberties to the will of the group. Like Alexis de Tocqueville, one of his great influences, Mill knew the danger of the tyranny of the majority and fought always to keep the rights of the individual at the center of his platform.

Being the true Victorian sage that he was, Mill was capable of a double vision when it came to utilitarianism. He saw always the true ideals and goals that lay behind the various versions of utilitarian thought, but saw equally well the dangers inherent in those same ideals and goals. Nowhere, perhaps, was this more evident than in Mill's critique of the positivist philosophies of Auguste Comte. Comte (along with the Saint-Simonians) held a philosophical view of history that traced in the movements of historical periods a natural progression from the theological stage (which stretched from the classical pagan era to the medieval Catholic period) to the metaphysical stage (Protestant Reformation to French Revolution) to the positive stage. In this final, positive stage (as yet to come), society would throw off the shackles of religious authority and opinion and move forward through the cultivation of science and technology.

At first, Mill shared in Comte's views; however, as Comte got more authoritarian and deterministic in his theories and began to call for a new religion of humanity, Mill pulled away from him. What Mill sought was full freedom and enlightenment, not the return of a new hierarchy run by sociologists and philosophers invested with a new kind of spiritual authority.

Mill considered Comte's latter work "a monumental warning to thinkers on society and politics, of what happens when once men lose sight, in their speculations, of the value of Liberty and Individuality."[1] Given the destructive power of twentieth-century totalitarianism, Mill proved quite prophetic!

---

[1] From chapter VI of *Mill's Autobiography*, Riverside Edition (Boston: Houghton Mifflin, 1969), 127–28.

He did, however, salvage from Comte one vital aspect of his historicism: namely, that history fluctuates between organic periods (when men accept both the political power and the moral ideals of their rulers) and critical periods (when men reject their old convictions but have nothing to put in their place). In an essay written when he was only twenty-five, "The Spirit of the Age," Mill adapted and extended Comte's views to contrast his own Age of Transition from the Natural Age that preceded it:

> Society may be said to be in its *natural state*, when worldly power, and moral influence, are habitually and undisputedly exercised by the fittest persons whom the existing state or society affords.

This was the case in medieval Europe, when the Catholic clergy were the most educated and enlightened men of their day; they inspired respect and faith in those they ruled and thus maintained peace. Oddly, Mill's view of medieval Catholicism and the beneficent effects of its moral authority are identical to Newman's, but with a vital difference. Whereas Newman sought to restore traditional authority in the modern world, Mill believed that the time was no longer ripe for such rule.

> Society may be said to be in its transitional state when it contains other persons more fit for worldly power and moral influence than those who have hitherto enjoyed them.

On this point Mill the Whig is clear: In his age, the Tory aristocracy (along with the clergy) has lost its moral authority and has ceased to possess the virtues most needed. Though they once possessed the will and the high ideals to rule, they have grown fat and lazy and have surrendered their political *and* moral prerogatives.

Who then is fit to rule? It is, as we saw in chapter 1, the middle class with its new ethic of hard work, common-sense rationalism, and utilitarian values. Mill was no anarchist; he believed firmly that authority is necessary in any age or period. Nevertheless, if society is to progress and to achieve happiness (which was

Mill's final goal, as it was that of his father), that authority must be invested in those best suited to rule. The Age of Aristocracy was over; the Age of Meritocracy had begun.

THE FEMININE TOUCH

Still, despite his meditations on the need for lawful and efficient authority, Mill's central legacy has been, and must ever be, that of a man who fought for liberty with a tireless passion. In keeping with this lifelong commitment, Mill wrote early articles in support of Canadian home rule and, while a member of Parliament (MP), spoke out as well for Irish home rule. Also during his tenure as an MP, Mill (who abhorred all forms of slavery) championed the North in the American Civil War at a time when most of the aristocrats in Parliament favored the agrarian South. He fought against the ill-treatment of blacks in Jamaica and the working class at home. He conducted himself in politics with complete honesty and candor (he refused only to discuss his religious opinions) and even fought for what we today would call campaign finance reform! He wrote influential essays on the freedom of speech and assembly, fought censorship in all its forms, and wrote a masterwork, *On Liberty*, that remains one of the classic defenses of freedom. Long before it became popular, Mill also fought for women's rights (especially for suffrage) and wrote a book on the subject that also remains a classic: *The Subjection of Women*.

Actually, if truth be told, Mill cowrote *The Subjection of Women* with a fellow Victorian who, aside from his father, was perhaps the greatest influence on his life. At the age of twenty-four, Mill met and fell in love with Harriet Taylor, an intelligent, spirited, free-thinking woman who was, like Mill himself, very much a product of her age. Harriet shared Mill's feelings but was, alas, already married. The two would-be lovers maintained a close relationship; however, out of regard for her husband (whom they both cared deeply for), they never consummated their affair—an arrangement that lasted for twenty years! (Mill, as we will see, was not the only

Victorian with a peculiar sex life, or lack thereof!) Harriet's husband died in 1849, and the two were wed in 1851, remaining happily married until Harriet's own death in 1858.

From Harriet, Mill received the feeling and sentiment he had never gotten from his father (or his mother, who was vastly inferior in intellect to her husband and had little affection for her son). Harriet, though, was no quiet or submissive companion; though she encouraged Mill in all his books and causes, she continually challenged him to refine his thoughts and test his assumptions. In his *Autobiography*, Mill depicts her as nothing less than a paragon of intellect and virtue: Though she shared the elevated passions of the poet Percy Shelley, wrote Mill, "in thought and intellect, Shelley, so far as his powers were developed in his short life, was but a child compared with what she ultimately became." Had women been allowed political careers, Mill asserted, she would have been "eminent among the rulers of mankind." And the litany goes on. Though his overpraise of Harriet borders, at times, on the ridiculous, it is clear that she was vital to Mill's growth and accomplishments. For it was she, more than anyone else, who demonstrated to Mill that a person could share his desire to reform the world and his dedication to utilitarian methods and principles while yet remaining a warm, balanced human being.

6

JOHN STUART MILL
Crisis and Resolution

IN THE FIFTH CHAPTER of his *Autobiography* (from which all of the quotes in this chapter will be taken), John Stuart Mill documents what he calls a "crisis in my mental history": a devastating emotional collapse that was part nervous breakdown, part clinical depression. Although Mill's crisis sprang most directly out of his unique educational experience, the fact and the nature of his crisis places him in a central Victorian tradition. Indeed, with the exception of Huxley and perhaps Browning, nearly every major Victorian writer suffered some type of internal crisis that forced him to reassess both his beliefs and his goals. How could it be otherwise in an Age of Transition? When the old verities are shaken, when the past seems cut off and the future unclear, how can such crises be avoided? The Victorian Age was, supremely, an Age of Crisis, and its key spokesmen embodied that crisis.

A DROWSY, STIFLED, UNIMPASSIONED GRIEF

Mill begins chapter V by stating that from the age of sixteen, he had but one passion, one object in life: "to be a reformer of the world." For many years this passion carried him on a wave of utopian optimism; then, in the autumn of 1826, when he had reached the age of twenty-one, disaster struck. Suddenly, with no apparent provocation, Mill fell into "a dull state of nerves," a state he rather oddly likens to the feeling of conviction of sin that precedes a religious conversion. Unable to shake himself out of this strange mood, Mill began (as was common for him) to analyze himself; specifically, he asked himself a question that he had never asked before: If you were to achieve all your goals, if you truly succeeded in reforming the world, would you be happy? The answer he gave himself was "no," an answer that immediately catapulted him into a state that today we would call clinical depression: that is, a state of cold, dead, passionless torpor.

Mill illustrates the nature of his dark mood by quoting four lines from Coleridge's "Dejection: An Ode" that read like a textbook description of clinical depression:

> A grief without a pang, void, dark and drear,
> A drowsy, stifled, unimpassioned grief,
> Which finds no natural outlet, no relief
> In word, or sigh, or tear. (21–24)

More than just a bout of low spirits, what Mill and Coleridge attempt to describe in their respective works is a kind of inner deadness from which the sufferer cannot rouse himself. Behind them both, one hears the lament of the melancholy Hamlet: "How weary, stale, flat and unprofitable / Seem to me all the uses of this world!" (I.ii.133–34). While trapped in such a state, the sufferer reaches outward in vain, for nothing from the external world can hope to bring restoration to a soul that is itself sullen, lethargic, and hollow. "I may not hope from outward forms to win," explains Coleridge later in the next stanza, "The passion and the life, whose fountains are within." It is a peculiarly Romantic (as opposed to Victorian) malady, this excessive self-consciousness that strangles on its own melancholy, but the young would-be utilitarian was caught inextricably in its grip and could find no release.

Desperately, impulsively, Mill sought solace from his depression in his books and his studies, but nothing availed. None of the remedies taught him by his father or his father's systems could restore his emotional health. I mentioned above that Mill uncharacteristically compares his state to that of a convicted sinner on the threshold of conversion. And indeed, anyone who has read any of the devotional literature that has accompanied the Great Awakenings and revivals of Christianity in America or Britain will be half expecting Mill to suddenly fall on his knees and (John Wesley style) receive Christ as his savior. But he never does. His final resolution *will* be spiritual in nature, but it will happen apart from any Christian doctrine or supernatural event—will constitute, instead, a sort of secular salvation. What else could it be? Mill's education, as we saw, ignored religion completely, and his father had instilled in him the unswerving belief that non-empirical, non-rational religious doctrines were ultimately of no value and could not be relied upon to resolve the problems of society or of the individual.

I just said that none of Mill's remedies seemed to work, but the situation was, in fact, much more dire. To his horror, Mill soon discovered that the very methods that he marshaled to combat his mental breakdown actually made the condition worse. For a utilitarian trained in logical, systematic thinking, analysis is the solution to all ills and conundrums, but when Mill tried to analyze himself accordingly, he learned that the same analysis that strengthens the mind, enervates the feelings and leaves them dry (the "paralysis of analysis" we would say). Worse yet, he found that analysis can become itself a kind of addiction, a vampire that feeds on itself. Significantly, though Mill does not make the connection, this "dissolving influence of analysis," as Mill terms it, is one of the key themes of Coleridge's "Dejection: An Ode," the poem that Mill quotes to describe his own condition:

> For not to think of what I needs must feel,
>   But to be still and patient, all I can;
> And haply by abstruse research to steal
>   From my own nature all the natural man—
>   This was my sole resource, my only plan:
> Till that which suits a part infects the whole,
> And now is almost grown the habit of my soul. (87–93)

There was a time when Coleridge could feed off his own inner resources with impunity, but now this one-time coping mechanism had grown into a self-destructive habit that was systematically eating up what few stores of restoration remained within.

As for Mill, the upshot of his own addiction to analysis ("abstruse research") was to leave him "stranded at the commencement of my voyage with a well-equipped ship and a rudder, but no sail, without any real desire for the ends which I had been so carefully fitted out to work for: no delight in virtue or the general good." For anyone such a state would be lamentable; for a Victorian it is deadly. The whole base of Mill's utilitarian goals was to create a society that would minimize pain and maximize pleasure; in his crisis, he feared that even if this goal were reached, the pleasures that resulted would, in the absence of the struggle exerted to achieve it, cease to be pleasurable. Human happiness, he cries out in despair, must rest on a firmer foundation, one that cannot be taken away or used up, one that will come from peace within rather than strife without. As an indicator of the angst Mill felt at this point in his life, he even worried that "the exhaustibility of musical combinations" would some day rob him of the pleasure he took in music. Again, at this point in the narrative, one half expects the clinically depressed Mill to "walk down the aisle" and give his life to Christ. But Mill is no John Newton (the author of "Amazing Grace"); neither is he St. Augustine. His testimony is a purely secular one, and it can end only with a secular epiphany.

STRIKING A BALANCE

Mill's resolution, when it finally came, came in three distinct stages. The first ray of hope broke through when Mill read, totally by chance, a passage from the memoirs of an eighteenth-century French writer named Marmontel. In the book, Marmontel recalls the death of his father and how that event forced on him the knowledge that, though only a boy, he *would* be able to be to his family what his father had been. When Mill read this passage, it brought him to the point of tears, convincing him that all feeling had not died in him but that he could still sympathize and even empathize with others. Indeed, part of Mill's problem was that, due to his education, he had no friends his age and thus felt that he was the only man in all England to be suffering such a crisis. Reading Marmontel helped bring Mill back into the human family and resensitized him to the simple pleasures that lay around him (it supplied him, we might say, with a support group).

The second stage of recovery was reached when Mill learned that by making happiness his direct, self-conscious end he was actually destroying his potential for happiness. Just so, it is one of those eternal rules of life that the vacationer who continually asks himself, "Am I having fun yet?" will never have any fun at all. The solution Mill found, simple but profound, was "to treat, not happiness, but some end external to it, as the purpose of life." It is when you forget about yourself and your personal need for happiness and concentrate, instead, on the happiness of others, that your own happiness suddenly appears.

During his crisis, Mill tells us, he tried reading the works of Byron, a melancholy, over-self-conscious Romantic, who, in his poetry, often expressed the same world-weariness that Mill felt; but he quickly abandoned this pursuit, for Byron's passionate self-pity only intensified his grief and angst. In such works as *The Giaour, Lara, Manfred,* and *Childe Harold's Pilgrimage* (all of which Mill mentions having read during his crisis), Byron conjures up partly autobiographical heroes who share his feelings of guilt and isolation and who parade those feelings across Europe from the plains of Waterloo to the highest peaks of the Alps. Moody and defiant, these characters (known collectively as Byronic heroes) have committed some taboo sin or tasted of some forbidden fruit, and the experience has left them wasted (old before their time) and alienated from the rest of humanity. However, rather than seeking forgiveness or attempting to reenter society, they choose to remain alone, wearing their suffering as a personal, self-inflicted crown of thorns. Though tempted for a short while by this excessive form of

Romanticism, the ever Victorian Mill soon cast it off, and embraced instead (though he had not yet heard of it) the anti-self-consciousness theory advocated by Thomas Carlyle (of which and of whom we will learn more in chapter 18).

Now this second stage may seem at first to contradict the first: how can one both regain his feelings and put them aside, both indulge the passions and restrain them? The answer, key to Mill's recovery, is balance: The feelings (contra utilitarianism) must be cultivated, but they must not (contra Byron) be enshrined as the end and goal of life. In seeking to advance the benefits of liberty, liberalism, and utilitarianism, Mill would likely have to sacrifice much of his personal time and energy, but he would not allow that sacrifice to become an end-in-itself, as it appeared to be for the Byronic hero. He would stop brooding and start doing. Inasmuch as he needed to pay attention to his inner feelings, he would look inward, but once that inward glance became too insular, too self-conscious, he would look outward again. It was a difficult balance to attain and to maintain, but Mill committed himself to achieving it. And achieve it he did, but only with the help of a third Romantic poet: William Wordsworth.

WORDSWORTH TO THE RESCUE

For all the genius of his two great mentors (James Mill and Jeremy Bentham), for all his own ceaseless struggles to learn and to grow, it was finally a decidedly non-urban poet, one who indulged overmuch in that very sentiment his father had taught him to avoid, that proved the one thing needed to pull Mill out of his crisis. Through reading closely with an open mind and heart the poetry of Wordsworth, Mill learned that there is a difference between the outward beauty of objects and the more subjective beauty that we project onto those objects. This subjective beauty that both rises out of and is colored by internal states of feeling constitutes a more permanent kind of joy that will be not eradicated but enhanced when utopia is achieved. And out of this "inward joy," this "culture of the feelings," Mill was able to draw "a sympathetic and imaginative pleasure, which could be shared in by all human beings, which had no connexion with struggle or imperfection, but would be made richer by every improvement in the physical or social condition of mankind." By the power of this sympathetic imagination, Mill could move out of himself toward others and share in their joy; by this same power he could accept the loss of his youthful freshness and innocence (what little his father had allowed him) and find what Wordsworth terms (in "Tintern Abbey," line 88) "abundant recompense."

Mill's solution, of course, has bearing not only on his own personal crisis but on that of his age. The Victorians, Mill's *Autobiography* establishes, need not throw off completely their Romantic heritage; feeling, far from being the foe of progress, is the very thing that enables us to enjoy its fruits. Too often, Mill asserts, Englishmen set as their goal the suppression and even deadening of their emotions. Mill, who learned the hard way, would instruct his fellow countrymen in how the cultivation of feeling and the sympathetic imagination are necessary to the formation of true character. Indeed, in an influential essay that he wrote on Bentham, Mill exposes as Bentham's one great flaw his total lack of sympathetic imagination:

> In many of the most natural and strongest feelings of human nature [Bentham] had no sympathy; from many of its graver experiences he was altogether cut off; and the faculty [i.e., sympathetic imagination] by which one mind understands a mind different from itself, and throws itself into the feelings of that other mind, was denied him by his deficiency of imagination.[1]

Though he could have been the greatest man of his age, Mill felt, Bentham's inability to move out of himself and to share in the

---

[1] "Bentham," Mill's *Essays on Literature and Society* (New York: Collier Books, 1965), 258.

feelings of others left him finally unable to compensate for his own personal flaws. It left him, to use one of Mill's more felicitous phrases, a "one-eyed man."

Though Mill continued to believe in and adhere to the basic tenets of utilitarianism as they were laid out by Bentham, his crisis and resolution taught him that Bentham's conception of man as being motivated solely by self-interest and the pleasure/pain principle was insufficient:

> Man is never recognized by [Bentham] as a being capable of pursuing spiritual perfection as an end: of desiring, for its own sake, the conformity of his own character to his standard of excellence.[2]

As is often true of humanitarians, Bentham had a great love for humanity in the abstract but no capacity to love or sympathize with individual human beings. By analogy, though his system had the potential to protect the material interests of a society, it left the spiritual interests poor and unfed. Bentham had little to no regard for poetry; Mill, on the other hand, whose resolution came through reading the poetry of Wordsworth, became a great defender of poetry and even asserts in his *Autobiography* that it is precisely those who possess unpoetical natures who most need poetry. Interestingly, Mill, who strongly linked poetry to the cultivation of inner feeling, came to think of poetry almost fully in Romantic terms; in fact, in an essay titled "What is Poetry?" Mill argued that true poetry is not so much heard as it is overheard.

Mill remained, to the end of his life, a committed disciple and champion of the utilitarian creed, but it was he, more than anyone, who humanized that creed, who helped it, as it were, to put on flesh and blood.

---

2 Ibid., 262.

7

⁓ · ⁓

TENNYSON'S IN MEMORIAM
The Poem that Embodied Its Age

⁓ALTHOUGH I HAVE SUGGESTED both 1837 (the crowning of Queen Victoria) and 1832 (the passing of the First Reform Bill) as possible dates for the beginning of the Victorian Age, perhaps the true emotional and spiritual date that marks the transition from Romantic to Victorian is 1833. For it was in this year that a tragic event occurred in the life of a man who not only would become England's greatest Victorian poet but would most embody the spirit of Victorianism. The poet is Alfred, Lord Tennyson (1809–92); the event is the death of his friend and future brother-in-law, Arthur Henry Hallam (1811–33).

THE GENESIS OF AN EPIC

Born in 1809, Tennyson was a shy, withdrawn young man who discovered early his talent and love for poetry. Growing up in the heyday of Romanticism, he at first modeled his poetry on Keats. His early poems showed promise, but he lacked the confidence and the encouragement to come out of his personal and poetic shell and to make full use of his natural gifts. This needed the confidence and encouragement he found in the person of a charismatic young man who befriended him during his college years at Cambridge. The young man's name was Arthur Henry Hallam, and he was that special kind of friend who helps to draw shy people out of their shell; this vital service he performed for the floundering, unsure Tennyson. As part of this "service," Hallam urged Tennyson to join the Apostles, a literary group of Cambridge students who met to discuss the aesthetic, spiritual, and scientific issues of their day. Unlike the founders of the Oxford Movement, the Apostles tended to be more in sync with the growing mood of liberalism. Thus, while Newman and his fellow Tractarians were seeking a return to the older values and ideals of a traditional high-church Anglicanism, Hallam was leading the Apostles toward a full and positive engagement with all that was most progressive and innovative in science, religion, and politics.

Thrown together in the white heat of conversation and debate, Tennyson and Hallam soon became fast friends. Hallam critiqued Tennyson's poetry and nursed him through some of the negative, even virulent, criticism that greeted his first volume of poems. The two even traveled together to the Pyrenees on one of those idyllic walking tours that had, several decades earlier, helped to cement the friendship of Wordsworth and Coleridge. As added glue to their friendship, Hallam was soon betrothed to Tennyson's sister, Emily. Lifelong happiness seemed to be in the grasp of the often moody Tennyson; a return to paradise seemed imminent.

Then, in 1833, disaster struck. At the age of twenty-two, Hallam died while on a visit to Vienna. Tennyson was devastated by the news. As a way of dealing with his grief, Tennyson began writing a series of short poems. At the time, he had no thoughts whatever of publication; to him the poems were an emotional necessity, a form of grief therapy. For the next ten years, while working (and publishing with some success) a series of poems on various subjects, Tennyson continued to work on his "Hallam poems." As the number of poems increased (eventually reaching 131), Tennyson began to give some thought toward publishing them in a series. Accordingly, he arranged the poems in what seemed the most logical order, added an epilogue (1842) and a prologue (1849), and published the epic-length work (under the title, *In Memoriam, A. H. H.*) in 1850.

Oddly, *In Memoriam* (to my mind, the single greatest meditation on the subject of grief) shares a similar genesis with a second work that I (and I am not alone on this) would dub the second greatest meditation on the grieving process: *A Grief Observed* (1961). This brief but deeply profound prose work was written by C. S. Lewis (1898–1963), the acclaimed author of *Mere Christianity, The Screwtape Letters,* and *The Chronicles of Narnia.* Though a bachelor until he reached his fifties, Lewis fell in love with and married Joy Davidman Gresham. The couple spent three happy years together as husband and wife, but their extended honeymoon ended abruptly in 1960, when Joy succumbed to a long bout with cancer. Lewis (a strong Christian who had two decades earlier written a book titled *The Problem of Pain* to help explain why a loving God allowed suffering in the world) was devastated by the death of his wife and began to question his own faith. As a way of dealing with his grief and his inner wrestlings, Lewis began to keep a journal. Like Tennyson, Lewis had no thought of ever publishing his journal entries; he wrote them solely as an emotional outlet, a private dialogue between God and his own tortured spirit. However, again like Tennyson, Lewis soon found that his scattered entries were shaping themselves into a book: one that might possibly encourage and enlighten others who were struggling with grief. Accordingly, Lewis too found himself committing to print an intensely personal work that was never intended for public eyes. But, of course, this is why *A Grief Observed* and *In Memoriam* are such powerful and timeless works; in both memoirs (for that, finally, is what they are), the writer speaks to us directly out of his confusion and pain. There is no attempt to cover up the severity of the grief or to moderate the initial questioning of God's mercy and providence. By the end, both works move back toward a position of peace, faith, and acceptance, but, until that resolution, it can be quite a "bumpy ride." What we encounter in both poem and journal is naked emotion, grief in the raw. To read and engage these works, to follow them from despair to hope, crisis to resolution, is to experience a true and lasting catharsis.

So did Lewis's readers feel in 1961; so did Tennyson's readers in 1850. *In Memoriam* proved an instant and lasting success and won Tennyson the position of poet laureate in 1850 (after the death of Wordsworth, the previous poet laureate), a position he held until his death, and one that he filled with dignity. Indeed, whereas most poets today would consider the role of "court poet" as a limiting one, if not a form of "aesthetic prostitution," Tennyson took seriously his role as the poet of his country. Tennyson was a patriot with a deep respect for the queen; his stirring poem "The Charge of the Light Brigade" is totally free from irony in its celebration of that heroic piece of folly. In honor of the death of Prince Albert, Tennyson added a moving, equally sincere dedication to Albert to his Arthurian *Idylls of the King*. The queen herself felt strong affection for the poet. Indeed, *In Memoriam*'s greatest compliment was surely paid it by the widowed Victoria, who told Tennyson that, next to the Bible, *In Memoriam* was her greatest consolation.

In addition to gaining him fame and the undying regard of Victoria (along with most of her subjects, who grew used to hearing the poem quoted from lecterns and pulpits all over the country), the publication of *In Memoriam* led to another personal milestone in the poet's life: his marriage. Although Tennyson had gotten engaged to Emily Sellwood in 1838, they did not consummate their vows until 1850. The external reason for Tennyson's delay was a financial one (he was a struggling poet and had little security to offer a wife); however, perhaps just as vital was his internal emotional need to "get over" the death of Hallam and to free his heart to love another. And his grief *was* intense. Though there is no evidence of a homosexual relationship between Hallam and Tennyson, they shared a deep friendship that was in some ways all-consuming. Hallam was friend, father, brother, and mentor to the lonely Tennyson. Before Tennyson could allow Emily fully into his heart, he had to leave behind—fully leave behind— his first and truest companion.

PARADISE LOST

In Tennyson's mind, the death of Hallam slowly became equated with the death of something else: namely, the death of Romanticism. When Hallam died, all that was innocent and fresh, all those Romantic hopes for a restored Eden, died too. In fact, while working on the early sections of *In Memoriam*, Tennyson also completed a meditation on the death of another famous Arthur *(King Arthur)* that would later be used in his Arthurian epic: *Idylls of the King*. In this stately, elegiac poem (titled, after Thomas Malory, *Le Morte d'Arthur*) the dying King Arthur calls on his last knight, Sir Bedivere, to take Excalibur (Arthur's sword) and cast it into the lake. As he passes on the sword, Arthur muses:

> . . . I think that we
> Shall never more, at any future time,
> Delight our souls with talk of knightly deeds,
> Walking about the gardens and the halls
> Of Camelot, as in the days that were. (17–21)

Though Arthur the King speaks here of Camelot, what we really have is Arthur Hallam reminiscing with Tennyson (who is Bedivere) about the glory days of the Apostles. The "days that were" refer as much to the innocent days of the Round Table and of chivalry as they do to the golden days of Cambridge when Tennyson, Hallam, and their friends discussed all that was most noble, beautiful, and true in their world.

Bedivere takes the sword but is unable to cast it into the lake. He desires, rather, to keep it for himself as a memento of Arthur and the glories of Camelot; he would rather live in his memories then move on to pastures new. Two times he reaches back his arm to cast the sword into the lake, but both times he finds himself unable to complete the deed. Finally, at the insistence of the King, he returns a third time and throws Excalibur into the lake, where it is caught and dragged under the water by the hand (clothed in white samite) of the Lady of the Lake. But even this miracle cannot stem Bedivere's grief. With heavy heart, he cries out:

> Ah, my Lord Arthur, whither shall I go?
> Where shall I hide my forehead and my eyes?
> For now I see the true old times are dead . . .
> And I, the last, go forth companionless,
> And the days darken round me, and the years,
> Among new men, strange faces, other minds.
> (227–29, 236–38)

The grief here is more Tennyson's than Bedivere's, the grief of the survivor who has lost his desire to move on and seek new experiences, new passions. But the gentle Arthur comforts *both* men with these words:

> The old order changeth, yielding place to new,
> And God fulfils Himself in many ways
> Lest one good custom should corrupt the world. (240–42)

Just as Bedivere here must learn the liberal Victorian moral of pressing forward, of trusting in change, in new ideals, in the future, so, in *In Memoriam*, must Tennyson learn the same.

But he must learn it on a higher, societal level, one that encompasses not only the individual grief of an isolated griever, but the corporate grief of an age whose old ways and beliefs have been stripped away. That is to say, whereas *In Memoriam* begins as a simple elegy of a man for his friend, it soon expands into a poetic requiem that sounds the full grief of the Victorian Age as it mourns its loss of faith. Tennyson the melancholy Romantic matures into Tennyson the spokesman of Victorian angst; as he moves through the stages of grief, he realizes that much more is at stake than his own peace.

Like most grievers, he struggles with whether he will see Hallam again in heaven, but this struggle leads him to question the immortality of the soul, which in turn leads him to take up the whole questioning of religious faith that dominated his age, especially in the face of the new science. He begins by agonizing over whether his friendship with Hallam was "worth it," whether it had true meaning and purpose, and ends by asking the larger Victorian question: Is there any meaning or purpose inherent in this species we call *Homo sapiens*, and is that species guided by a loving hand? Is there any point in moving on, in building relationships and institutions that will only crumble in the end? Tennyson asks this question both of himself and on behalf of his society, and in attempting to answer it, he transforms his poem from a tribute to one man to an embodiment of an age.

TENNYSON AGONISTES

The poet of *In Memoriam* is, supremely, a wrestler (I like to call him Tennyson Agonistes), and in his wrestling with personal and societal issues, he comes also, like Jacob, to wrestle with God. For *In Memoriam*, aside from being an elegy for a man and his age, fits into the ancient genre of theodicy: a genre that attempts to meditate on the justice (or injustice) of God. This genre first appears in the biblical book of Job, an extended poem that seeks to understand why the innocent suffer and why God seems silent when his righteous followers are in pain. Other theodicies (like those of St. Augustine) take up the question of the origin of evil; Dante's *Divine Comedy* is in part a theodicy that seeks to fathom God's system of punishment and reward.

However, in crafting his theodicy, Tennyson was most conscious of two English poets who each wrote an epic theodicy that attempted to answer universal questions in the terms of his age. The first of these poets is John Milton, whose seventeenth-century theodicy *(Paradise Lost)* attempts, to quote the poem, to "justify the ways of God to man" (I.26). Milton accomplishes this through exploring the fall of Satan and of man, but he does so through the prism of the British Civil War and the questions of monarchy and hierarchy that event raised. The second is Alexander Pope, whose eighteenth-century theodicy *(An Essay on Man)* attempts, like *Paradise Lost* before it, "to vindicate the ways of God to man" (I.16). Still, despite its purpose, Pope's poetic theodicy is a vastly different work from Milton's. Pope tells no epic tale of temptation and fall; rather, he offers a rational explication of the natural order of the universe and builds a system that embodies the concerns of *his* age: the Enlightenment. Tennyson, in imitation of these two mighty predecessors, recast his theodicy in terms of all those Victorian issues, all those crises of faith that we have already discussed in the preceding chapters.

But this is not all Tennyson learned from Milton and Pope. He learned too the need to choose a poetic form that would most perfectly embody the nature of his nineteenth-century theodicy. In *Paradise Lost*, the poetic form is "blank verse," a form that consists of an unrhymed series of ten-syllable lines in which the even syllables are stressed (Shakespeare uses this form for his soliloquies). Without any rhymes to impede the flow of the lines, Milton's epic blank verse moves forward in a stately, grandiose fashion that is, at once, meditative and sweeping; indeed, blank verse, as Milton found, comes closest to capturing the rush and power of Homer's epic line. Pope, for his theodicy, chose as his form the heroic couplet: two lines (each of which, like blank verse, has ten syllables and five stresses) that are linked by a rhyme. Here is an example from *An Essay on Man*:

> Say first, of God above, or man below,
> What can we reason, but from what we know?

Though these heroic couplets are linked together in a series, there is always a strong stop at the end of each couplet, marked by a period, a semicolon, or a colon (only occasionally a comma).

Unlike the free-flowing blank verse of Milton, Pope's heroic couplets read like a mathematical proof that moves logically, step-by-step, from proposition to proposition to conclusion. In the movement of his heroic couplets, we can feel the balance, the order, the rationality that Pope's Age of Enlightenment prized and that he hoped to embody in his theodicy.

For his theodicy, Tennyson chose a four-line stanza with shorter, eight-syllable lines that rhyme, not ABAB or AABB as one would normally expect, but ABBA. Here is an example:

> Thou wilt not leave us in the dust:
> Thou madest man, he knows not why,
> He thinks he was not meant to die;
> And thou hast made him: thou art just.

In this strange, "mirror-image" stanza, Tennyson embodies, I believe, the movement from faith (the first "A" rhyme) to doubt (the two "B" rhymes) back to faith (the second "A" rhyme); and this movement, as we shall see in the chapters that follow, is the very movement of the poem itself. Tennyson, I said above, is a wrestler, and the stanza form he uses strikes the ear of its reader with the subtle but insistent sounds of struggle, of a battle being waged and finally resolved. It is the music of his era, and Tennyson will conduct that music into the greatest symphony of the Victorian Age.

8

TENNYSON'S *IN MEMORIAM*
A Beam in Darkness

THOUGH THE PROLOGUE to *In Memoriam* appears first in the poem, it was actually the last section to be written, and thus expresses a faith and a resolution that the poem will not achieve for much of its length. Still, Tennyson clearly meant for us to read his Prologue first, perhaps because he wanted to mimic in his overall poem that movement from faith to doubt to faith that he "hardwired" into the ABBA construction of his stanza form. For this reason, I will begin my analysis of the poem by considering how the Prologue sets the stage for the key issues the work will explore.

VASTER MUSIC

The first stanza of the Prologue begins with both a definition and an affirmation of faith:

> Strong Son of God, immortal love,
>> Whom we, that have not seen thy face,
>> By faith, and faith alone, embrace,
> Believing where we cannot prove. (1–4)

Tennyson alludes here to the biblical definition of faith as "the evidence of things not seen; the assurance of things hoped for" (Heb 11:1; KJV). The mysteries of God, which will be sounded in Tennyson's theodicy, are finally beyond the propositional and observational proofs of science. Neither the vast narrative structure of Milton's epic nor the enlightened order of Pope's cosmic system will do in the Victorian Age of doubt. In many ways, Tennyson is closer to the Jansenist Pascal before him ("the heart hath reasons") and to the existential Kierkegaard ("leap of faith") who was almost his exact contemporary.

Tennyson lived and breathed in a post-Enlightenment Age when faith and reason were slowly parting company, an age when grace, if seized at all, tended to be seized in a finally antirational way. Given such an age, the best Tennyson can assert is this:

> We have but faith: we cannot know,
>   For knowledge is of things we see;
>   And yet we trust it comes from thee,
> A beam in darkness: let it grow. (21–24)

At the outset, Tennyson (who, though a believer, was in many ways closer to Huxley than Newman), accepts the liberal distinction between knowledge and faith, empirical facts and intuitive beliefs. His religious reconciliation, when it comes (see chapter 11), will lack the more rational certainty of Newman's. What the doubting Tennyson seeks is not a new defense of Christian doctrine, but a "beam in darkness," a faint ray of hope that he trusts will grow in power and intensity as he struggles his way through grief.

In the Victorian Age of transition, where the role and nature of all authority (even divine) are tenuous and unclear, Tennyson (like Job) can fall back only on a "bend of the knee" to a force he cannot fully understand:

> Thou wilt not leave us in the dust:
>   Thou madest man, he knows not why,

> He thinks he was not meant to die;
> And thou hast made him: thou art just.
>
> Thou seemest human and divine,
> The highest, holiest manhood, thou.
> Our wills are ours, we know not how;
> Our wills are ours, to make them thine. (9–16)

His assertion here of God's justice, of the divinity of Christ, and of our need to submit to God is simply that: an assertion. By the end of the poem, this assertion will have accumulated persuasive force, but it will be an emotional force ("felt along the heart" to quote Wordsworth's "Tintern Abbey") rather than a rational one. Still, though Tennyson shares here the liberal uncertainty in religious matters that dominated his age, he, like all of the great Victorian poets and sages, is critical of the pretensions of his age.

Right from the outset, Tennyson confesses that his age is not all-knowing:

> Our little systems have their day;
> They have their day and cease to be;
> They are but broken lights of thee,
> And thou, O Lord, art more than they. (17–20)

Tennyson recognized that many of the systems hailed by the Victorians as the solution to all the ills of the world (utilitarianism, the new science, technology, etc.) were really philosophical "fads" that would soon pass away. God's wisdom is greater than man's, and, though Tennyson did not share Newman's faith that God's wisdom could be channeled relatively unproblematically through the Church, he knew that true wisdom is found only in God's perfect Light. Man's ego alone convinces him that he is self-sufficient.

What Tennyson desires then is not a return to an authoritarian church (Newman), nor the elimination of all spiritual language (Huxley), nor the refounding of society along lines of utility (Mill), but a reunification of head and heart, a higher balance between body and soul:

> Let knowledge grow from more to more,
>   But more of reverence in us dwell;
>   That mind and soul, according well,
> May make one music as before, (25–28)

Tennyson was an advocate of the new science and studied it diligently (as we shall see in a later chapter, he is one of the most scientifically informed poets who ever lived); yet, he knew in his heart that scientific and philosophical rationalism can often kill the awe, wonder, and mystery both of man and of nature. In this, he never quite lost his first love for the poetry of John Keats. Keats, in a long narrative poem titled *Lamia*, memorably captures the dangers of rationalism:

> Do not all charms fly
> At the mere touch of cold philosophy?
> There was an awful rainbow once in heaven:
> We know her woof, her texture; she is given
> In the dull catalogue of common things.
> Philosophy will clip an Angel's wings,
> Conquer all mysteries by rule and line,
> Empty the haunted air, and gnomed mire—
> Unweave a rainbow. (II. 229–37)

Though Keats and Tennyson were both fans of Newton and his genius, they both realized as well that when Newton gave his physical explanation for the phenomenon of the rainbow he robbed the world of one of its great mysteries. Though neither poet (especially Keats) could be called an orthodox Christian, both lamented the loss of the sacred, of the holy, of the numinous that accompanied Europe's transition into the modern (post-Enlightenment) world. Both would use their poetry, at least in part, to restore some of that lost wonder.

In a later poem *(Maud)*, Tennyson refers to the "sad astrology" of modern science, sad because it disrupted (and deharmonized) that sympathetic universe that Dante celebrates in his *Divine*

Comedy. Tennyson would seek, in *Maud*, in *In Memoriam*, and in several other major works, to reestablish that older harmony; however, being a Victorian forced to live in a post-Romantic, post-Hallam world, he could not (like Keats) accomplish this by a simple return to a state of edenic innocence. No, the Victorian Tennyson would have to forge instead a new and greater harmony. If the attentive reader compares stanza 7 of the Prologue (lines 25–28, quoted above) to the rest of the stanzas, he will notice a subtle but vital distinction. Whereas all of the other stanzas end with a strong stop (either a period or, in the case of stanza 1, a semicolon), stanza 7 ends with a comma. That is to say, the syntax of the stanza does not end with its last line ("May make one music as before,"), but spills over on to the next stanza, which begins, "But vaster" (29). The message latent in this formal deviation is clear. Tennyson the Victorian would not go backward to Eden but forward to a richer, more complex paradise. He would reclaim that mystery sacrificed on the altar of rationalism and utilitarianism, but he would do it by moving past (not throwing out) the Anglo-Catholicism of Newman, the new science of Huxley, and the utilitarianism of Mill.

In the Christian (eschatological) view of history, the Fall from the Garden of Eden, though terrible and tragic in itself, is viewed as a good thing, for it leads, in the fullness of time, to a greater outpouring of divine love (the Incarnation and Crucifixion) and to a new paradise (the New Jerusalem) far superior to Eden. The early Church Fathers referred to this strange yet wonderful paradox as *felix culpa* (Latin for "blessed guilt" or "happy fault"), and instructed their congregations to look to the end (the eschaton) with faith and hope. In a parallel way, Tennyson felt that the loss of traditional Christianity (with its fixed verities and stable systems) would give way, in time, to a more mature, more vibrant faith able to incorporate and synthesize new doubts and discoveries. Science and industry would work together with this new faith to produce that vaster music that would restore mystery to the world even as it eradicated all the old wrongs. Such is the strong faith that underlies the Prologue; however, as noted above, this faith dominates the Prologue only because it was written last. At the true beginning of *In Memoriam*, the situation and the tone are far less hopeful.

THE FAR-OFF INTEREST OF TEARS

The Tennyson we encounter in the first poem (or section) of *In Memoriam* is a man nearly overwhelmed by grief. In the first two stanzas, he wonders if all his grief and pain, far from being a *felix culpa* that will pave the way for greater victories, are not merely that—grief and pain in a world of grief and pain:

> I held it truth, with him who sings
> To one clear harp in divers tones,
> That men may rise on stepping stones
> Of their dead selves to higher things.
>
> But who can so forecast the years
> And find in loss a gain to match?
> Or reach a hand through time to catch
> The far-off interest of tears? (1–8)

Yes, before the death of Hallam, he trusted that death gave way to new life and that the act of dying was but a stepping-stone for higher realities, greater progress, but now he is no longer so sure. Most people can handle suffering and pain when it seems to have some point or purpose, when it yields the rewards of a stronger faith or a calmer spirit, but when that same suffering seems empty, hollow, and meaningless, it becomes almost unbearable. Significantly, Tennyson uses a free-market, capitalist metaphor to suggest that his investment (his tears) will yield no interest or dividends (faith and peace).

Yes, it is only pain, futile and purposeless, and Tennyson, as so many grievers do, ends the first section of his poem by indulging in a very improper, self-destructive form of "grief management":

Let Love clasp Grief lest both be drowned,
  Let darkness keep her raven gloss.
  Ah, sweeter to be drunk with loss,
To dance with Death, to beat the ground,

Than that the victor Hours should scorn
  The long result of love, and boast,
  "Behold the man that loved and lost,
But all he was is overworn." (9–16)

The temptation here is to give oneself over to pagan revelry and
excess, to drown one's sorrows not just in the physical intoxication of alcohol, but in the spiritual intoxication of nihilism. Better to lose oneself in some barbaric ritual than face rationally an
unbearable truth: that is, that one can give one's whole heart to
another, lose that other, and then have nothing to show for it.

Interestingly, in section 2, Tennyson suddenly shifts to a new
form of "grief management" that, though it is 180 degrees
removed from his previous form, is equally self-destructive. The
poem is brief, and deserves to be quoted in full:

Old yew, which graspest at the stones
  That name the underlying dead,
  Thy fibers net the dreamless head,
Thy roots are wrapped about the bones.

The seasons bring the flower again,
  And bring the firstling to the flock;
  And in the dusk of thee the clock
Beats out the little lives of men.

O, not for thee the glow, the bloom,
  Who changest not in any gale,
  Nor branding summer suns avail
To touch thy thousand years of gloom.

And gazing on thee, sullen tree,
   Sick for thy stubborn hardihood,
   I seem to fail from out my blood
And grow incorporate into thee. (1–16)

The setting here is the grave of Hallam, and the grieving poet considers an ancient yew tree whose roots seem to intertwine with the body below as its branches embrace the tombstone above. For Tennyson, the tree becomes a symbol of that which is eternal and unchanging, which continues to live and to grow, even in the shadow of human death and decay. It is a triumphant image of permanence, and yet it is as well a sad image of an object that though it cannot die can neither feel nor love; it is, like the marble tombstone itself, coldly eternal. Ironically, this type of resolution would have appealed strongly to John Keats, who, in such poems as "On Seeing the Elgin Marbles" and "Ode on a Grecian Urn," yearned to merge with timeless works of art and leave behind our fleeting world of change. (I would even suggest that lines 13–16, above, are meant to echo the first five lines of "On Seeing the Elgin Marbles.")

But, of course (need I say it again), Tennyson is not Keats. If he is to be the poet and man he was destined to be, he must leave behind all Romantic, Keatsian "strategies" and press onward to a more Victorian resolution. Indeed, at a more mature stage in his grief, the poet *will* learn to reject such images in favor of the pain that feels and the death that lives. Nevertheless, at this point, his only desire is to merge with the tree. As often happens to grievers, his desire here is simply to stop feeling, to turn himself to stone. One of the reasons *In Memoriam* continues to speak so powerfully to those in grief (and remember, the true pain of being mortal is not so much the pain of our own death as it is the pain of losing those we love) is that it deals so honestly with the emotions and temptations that bombard the griever. In fact, those familiar with the psychological stages of grief outlined in Elisabeth Kübler-Ross's famous books, *On Death and Dying* will find that these can be applied effectively to *In Memoriam*.[1]

---

[1] See chapters III–VII of *On Death and Dying* (New York: Macmillan, 1969).

Let us close by looking at one last section (#7) that not only marks another stage in the grieving process but reveals the poet at the very nadir of despair and hopelessness. Again like so many grievers, Tennyson feels compelled to visit the home of the deceased:

> Dark house, by which once more I stand
> Here in the long unlovely street,
> Doors where my heart was used to beat
> So quickly, waiting for a hand, (1–4)

Tennyson, like many a mourner before and after him, tries to delude himself into believing that Hallam will magically come out of the house, that things will be as they were. But the hand he so vainly seeks does not come:

> A hand that will be clasped no more—
> Behold me, for I cannot sleep,
> And like a guilty thing I creep
> At earliest morning to the door.
>
> He is not here; but far away
> The noise of life begins again,
> And ghastly through the drizzling rain
> On the bald street breaks the blank day. (5–12)

I know of no profounder statement of grief in all literature. The poet himself is sickened at his own tormented desire to recall the dead and speaks of himself almost as an insect. The new dawn that breaks at the close of the poem promises neither light nor hope; all is dark and drear. By the end of the section, the poet who came to the house seeking companionship finds himself completely isolated from the world around him. Life and activity continue, but he cannot share in it—nor does he even desire to. Despair has beaten him down, a spiritual and emotional condition that is rendered concrete by Tennyson's choice to weigh down the final line with five strong beats instead of the expected four: "On the BALD STREET BREAKS the BLANK DAY."

But this is not the worst of it. Though the syntax of lines 9–10 reads, "He is not here; but far away the noise of life begins . . ." we cannot help but read the line thus: "He is not here but far away." Read that way, it marks the dark antithesis to the words of the angels that greet Mary and the other women when they come in search of the body of Jesus: "He is not here, but is risen" (Lk 24:6). There is to be no hope of resurrection, no promise of new life after the grave; the poet of section 7 is trapped in a Good Friday world that lacks the will or the faith to reach Easter Sunday. There is no beam in darkness; there is only darkness.

9

TENNYSON'S *IN MEMORIAM*
From Romantic to Victorian

ALTHOUGH THE EARLY SECTIONS of *In Memoriam* detail the grief and sorrow of a poet who is fully Romantic in his emotions and sensibilities, as the epic progresses this Romantic focus begins to shift. For the first twenty sections and for many scattered sections after that, Tennyson is content to grieve in a Romantic mode. However, beginning with section 21, a second, Victorian consciousness appears in the poem and initiates a long, slow wrestling match with the melancholy, Keatsian, excessively self-conscious griever of sections 1, 2, and 7. The struggle will be a difficult one, and it will move the poet (and his readers) through as many shifting moods and heightened emotions as an Italian opera, but in the end, it is the second wrestler who will win the contest. Let us, then, join the match and meet its two contestants.

IN DEFENSE OF PRIVATE SORROW

Section 21 begins, like section 2, with the grieving poet standing, figuratively, before the grave of Hallam. As before, his tendency is to handle his grief in a distinctly Romantic fashion:

> I sing to him that rests below,
> And, since the grasses round me wave,

> I take the grasses of the grave,
> And make them pipes whereon to blow. (1–4)

The metaphorical and allegorical setting here is purely pastoral; it evokes a Romantic longing for Eden, a nostalgia for a lost Paradise of grassy fields and warbling brooks. The poet is, in Keatsian fashion, isolated, cut off from the bustle and din of the city. The song he would sing to honor the dead is spontaneous and personal rather than measured and societal. And yet, even in this seemingly Romantic stanza, there is a touch, a hint, of the Victorian poet emerging within the melancholy griever.

The poet is not being as spontaneous or personal as he might at first appear. He is writing, in fact, within a set tradition that defines, in part, what shape his grief can and must take. Back in the third century B.C., three Greek poets—Theocritus, Moschus, and Bion—working on even earlier traditions, invented a new poetic genre that would come to be known as the "pastoral elegy," a genre that the great Latin poet Virgil would memorialize and perfect in his brief but moving *Eclogues*. In these delicate, lyrical poems (written many years before Virgil took up the titanic struggle of crafting his epic *Aeneid*), the lost Golden Age (generally set in the green valleys of Arcadia) is celebrated, even as an elegiac sense of its imminent loss hangs over the poetry. As in Theocritus, that loss of a simpler way of life is often expressed in the form of a lament for a shepherd who has died young. Other famous pastoral elegies include: Spenser's *The Shepheardes Calender*, Shakespeare's *The Winter's Tale* IV, Pope's *Windsor Forest*, Milton's *Lycidas*, and Shelley's *Adonais*. By the time the genre reached Tennyson, it had become a fixed part of the tradition; one could hardly write a respectable elegy without factoring in to it a pastoral note of innocence (and Eden) lost. That is to say, even at this early point in the poem, Tennyson is aware that he is more than merely an individual griever; he is, rather, a poet writing within a certain tradition that has certain set conventions.

Still, the dominant mood remains Romantic, until, in the second stanza, Tennyson allows a contrasting, finally Victorian voice to enter into his section (and his poem). This voice comes in the form of three passing travelers who comment on the poet's grief:

> The traveler hears me now and then,
>   And sometimes harshly will he speak:
>   "This fellow would make weakness weak,
> And melt the waxen hearts of men."
>
> Another answers: "Let him be,
>   He loves to make parade of pain,
>   That with his piping he may gain
> The praise that comes with constancy." (5–12)

To the first traveler, an unsympathetic, overly masculine boor, Tennyson is a crybaby, a womanish man whose tears threaten to destroy the stiff-upper-lip of the British soldier. To the second traveler, on the other hand, the poet is a phony, one who pretends to a grief he does not truly feel so that others will marvel at his loyalty and praise him for his selfless love.

But the third traveler (to whom two stanzas are given and with whom Tennyson is clearly most concerned) is, it seems, a Victorian businessman, a busy utilitarian out to reform the world:

> A third is wroth: "Is this an hour
>   For private sorrow's barren song,
>   When more and more the people throng
> The chairs and thrones of civil power?
>
> "A time to sicken and to swoon,
>   When Science reaches forth her arms
>   To feel from world to world, and charms
> Her secret from the latest moon?" (13–20)

Our zealous Victorian has nothing but scorn for the Romantic melancholy. How can Tennyson, the traveler rages, waste time mourning a single dead man when thousands cry out for needed political reform and when science and technology promise to unlock all the secrets of nature? To the Victorian, Tennyson's private grief is but a cover for selfishness and egocentrism. No longer is the individual to be privileged over the group; the time has come to reprioritize. In chapter 6, we saw that Mill, during his mental crisis, discovered he had to forsake the Romantic poetry of Byron with its overemotionalism and its intense self-pity. So here the poet is counseled to put aside individual sorrow for the sake of something greater, a wider social vision.

The concerns and values of the rising Victorian Age press themselves on the grieving poet, but he is not yet ready to adopt them. Though that second, latently Victorian voice has spoken, the first voice as yet lacks ears to hear the message. Accordingly, his response to the travelers is fully Romantic in image and ethos:

> Behold, ye speak an idle thing,
>   Ye never knew the sacred dust.
> I do but sing because I must,
> And pipe but as the linnets sing:
>
> And one is glad; her note is gay,
>   For now her little ones have ranged;
>   And one is sad; her note is changed.
> Because her brood is stolen away. (21–28)

Every major Romantic poet (from Wordsworth and Coleridge to Byron, Shelley, and Keats) wrote at least one poem in which he envied the freedom, the spontaneity, and the un-self-conscious singing of a skylark or a nightingale or any of a number of birds. Most notable among these poems are Keats's "Ode to a Nightingale" and Shelley's "To a Skylark," the second of which begins with this soaring stanza:

> Hail to thee, blithe Spirit!
>   Bird thou never wert,
> That from Heaven, or near it,
>   Pourest thy full heart
> In profuse strains of unpremeditated art (1–5)

Shelley, like all the Romantics, preferred to define himself poetically as a vessel through whom inspiration sang. Birds such as the nightingale or the skylark were treasured by such poets, for their songs seemed to flow out of them like a swift river whose current can be neither stemmed nor controlled. So here, Tennyson compares himself to a bird (the linnet) that cannot help but sing. She does not do it for any higher social purpose, but because she must. Like the David of the Psalms, she sings when she is happy and when she is sad, for singing is her natural mode of self-expression—and she indulges that mode, not for society, but for herself.

Exorcising Hamlet

The pastoral mood of #21 wends its way through five sections until suddenly, in #27, it breaks from its moorings in Romantic melancholy and soars upward to embrace the Victorian spirit of progress. In the opening sections of the poem, Tennyson wondered if it was all worth it. Would it not have been better to have never known the friendship of Hallam than to have lost it so tragically? Here, in #27, he finally breaks free from his self-pitying, Byronic orientation to assert boldly:

> I envy not in any moods
>> The captive void of noble rage,
>> The linnet born within the cage,
> That never knew the summer woods; (1–4)

He no longer wishes he had been born a "bird in a gilded cage," shielded from the harsh realities of the outside world. He prefers freedom with all the dangers attendant upon it to a naïve, protected existence that withdraws from struggle and confrontation. Neither does he envy the plight of the political prisoner (or perhaps POW) who accepts his bars and grows complacent, preferring rather to wait out his confinement than to risk all on a desperate attempt at escape.

Tennyson continues and elaborates on this bold new resolution in the second stanza:

> I envy not the beast that takes
> His license in the field of time,
> Unfettered by the sense of crime,
> To whom a conscience never wakes. (5–8)

He will not lose himself in the natural, Romantic world of the "noble savage," but will accept the full responsibility and pain that come with mature, moral choice. It is good, proclaims Tennyson confidently, to have a conscience, to be a man, even if that conscience causes us to suffer mental, emotional, and spiritual anxiety. From this point on, it becomes clear to Tennyson that the way of resolution will come not through a return to the innocence of childhood but through the development of adult discernment.

And part of that maturity and discernment will be the realization that we cannot hide from experience, that we must, instead, seek it out and face it. There is another thing he does not envy:

> Nor, what may count itself as blest,
> The heart that never plighted troth
> But stagnates in the weeds of sloth;
> Nor any want-begotten rest. (9–12)

In this life we must take risks, must be willing to be vulnerable. If we are to grow, we must not, like that great proto-Romantic, Hamlet, become sullen and apathetic. When the ghost of his father appears to him and calls on him to avenge the father's cruel and treacherous murder, Hamlet accepts the call immediately but then expresses that acceptance in the form of an almost ludicrously inappropriate simile:

> Haste me to know't, that I, with wings as swift
> As meditation or the thoughts of love,
> May sweep to my revenge. (I.v.29–31)

"I find thee apt," responds the ghost, but then, recognizing that his son's simile lacks the active and martial vitality necessary if he is to carry out his commission, follows with a warning:

And duller shouldst thou be than the fat weed
That roots itself in ease on Lethe's wharf,
Wouldst thou not stir in this. (32–34)

The third stanza of section 27, I would argue, is meant to echo
the ghost's warning to his lethargic and indecisive son. Tennyson
well knew that the Romantics shared Hamlet's besetting sin: what
the Church Fathers called sloth. There is in the character of Hamlet (as there was in the soul of most of the Romantic poets) a
strong temptation to spiritual acedia or torpor that dooms the
would-be hero to choose thinking over acting, smoldering angst
over swift resolve, self-protective hysteria over direct engagement.

By the twenty-seventh section of *In Memoriam*, Tennyson has
learned that Hamlet's way is a dead end, that it saves us from imme-
diate pain only to destroy us in the long run. The risk must be taken
if life is to be lived fully. The pain of loss must not cause us to close
ourselves off from the possibility of losing again. If Tennyson is to
leave the "Hamlet temptation" behind and progress forward, then
he must not say (or even wish) that he had never met Hallam.
Rather, he must say:

I hold it true, whate'er befall;
    I feel it, when I sorrow most;
    'Tis better to have loved and lost
Than never to have loved at all. (13–16)

I'm sure all of you have heard those last two lines before, but most
of you probably thought that they referred to a male-female love
affair, rather than to a male-male friendship. For Tennyson the
lines are a triumphant assertion of the risk-it-all mentality of the
Victorian explorer who would rank ignorance as a far greater evil
than pain. It is an assertion that is easy to acknowledge in the
abstract but is not so easy to proclaim after one has been wounded
emotionally. In his *Autobiography*, the Victorian Mill clearly states
that despite the pain of his mental crisis, he does *not* regret the
education that led to the crisis; for that education was the very

thing that prepared him to be the great social thinker and reformer that he became. In section 27, Tennyson realizes the same.

Indeed, I do not speak facetiously or callously when I say that were it not for the death of Hallam, Tennyson would most likely *not* have developed into the great poet that he became. He would have remained a Romantic imitator of Keats rather than maturing into the Victorian Age's single greatest voice.

ECHOES

Those with good ears may note that the final two triumphant lines of #27 echo an earlier section (#1) in which Tennyson fears that the forces of time and death will boast: "'Behold the man that loved and lost / But all he was is overworn.'" This parallel is not accidental; it is, in fact, central to the wider structure of the poem. Tennyson was well aware of the necessarily fragmented and episodic nature of his epic and attempted to overcome that obstacle by repeating key themes, words, and images throughout the poem. As in an opera by Wagner, Tennyson uses these repeated themes, words, and images as literary leitmotifs that add a vibrant dimension of referentiality and structural cohesion to the work. Like a medieval tapestry, then, *In Memoriam* is composed of carefully woven, crisscrossing threads; however, like the motives of a classical symphony or the riffs of a jazz piece, those threads shift, develop, transpose, and eventually resolve themselves.

Perhaps the most consistent and powerful leitmotif in the poem is the image of hands reaching up, out, or down: in #1, the hands reach "through time to catch / The far-off interest of tears"; in #7, the poet waits for a hand "that can be clasped no more." Persistently, and insistently, the hands metaphor will appear and reappear in the poem until it is finally resolved, as we shall see in chapter 11, in #124. These subtle leitmotifs that dot the landscape of the epic mark the clearest method used by Tennyson to lend structure and balance to his work. But they are not the only method. Like Beethoven, Tennyson consciously broke his "symphony of grief" into a series of movements that have their own beginning, middle, and end, while yet connecting to the greater poem. At times these movements are literary in focus (sections 21 through 27, as we saw, mark a pastoral movement not unlike the pastoral movement of Handel's *Messiah*); at times, they are more thematic (taking up a single event, such as the return of Hallam's body by ship to England, or a single issue, such as Tennyson's hopes and fears concerning the nature of the afterlife and whether or not he will be able to "catch up" to Hallam's soul as it ascends higher into the spiritual realms). Although my six-chapter study will attempt to highlight the most famous and most central sections of *In Memoriam*, Tennyson's epic really must be read in full to appreciate its overwhelming complexity and its vast scope: A poetic vista that takes in almost every facet both of grief and of spiritual speculation.

However, the simplest, yet most effective, way by which Tennyson orders and structures the movements of his epic is to shape the progress of the poem (and the grief itself) around three key dates: namely, the three Christmases following the death of Hallam. As anyone who has mourned a lost relative or friend knows, the grief is most intense around the holidays, especially those holidays (such as Thanksgiving in America or Christmas in any Christian country) when people gather for food, drink, and fellowship. Of course, several of the sections memorialize other dates, such as the New Year or the anniversaries of Hallam's death, but the three successive Christmases function most powerfully in the poem as a marker for Tennyson's emotional state and as a link to the wider spiritual issues of the poem.

The poem just analyzed, #27, marks the end of the first major movement of the poem; #28 accordingly takes place at the first Christmas since Hallam's death. And, as might be expected, there is a falling back in this poem toward the Romantic focus of the earlier sections. Progress is never wholly upward; there are always hills and valleys. Still, as the poem progresses from movement to movement, Christmas to Christmas, Tennyson's faith strengthens, and he embraces more and more the forward-looking ethos of Victorianism. Casting aside the sloth of Hamlet and taking up instead the challenge of the third traveler in #21, Tennyson Agonistes wrestles his way into the Victorian Age.　　　　　⌒

10

TENNYSON'S *IN MEMORIAM*
Crisis of Faith

AT ABOUT THE MIDWAY POINT of *In Memoriam*, Tennyson offers a series of three connected sections (54–56) that, to me, present the fullest, most concise expression of the wider Victorian crisis of faith. In the space of three poems, Tennyson manages to incarnate the whole diverse panoply of intellectual, emotional, and spiritual distresses that would rock the minds, hearts, and souls of his fellow Victorians when the wider implications of the new science began to be felt. The poems capture nothing less than the social crisis of an entire age, but they embody that moment in terms of the personal crisis of a single individual.

I CAN BUT TRUST

The crisis begins in the first stanza of section 54 with a feeble attempt on the part of the griever to assert some kind of faith in a greater benevolent design in the universe:

> O, yet we trust that somehow good
> 　　Will be the final goal of ill,
> 　　To pangs of nature, sins of will,
> Defects of doubt, and taints of blood; (1–4)

Though he sees only pain, misery, and death around him, the poet longs to believe that this present, temporary evil will somehow prepare the way for the triumph of life, joy, and love.

He longs to discern a hidden, cosmic plan that will lend meaning and purpose to such faith-crushing anomalies as hereditary diseases, irrational acts of evil, and human inconstancy. He wants, that is, to be able to view the evil and suffering he sees around him as a *felix culpa,* a blessed guilt that will lead, in the fullness of time, to a greater good.

He continues to express this longing, this desperate hope in the two stanzas that follow:

> That nothing walks with aimless feet;
>   That not one life shall be destroyed,
>   Or cast as rubbish to the void,
> When God hath made the pile complete;
>
> That not a worm is cloven in vain;
>   That not a moth with vain desire
>   Is shriveled in a fruitless fire,
> Or but subserves another's gain. (5–12)

I once saw on a secretary's desk a plaque with the following inscription: "I know I'm special, cuz God don't make no junk." Though the language here is more sophisticated and profound, the sentiment is identical. The grieving poet needs to believe that nothing that happens on this earth is arbitrary, that even the death of the smallest of animals fulfills a role in the greater plan of God. After all, did not Jesus promise that God remembers each sparrow and numbers each hair on our heads (Lk 12:6–7)? Most people can handle pain and grief when they can see some reason for it, some higher good that it will accomplish; but when the death appears aimless and fruitless, when it promises neither tragic wisdom nor redemptive suffering, then who can bear up under it?

It is this lack of a clear vision of providential purpose that leads the poet to despair:

> Behold, we know not anything;
>   I can but trust that good shall fall
>   At last—far off—at last, to all,
> And every winter change to spring.
>
> So runs my dream; but what am I?
>   An infant crying in the night;
>   An infant crying for the light,
> And with no language but a cry. (13–20)

How can his limited sight pierce through the centuries of pain to come and see the light on the other side? Even if it does come, even if the cold, desolate winter does finally thaw, it will be far off. The poet can know nothing and can trust nothing for sure; even his great and noble theodicy *(In Memoriam)* that seeks to find an answer to grief is nothing but the cry of an infant. In the face of that most dreaded prospect, that life is a meaningless joke, the poet is weak, confused, and blind. Where now, the reader asks, is that "beam of darkness" Tennyson calls for in the Prologue?

SURVIVAL OF THE FITTEST

But alas, this is not the worst of it; in the section that follows, the poet realizes to his horror that the fundamental teachings of the new science only confirm his existential despair.

Yes, section 55 (like section 54) begins with a small ray of hope, but this time that hope is exhausted in a mere one stanza (rather than the three of #54):

> The wish, that of the living whole
>   No life may fail beyond the grave,
>   Derives it not from what we have
> The likest God within the soul? (1–4)

As in #54, Tennyson tries vainly to assure himself of something for which he seems, at present, to have little evidence. Does not our whole inner being cry out that we are immortal, that our lives will not end with death and the grave? Are we not incapable of imagining our own extinction or that of another? And if this is so, if this inability to accept our own mortality is real (not a mere delusion), then what can be its origin? Surely, offers the desperate poet, the origin of that voice that whispers to us these promises must be our soul, that part of us which is linked directly to (and made of the same immaterial substance as) God.

But this faint hope quickly disintegrates in the face of the new science:

> Are God and Nature then at strife,
>   That Nature lends such evil dreams?
>   So careful of the type she seems,
> So careless of the single life,
>
> That I, considering everywhere
>   Her secret meaning in her deeds,
>   And finding that of fifty seeds
> She often brings but one to bear; (5–12)

What Tennyson here shudders at (what so strongly contradicts what God, through the voice of Tennyson's soul, seems to promise) is that part of Darwinian evolution known, variably, as natural selection or the survival of the fittest: the notion that evolution works through a weeding-out process by which the strong adapt and survive and the weak perish. (The phenomenon can be actually observed on a micro-level in strains of bacteria that adapt to new antibiotics; Darwinians, now and then, theorize that the same process occurs as well on the macro-level.) To the poet in crisis what this scientific theory suggests is that nature is a wholly amoral and indifferent mistress who is willing to sacrifice (without remorse) forty-nine seeds as long as one survives. Indeed, she does not care for the individual at all, only for the species (type) of which that individual is a part.

The precise numbering used here is surely meant as a telling contrast to the loving shepherd of Luke 15:3–7, who will abandon ninety-nine sheep in order to seek out the one that is lost. From his childhood, the poet had trusted in the Bible's depiction of a caring, involved God who respects the dignity and integrity of each individual; now both science (natural selection) and his own tragic experience (the unnecessarily early death of Hallam) suggest the very opposite. Such is the implication of Darwinian evolution, and Tennyson, as poetic spokesman of his age, must wrestle with this implication and find some kind of answer or resolution.

But here I must pause. When I make reference to Tennyson's response to Darwinian evolution, I speak, of course, anachronistically, for, incredible as it may sound, Tennyson composed this section of the poem at least twenty years before Darwin published his *Origin of Species* (1859). I noted in an earlier chapter that Tennyson was perhaps the most scientifically informed poet who ever lived, and here (as in many other sections of *In Memoriam*) he proves himself to be just that. Tennyson kept carefully abreast of the new discoveries in astronomy and geology, and, long before the theories of Darwin and the popularizing of those theories by T. H. Huxley had made headlines, Tennyson was already struggling with the implications of an immensely old universe.

His chief source for the scientific speculations that pervade *In Memoriam* is considered by nearly all critics to be Sir Charles Lyell's *Principles of Geology* (1830–33), a work that postulated that the earth itself (like a sandy shore) has been formed over eons of slow and gradual erosion and accretion. As a scientist, Lyell held a uniformitarian (rather than a catastrophic) view of the geological history of the earth. It was not the Genesis flood and its aftermath that formed the mountains and valley, but an infinitesimally slow process that has remained uniform over millions of years. This uniformitarian theory has perhaps never been more powerfully expressed than in a haunting, lyrically beautiful stanza from the 123rd section of *In Memoriam*:

There rolls the deep where grew the tree.
　Earth, what changes hast thou seen!
　There where the long street roars, hath been
The stillness of the central sea. (1–4)

It is precisely stanzas such as these that have won Tennyson his reputation for being a poet who not only understood science in the abstract but felt its deeper, poetic meaning as well. Yes, Tennyson knew his science well, and, like a good Victorian, he seems to have considered it one of his duties as a poet not just to struggle with the crises of his age, but to actually predict in advance what those struggles would be and to deal with them, first, in his poetry. In *In Memoriam*, Tennyson is more than a Victorian everyman; he is a forerunner, a John the Baptist paving the way for a triumphant society that will rise above its limitations and fears.

Of course, in #55, there is as yet little of that triumph; the poem, in fact, ends on a note of despair, desperation, and utter impotence:

I falter where I firmly trod,
　And falling with my weight of cares
　Upon the great world's altar stairs
That slope through darkness up to God,

I stretch lame hands of faith, and grope,
　And gather dust and chaff, and call
　To what I feel is Lord of all,
And faintly trust the larger hope. (13–20)

In Genesis 28:12–13, Jacob sees a vision of a ladder that stretches from earth to heaven, and on that ladder he sees angels ascending to and descending from the throne of God. Tennyson here sees a similar ladder, but at the top is not the Father of all Lights, but darkness, emptiness, and ignorance. How can the Victorian faith in progress (or *any* faith) hold out against such darkness? Indeed, so crushed is Tennyson as he stares into the face of this seemingly godless abyss that he falls back (I would argue) on one of the most despairing lines in Romantic poetry to help him express his own despair. I refer to a line from the fourth stanza of Shelley's "Ode to the West Wind" in which the isolated and angst-ridden poet cries out:

> I fall upon the thorns of life! I bleed!

Tennyson, faltering for a moment in the midst of his gradual embrace of Victorianism, seems as if he too will be crushed by the thorns of his own inner torment and inability to reconcile himself with a universe that seems black and empty.

In the previous chapter, we discussed the recurring image of hands reaching out; here that image reappears amidst great anguish and pathos, the visual equivalent of the infant's cry in the night. Here is the Victorian dark night of the soul, the horror of a blind, impersonal universe.

EXTINCTION

Yet still we have not reached the worst, for natural selection holds an even darker implication that the poet must wrestle with as well:

> "So careful of the type?" but no.
>   From scarped cliff and quarried stone
>   She cries, "A thousand types are gone;
> I care for nothing, all shall go.
>
> "Thou makest thine appeal to me:
>   I bring to life, I bring to death;
>   The spirit does but mean the breath:
> I know no more." (1–8)

Not only does nature care nothing for the individual; she does not even care for the type. Whole species have gone extinct before (from the dinosaur to the dodo bird), and many more will follow. Far from the benevolent mother she was to the Romantics, nature here becomes a cruel, devouring beast who seems to take pleasure in destruction. She cannot be appealed to or appeased by our prayers, and she stands as a brutal reminder that what we call our soul is but a breath of wind.

What then of Man, asks the poet? Can it be possible? Shall he,

> Man, her last work, who seemed so fair,
>   Such splendid purpose in his eyes,
>   Who rolled the psalm to wintry skies,
> Who built him fanes of fruitless prayer,
>
> Who trusted God was love indeed
>   And love Creation's final law—
>   Though Nature red in tooth and claw
> With ravine, shrieked against his creed—
>
> Who loved, who suffered countless ills,
>   Who battled for the True, the Just,
>   Be blown about the desert dust,
> Or sealed within the iron hills? (9–20)

Can it be that Man, with all his accomplishments, all his dreams and struggles, will end up an extinct species? Is the noble human race destined to be just another stratum in the fossil record? All the causes for which we fought, the mighty cathedrals that we built, the books of philosophy over which we labored: How is it possible that all these will be wiped away and the entire memory of *Homo sapiens* erased from the earth? If nature is indeed "red in tooth and claw" (a terrifying image that reverberated throughout the Victorian Age), what hope is there for our race?

No, concludes Tennyson, if extinction is our final end, we are truly

> A monster then, a dream,
> A discord. Dragons of the prime,
>   That tare each other in their slime,
> Were mellow music matched with him. (21–24)

In #27, Tennyson chooses to be a man with conscience and choice rather than a beast of the field. Here, he wonders if the beasts are not our betters, for at least they never held any pretensions to being a chosen race with a specific destiny and a soul (or selfhood) that would endure forever. If extinction is our goal, then our greatest nobility is, in fact, our greatest torment and shame. If all that lies ahead of us are the stone quarries, the iron hills, and the tar pits, then we are truly a cosmic farce, the bad joke of the universe. At least the dinosaurs never fancied themselves the Crowns of Creation. At least they never deluded themselves into believing that such a thing as love existed and that that love had created their world.

Tennyson closes his darkest section with a faint ray of hope:

> O life as futile then, as frail!
>   O for thy voice to soothe and bless!
>   What hope of answer, or redress?
> Behind the veil, behind the veil! (25–28)

The "thy" here refers not to God but to Hallam. If only Hallam could speak one word to him, he would know then that our soul is immortal, that something will survive the onslaught of nature. If the sought-for voice is heard, then love, purpose, and design need not be meaningless, hollow words. If he speaks, hope is possible; *all* is possible.

If not, we are left only with the words of the Apostle Paul: "If in this life only we have hope in Christ, we are of all men most miserable" (1 Cor 15:19; KJV).

II

TENNYSON'S IN MEMORIAM
Faith in Religion Restored

I N SECTION 56, Tennyson looks directly in the face of Darwinian theory, with its dark implication that man himself, as a species, may someday go extinct, and it fills him with dread. In response, the grieving poet calls out, in pain and desperation, for a single touch from the soul of Hallam. Modern intelligent-design theorists (particularly Michael Behe) have recently revived one of the strongest arguments against natural selection. The argument (known as irreducible complexity) states that if a single biological system (for example, the eye or the cell) can be identified that could not have been produced by a slow process of unguided, incremental change, then the theory must be abandoned. In parallel fashion, Tennyson realizes, at the end of #56, that an authentic word from Hallam would shatter (at least for him personally) the implication that our souls (like our bodies) are mortal and that all there is in the universe is nature (matter) and the void. In section 95 (the climax of *In Memoriam*), that longed-for word finally comes.

LOVE'S DUMB CRY

The setting for this, the loveliest and most moving section of the poem, is a gathering of the Tennyson family at Somersby. The time is roughly two years after the death of Hallam.

In the opening four stanzas, Tennyson describes, in precise detail, a calm, peaceful night in which all of the natural and animal world seems in perfect harmony. So still, in fact, is the evening that the candles burn "unwaveringly"; so uncannily silent that the poet can hear, far off in the distance, the sound of the brook warbling gently. Tennyson and his family linger late on the green lawn, singing together in joyous unison:

> While now we sang old songs that pealed
>   From knoll to knoll, where, couched at ease,
>   The white kine [cattle] glimmered, and the trees
> Laid their dark arms about the field. (13–16)

The mood evoked by the opening stanzas of the poem is one of utter tranquility, culminating in lines 15–16 with their almost pantheistic suggestion that nature is embracing herself. The stage is indeed set for a mystical exchange that will give the lie to sections 54–56.

For awhile, the singing and fellowship continue. Then, slowly, the others depart, leaving the poet alone in his solitude:

> But when those others, one by one,
>   Withdrew themselves from me and night,
>   And in the house light after light
> Went out, and I was all alone, (17–20)

This gradual, twenty-line build-up (a build-up that is as long as most of the other sections of the poem), stills, almost hypnotizes, the reader, preparing him (like Tennyson) for the vision to come. But it does something else. It calls up certain events that Wordsworth recalls in his own epic autobiographical poem, *The Prelude*, events that mark a moment of mystical intercourse between man and nature. In these moments (Wordsworth calls them "spots of time," XII.208), the young poet, after being cut off from his companions, experiences a vision of both the beauty and the awe, the richness and the starkness, of nature, a vision that overwhelms his senses and fills him with a feeling of "visionary dreariness." In that mystical moment, time is suspended, and the full weight of the power of nature sinks deep into the psyche of the poet, where it remains like a seed that can be called up and reexperienced whenever the adult poet needs to be restored and revivified.

In section 95, Tennyson has such an experience, an experience that allows him to transcend *both* the over-self-consciousness and self-pity of his earlier Romantic mode and the restless Victorian need to move ever forward. In place of both extremes, the poet finds something of permanence. This mystical process of discovery begins in line 21, as the poet, tranquil and alone, is suddenly seized by a strange passion:

> A hunger seized my heart; I read
>   Of that glad year which once had been,
>   In those fallen leaves which kept their green,
> The noble letters of the dead. (21–24)

The "glad year" to which Tennyson refers is not a literal year but a symbol for his many years of friendship with Hallam; the reference to "leaves" and "green" recalls the pastoral imagery of #21; the book in which he reads is the book of his own nostalgic memories. This time, however, his recollections do not lead simply to Wordsworthian reverie or Keatsian tears or Byronic grief; the poet has moved beyond them all.

This time he attacks the memories with a force, an urgency, and a will that allow him to rise above simple remorse:

> And strangely on the silence broke
>   The silent-speaking words, and strange
>   Was love's dumb cry defying change
> To test his worth; and strangely spoke
>
> The faith, the vigor, bold to dwell
>   On doubts that drive the coward back,
>   And keen through wordy snares to track
> Suggestion to her inmost cell. (25–32)

With memory comes courage, a courage that is grounded in love and that is stronger and more enduring than time. Tennyson may have in mind one of Shakespeare's most beloved sonnets:

> Let me not to the marriage of true minds
> Admit impediments; love is not love
> Which alters when it alteration finds,
> Or bends with the remover to remove.
> O, no, it is an ever-fixed mark
> That looks on tempests and is never shaken;
> It is the star to every wand'ring bark,
> Whose worth's unknown, although his height be taken
> Love's not Time's fool, though rosy lips and cheeks
> Within his bending sickle's compass come;
> Love alters not with his brief hours and weeks
> But bears it out even to the edge of doom.
> If this be error and upon me proved,
> I never writ, nor no man ever loved. (Sonnet 116)

For Tennyson (as for Shakespeare), true love (if it deserves the name of true love) must be constant, unchanging, and eternal. Change, upheaval, even death cannot rob it of its purity or its tenacity. The love shared by Tennyson and Hallam was a true one (as fixed and as steadfast as the North Star alluded to in Shakespeare's sonnet), and that love itself now challenges the poet to test its worth and see what it is made of.

But Tennyson, the Victorian wrestler, does not stop there. Along with this unshakable, time-defying love comes a stronger, purer faith that is not afraid to doubt, to search for truth even in the midst of error. In the next section (#96), Tennyson expresses this more clearly in two lines that are often quoted: "There lives more faith in honest doubt, / Believe me than in half the creeds" (11–12). True faith (like true love), asserts Tennyson, is neither blind nor rose-colored; just so, the one who possesses such a faith does not prove his integrity by withdrawing from the issues of his day but by engaging them directly. *In Memoriam*, as a document of the Victorian Age, calls for a religion unafraid to address the challenges of the new science. To faith, hope, and love must be added the classical virtue of courage.

Indeed, it is only when Tennyson screws up his courage, when he turns around and looks death, doubt, and despair in the face that the moment of vision comes:

> So word by word, and line by line,
>   The dead man touched me from the past,
>   And all at once it seemed at last
> The living soul was flashed on mine.
>
> And mine in it was wound, and whirled
>   About empyreal heights of thought,
>   And came on that which is, and caught
> The deep pulsations of the world,
>
> Aeonian music measuring out
>   The steps of Time—the shocks of Chance—
>   The blows of Death. At length my trance
> Was canceled, stricken through with doubt. (33–44)

Slowly, bit by bit, the souls of Tennyson and Hallam reach out toward each other, until, with a flash, they touch, meld, and become one. In many of the "spots of time" episodes that are scattered throughout the *Prelude* (as well as in many of his free-standing lyrics), Wordsworth uses the word "flash" to mark the exact mystic moment when the natural world entered into his psyche. So here, Tennyson uses the same word to identify that "eternal second" when Hallam's spirit and his own were reunited.

In a flash, the two souls, so long separated, are drawn together and whirled throughout the cosmos. And suddenly, in that supranatural moment, the poet who prayed (in the Prologue) that "heart and soul [would] make one music as before," hears (indeed, experiences firsthand) something even greater: that universal harmony, that song of the old sympathetic universe he feared had been lost forever. In his spiritual journey he receives, finally, that higher vision he sought in his deepest crisis (54–56); he sees, that is, a fate and purpose higher than death, chance, and time. More than that, he touches the very beating heart of the universe, touches on something so great, so beyond his comprehension that he can only give it the name "that which is." (Wordsworth, in a similar mood, calls it "something far more deeply interfused." "Tintern Abbey," line 96.)

But the vision cannot be sustained, for doubt (the typical, cowardly kind) steps in; like Peter walking on the water, the poet soon slips back into his heavy, earthly element (Mt 14:22–32). And as he does, he mourns his inability to express fully what he saw:

> Vague words! but ah, how hard to frame
> In matter-molded forms of speech,
> Or even for intellect to reach
> Through memory that which I became. (45–48)

Tennyson, I would argue, echoes in lines 45–46 the very words that Dante speaks in the last canto of the *Divine Comedy* after he has looked directly on the face of God. Wishing to put the experience into words yet knowing simultaneously that he cannot, Dante exclaims in frustration: "How speak trans-human change to human sense." Like Dante before him, Tennyson here suggests that manmade, physical-based words cannot possibly plumb the depths of the divine, spiritual wisdom he encountered. More than a mere "spot of time," the poet's vision has pervaded him at a level deeper even than memory. Indeed, his experience was more than a matter of seeing or hearing or feeling. It was a matter of *becoming* something greater, something more than a middle-aged Victorian gentleman.

Tennyson has heard the voice, has felt the touch he cried out for at the end of #56. Technically speaking, the section could have ended here, but, wonderfully, it does not. In the next stanza, Tennyson reechoes, word for word, an image used earlier in stanza four (see lines 13–16, quoted above):

> Till now the doubtful dusk revealed
> The knolls once more where, couched at ease,
> The white kine glimmered, and the trees
> Laid their dark arms about the field. (49–52)

The section has come full circle, but not quite. At the end of his inner journey, Tennyson arrives back where he started, but at a higher level. It has been done for him just as he asked it to be in the Prologue: "That mind and soul, according well, / May make one music as before, / But vaster." As at the close of all true visions, all is the same, and yet all has changed.

And then it comes, the final confirmation of the lasting truth and reality of his vision:

> And sucked from out the distant gloom
> A breeze began to tremble o'er
> The large leaves of the sycamore,
> And fluctuate all the still perfume,

> And gathering freshlier overhead,
> Rocked the full-foliaged elms, and swung
> The heavy-folded rose, and flung
> The lilies to and fro, and said,

> "The dawn, the dawn," and died away;
> And East and West, without a breath,
> Mixed their dim lights, like life and death,
> To broaden into boundless day. (53–64)

The breeze that blows gently through the final three stanzas is almost a felt presence; the peace that descends on Tennyson (and us) lies almost beyond words. All seems to hang breathlessly on a frozen, threshold moment of time. On the simplest level, what happens at the end of the section is that the dawn rises (Tennyson's timeless trance has lasted the whole night long), and, for a brief, fragile moment, moon and sun, night and day, darkness and light, West and East, touch and embrace.

But that is not all that happens. Two other contraries meet in that magical moment of suspension: death and life, Hallam and Tennyson. The meeting, of course, is a brief one, but it is enough. When the moment ends, and the opposites go their way, it is not to reestablish an eternal separation, a cosmic estrangement, but "to broaden into boundless day." I would encourage you to speak that line out loud very slowly. It is the verbal equivalent of a cool breeze on a hot, humid day; it carries with it the very depth and breadth of infinite space. And, of course, it is more. It marks the very antithesis of that terribly heavy, funereal line that ends #7: "On the bald street breaks the blank day." The weight has finally lifted; the wait has finally passed.

TENNYSON'S TESTIMONY

Though #95 restores and emboldens Tennyson's faith in the immortality of the soul and the meaningfulness of the universe, it is not until section 124 that the poet attempts to put the exact nature of that faith into words. For it is in this section that we are given nothing less than Tennyson's spiritual testimony.

The poet begins in stanza one by invoking, haltingly, the dual mystery of the Christian God (the Trinity and the Incarnation), and then proceeds, in a famous statement that is "pure Tennyson," to explain where he did *not* find God:

> I found him not in world or sun,
>   Or eagle's wing, or insect's eye,
>   Nor through the questions men may try,
> The petty cobwebs we have spun. (5–8)

Once, after looking through a microscope at the myriad of miniature life forms that dwell in a drop of water, Tennyson purportedly exclaimed: "Strange that these wonders should draw some men to God and repel others. No more reason in one than in the other." Tennyson (both as believer and as poet) refused in the end to subscribe either to the argument by design (that sees in the design of nature the hand of a Creator) or to natural theology (that would deduce evidence for a benevolent, merciful God in the benign aspects of the natural world). On the contrary, he believed that, when it came to faith, science was neutral and finally irrelevant.

Tennyson asserts as much in the stanza quoted above, and then, shockingly, extends his rejection of science as a clear avenue to faith in God to include the efforts of philosophy and theology ("petty cobwebs") as well. Neither in scientific nor in doctrinal theories was Tennyson willing (or able) to rest his faith. Rather, he asserts:

> If e'er when faith had fallen asleep,
>   I heard a voice, "believe no more,"
>   And heard an ever-breaking shore
> That tumbled in the Godless deep,
>
> A warmth within the breast would melt
>   The freezing reason's colder part,
>   And like a man in wrath the heart
> Stood up and answered, "I have felt." (9–16)

"The heart hath reasons," said Pascal (*Pensées,* 423), "that the mind knows nothing about." Rational proofs are sufficient neither to support nor to debunk the claims of religion. The most Tennyson can claim in his Victorian, post-Enlightenment world (a world that, as we saw in chapter 8, has separated rational knowledge from emotional faith, empirical facts from intuitive beliefs) is that he has felt the truth and presence of God, has experienced it in his heart.

Yes, he has felt it passionately, a warmth that can stand resolutely against all existential despair, all fear of the void, and he will assert that warmth like a man in wrath. Or rather, no, not quite that strongly:

> No, like a child in doubt and fear:
>   But that blind clamor made me wise;
>   Then was I as a child that cries,
> But, crying, knows his father near; (17–20)

He is still, as in #54, "an infant crying in the night," but now, for the first time, as he cries out in the dark night, he feels the nearness of his (heavenly) father. In a *Grief Observed*, C. S. Lewis, mourning for the tragic death of his wife, offers a similar, tenuous image of a griever regaining his faith. Picture a man, writes Lewis, locked in a dark dungeon and nearing the point of total despair. Suddenly, far off in the distance, he hears the sound of a bird and realizes, with a flash, that he is not in a dungeon at all, but out in the open air. The knowledge does not change his situation, he is still lost in the dark, but now he knows that he is neither alone nor in prison.[1]

Like Lewis, Tennyson realizes that he is not alone, that his father is near, and, with that vital realization, he can end his testimony on a note of triumph that resolves one of the key images of the work:

> And what I am beheld again
>   What is, and no man understands;
>   And out of darkness came the hands
> That reach through nature molding man. (21–24)

Finally, after all the groping and reaching, after all the poet's frustrated attempts to stretch his hands out toward Hallam, toward God, toward hope, it is another set of hands (those of God) that reach down for him with a loving embrace: arms that descend out of the darkness, bringing light. But they are not detached hands, coming only in moments of crisis. They are, rather, hands that have worked and will continue to work through nature, and even through evolution, to shape and to mold man.

---

[1] C.S. Lewis, *A Grief Observed* (New York: Bantam, 1976), 74.

12

TENNYSON'S *IN MEMORIAM*
Faith in Science Restored

By SECTION 95, Tennyson's faith in religion (particularly in the immortality of the soul) is restored. Indeed, so powerful is that restoration that, were Tennyson writing merely a personal lyric on the loss and recovery of his faith, the epic could have ended with the last glorious line of #95. However, by this stage in the poem, a solely personal resolution will not suffice. Tennyson Agonistes, the Victorian wrestler, has, long before #95, raised the stakes of his poem to include not only the doubts within his own soul but the doubts and the fears and the confusions of his entire society. More is at issue than Tennyson alone; many more questions must be answered before the duty-bound poet can lay down his pen. There remains the need for a fuller answer to the challenges of the new science. In section 118, therefore, Tennyson extends his personal, spiritual restoration to include a direct engagement with the uniformitarian theories of Lyell.

THE APE AND THE TIGER

Section 118 begins with a resolution on the part of the restored poet to take a second, more in-depth look at evolution and all that the process implies:

Contemplate all this work of Time,
 The giant laboring in his youth;
Nor dream of human love and truth,
 As dying nature's earth and lime; (1–4)

Far from a blind, mechanical, arbitrary process run by a ravenous Nature "red in tooth and claw" (#56), evolution here transforms itself into a Herculean figure struggling to perfect and purify itself. No, asserts the poet as he looks, *really* looks, at the whole vast process, human life with all its dreams and accomplishments is not just so much refuse in the garbage pile of the cosmos. We must not think that we are merely nature's compost,

But trust that those we call the dead
 Are breathers of an ampler day
 For ever nobler ends. . . . (5–7)

I have always loved the phrase, "ampler day"; it has the same effect on me as the last line of #95: "To broaden into boundless day." Both phrases convey a feeling of fresh air and wide-open, infinite spaces; both are like the breath of spring after a long and heavy winter.

Tennyson, the poet's poet, knows exactly the effect that the phrase will have on his reader, but he means it to have more than solely an emotional impact. Tennyson has a message, one he has learned through the discipline of pain and grief, one that he would share with his age. Put simply, this is his message: As our bodies evolve, so too must our souls; as nature presses upward and outward to perfect itself, so too does the spirit of man struggle to move beyond its limited mode of existence to a fuller, richer one. Rather than cancel each other out, the two progressions (the natural and the supernatural) complement and reinforce each other: one is a parallel, a type, a figure for the other.

Not only religion, but the scientific observations and theories of the geologists, the astronomers, and the paleontologists speak forcefully of a greater purpose that is working itself out on our planet:

> . . . They say,
> The solid earth whereon we tread
>
> In tracks of fluent heat began,
>   And grew to seeming-random forms,
>   The seeming prey of cyclic storms,
> Till at the last arose the man; (7–12)

Yes, at first glance, evolution (and uniformitarianism) may seem arbitrary and even chaotic, but to the one who looks closer, an underlying purpose is evident: one that runs unswervingly from the volcanic eruptions and lava flows of the unformed earth, to the vast deserts of the ice age, to the formation of man himself. Though there are setbacks and momentary returns to chaos that may confuse and disorient the untrained, slothful eye, the direction of all this geological and biological ferment has ever been, and ever shall be, upward and forward.

And that forward thrust, Tennyson makes clear, exists on both a natural and an anthropological level:

> Till at the last arose the man;
>
> Who throve and branched from clime to clime,
>   The herald of a higher race,
>   And of himself in higher place
> If so he type this work of time
>
> Within himself, from more to more;
>   Or, crowned with attributes of woe
>   Like glories, move his course, and show
> That life is not as idle ore, (12–20)

What Tennyson asserts here is that just as the natural world has evolved from lower, brute forms to greater complexity, so is man evolving from his primitive state toward a state of greater beauty. Or, to put it another way, just as Man *(Homo sapiens)* is the crown of natural evolution, so is mankind itself developing upward toward a Crowning Race of men who will be to primitive man what man is to the ape. The evolution of man, that is, is a type of the greater evolution of nature. Indeed, even in the unique development from infancy to adulthood of each individual we may spy yet another type of the wider evolutionary process.

In typical fashion, Tennyson here expresses poetically what has been a key concept in the formation of evolutionary science: ontogeny ("the development of an individual organism") recapitulates phylogeny ("the historical development of a tribal or racial group"). To claim that the former recapitulates (or reenacts) the latter is to claim that the entire developmental history of a species is played out in miniature in the life cycle of each member of that species. This assumption is key to much modern speculation on the origin and development of man. For example, when anthropologists try to account for the evolution of speech in primitive man, they will often use as an explanatory parallel the evolution of speech in modern human infants. Even evolutionary-minded theologians and cultural anthropologists use the same reasoning. Thus, though the Bible claims that all men started as monotheists and then fell away into idolatry, pantheism, and animism, the modern claims that the process worked the other way. And, to reinforce their evolutionary view, they point to the way human children tend to progress from a pantheistic, idolatrous view of religion and nature to a more mature monotheism. This assumption, that micro reflects macro, also appears in the scientific claim that unobserved extra-species development (macro-evolution) is supported by observed intra-species adaptations (micro-evolution).

But Tennyson's goal here, of course, is not to prove the validity of an evolutionary schema; he seeks instead to find in the theory of evolution both a resolution for his grief and a vision of hope for himself and his age. And he finds that resolution and that vision in this simple but profound paradigm of a three-tiered evolution (individual, species, terrestrial), each level of which promises growth and progress. But what is to be the method of that process? Like the evolution of the earth (which necessitated periods of intense heat and pain), the evolution of Man will (nay, *must*) involve suffering. No, exclaims Tennyson, the life of man (both as individual and as species) "is not as idle ore,"

> But iron dug from central gloom,
>   And heated hot with burning fears,
>   And dipped in baths of hissing tears,
> And battered with the shocks of doom
>
> To shape and use. Arise and fly
>   The reeling Faun, the sensual feast;
>   Move upward, working out the beast,
> And let the ape and tiger die. (21–28)

Man *will* be purified and perfected, he will, in time, reach and become the Crowning Race, but first he must, as it were, be tried like gold in the fire. Only by such a process can the dross of primitive man be washed out; only thus, through pain and suffering, can the savage, bestial side of man ("the ape and the tiger") be worked out. And, of course, if pain is needed to effect the evolution of the species as a whole, so must it be applied to each individual in turn, if that individual is to grow and develop. The grief Tennyson has struggled with throughout *In Memoriam* is itself a type of the more general sorrow that the human race must suffer if it is to continue on the rising path of progress. Though Tennyson was far less credal or orthodox in his faith than Cardinal Newman, he arrives here (via new science rather than traditional Catholicism) at the same vision of our world as a "moral factory for the melting, refining, and moulding . . . of the raw material of human nature." The parallel is a surprising one, and yet, at the same time, not so surprising: both Tennyson and Newman were, after all, raised in an age that worshiped progress and upward growth as God-ordained mandates.

All along Tennyson has known it, known that we as individuals and as a species must make our way up the rising path, known too that one cannot ascend the path without suffering. All that he has known, but now, at last, he has come to understand it. For mankind to grow, there must be death; for Tennyson to grow, Hallam must die. On all three levels (individual, species, terrestrial), the password is "progress": a password that is so vital to Tennyson (and his age) that the poet actually inscribes it into the very form of section 118. I'm sure you have noticed by now that in almost all cases, the individual stanzas that make up *In Memoriam* end with some kind of punctuation mark, whether a period, a comma, or a semicolon. Tennyson quite consciously breaks this pattern in #118. Stanzas two, four, and six do not end with a punctuation mark, causing the syntax and the thought patterns of each stanza to run directly into the stanza that follows it (in poetry, this literary device is called an enjambment). What better way to express three-tiered progress than to effect in the form of the poem itself a three-fold shattering of normal limits and boundaries and a pressing outward and upward of meaning and life. Stanzas two, four, and six progress directly, inexorably into stanzas three, five, and seven. Nothing can stop them. The end point must be reached.

THE CROWNING RACE

In the Epilogue to *In Memoriam*, Tennyson further develops this three-tiered evolution to present his reader with both a metaphor for the process and a vision of what the Crowning Race of Man will entail. The Epilogue takes place on the wedding day of another of Tennyson's sisters, Cecilia. Tennyson's choice to end his epic with a wedding is significant, for by so doing he casts his work in the same mold as the Bible itself: which begins with a death (the Fall of Man) and ends with a wedding (the Great Marriage of Christ the Bridegroom and his Bride, the Church; see Rev 22). That is to say, both the Bible and *In Memoriam* are essentially comedies, for they end not with a death, but with a marriage (the same is true, allegorically speaking, of *The Divine Comedy*). Our universe, finally, is a comic one, for it is moving toward love and consummation, rather than separation and death: even science, Tennyson discovers, shares this intimation of a glorious end. Indeed, the Epilogue ends on a profound theological and philosophical note that is also, oddly, scientific. That closing note comes in the form of an image that reconciles creation and evolution:

> A soul shall draw from out the vast
> And strike his being into bounds,
> And, moved through life of lower phase,
> Result in man, be born and think,
> And act and love, a closer link
> Betwixt us and the crowning race. (123–28)

The metaphor is condensed but clear; its source, the new field of embryology. As we have seen many times now, Tennyson was a poet who knew and understood science, and who kept himself abreast of new theories and developments. In the case of the lines quoted above, Tennyson alludes to the discovery that the fetus, at various stages of gestation, has animal characteristics (fish, reptile, and so on). Adapting this discovery for his own poetic use, Tennyson suggests, quite intriguingly, that just as the creation of a child in its mother's womb takes the growing embryo on an evolutionary journey through lower animal forms, so man himself, though a special and purposeful creation of God, developed physically through evolutionary stages. (This fetal development, incidentally, adds yet another tier to the three levels of progress.) Once again we spy, as we did at the end of #118, the divine hands of God reaching through nature to mold and shape mankind.

However, here, at the close of his epic, Tennyson desires to draw our vision beyond these crude origins to take in a glorious vision of that longed-for Race that will mark the final crown of evolution:

Of those that, eye to eye, shall look
   On knowledge; under whose command
   Is Earth and Earth's, and in their hand
Is Nature like an open book;

No longer half-akin to brute,
   For all we thought and loved and did,
   And hoped, and suffered, is but seed
Of what in them is flower and fruit; (129–36)

Tennyson, in keeping with the positivistic, utilitarian dreams of his age, pictures the final state of man as a utopic one, one in which man has finally conquered and controlled nature. At this end point of his evolutionary growth, man has tamed not only the beast without but the one within as well: the ape and tiger of #118 have been worked out for good. Best of all, in the glow of this coming human victory, Tennyson is enabled to look again at the tragedies and triumphs of our present humanity and see in them not meaningless suffering nor the vanity of human pretension, but so many life-giving seeds that will someday sprout and flower. Truly, as Jesus proclaims in his last public discourse (Jn 12:24), it is better that the grain of wheat die, for, unless it die, it cannot bear fruit.

Hallam, Tennyson has come to realize, was just such a seed. But he was also something greater:

Whereof the man that with me trod
   This planet was a noble type
   Appearing ere the time was ripe,
That friend of mine who lives in God,

That God, which ever lives and loves,
   One God, one law, one element,
   And one far-off divine event,
To which the whole creation moves. (137–44)

Hallam, as the old cliché goes, was born ahead of his time. For Tennyson, however, this old cliché takes on a new meaning when applied to his departed friend. Hallam was, quite literally, a pre-figuring of that great and noble Crowning Race. The world was not ready for Hallam, for his mixture of gentleness and strength and for the wide but focused scope of his mind. Only when utopia comes will his virtues be recognized and appreciated. And so, for now (like the sleeping King Arthur on the isle of Avalon), he rests with God: not just a misty, personless God, nor even a removed deistic God, but one who is actively propelling history forward on its progressive way.

In theology, the study of the end times is called eschatology, and Tennyson's vision here is truly eschatological, for it envisions not just the end but the purpose and meaning of that end. And that purpose is nothing less than love, unity, and perfect consummation. In fact, the last stanza mirrors the closing lines of Dante's *Divine Comedy* with its vision of a universal harmony bound together by love. Yes, Hallam's death did signal a physical break in human relationship and intimacy, but that loss is nothing when viewed against the greater love that is to come.

II

TENNYSON AND THE VICTORIAN SPIRIT OF PROGRESS

.

13

THE EDUCATION OF
ALFRED, LORD TENNYSON

IN PART I OF THIS BOOK, I presented Tennyson as the fullest example of a Victorian who (like Newman and Mill) suffered a crisis of faith and resolved it; in Part II, I shall take up Tennyson again but from a somewhat different perspective. I shall begin in this chapter by surveying the early life and career of Tennyson in an attempt to achieve a fuller understanding of the man who would become Victorian England's most celebrated poet. Then, in chapters 14 to 17, I shall trace (as I did in my study of *In Memoriam*) Tennyson's shift from Romantic to Victorian by looking at a series of shorter poems that he composed just before and shortly after the death of Hallam in 1833. In the former poems, we shall uncover Tennyson's struggles with his own isolation as a Romantic poet and the dangers attendant upon such isolation; in the latter, we shall see how he broke out of this isolation to embrace a force greater than himself: the Victorian spirit of progress. Then, in chapters 18 and 19, I shall (as in Part I) compare and contrast Tennyson's poetry with the work of two Victorian prose writers (Thomas Carlyle and John Ruskin); in the essays of these two grand sages, we shall encounter a strong critique of the progressivist spirit Tennyson championed. Next, in chapters 20 to 22, we shall return to Tennyson, and take up his later, slightly darker works: poems in which the poet offers his own critique of Victorian society.

Central to these chapters will be a close analysis of two books from Tennyson's epic reworking of the legends of King Arthur: *Idylls of the King*. As a contrast to Tennyson, in chapters 23 and 24, I present another poet, Matthew Arnold. Unable in his poetry to shift from Romantic to Victorian, Arnold turned instead to a critical, prophetic type of prose that proved as powerful an embodiment of Victorianism as the poetry of Tennyson.

YOUNG MAN TENNYSON

Alfred Tennyson was born in 1809 to George Clayton Tennyson and Elizabeth Fytche.

His father was a stern and unhappy man who had been disinherited by his rich, controlling father in favor of his younger, more charismatic brother, Charles. That is not to say George's father did not give him financial assistance—George and his family remained somewhat comfortably in the middle echelons of the British squirearchy—but he gave it to him more as a charitable handout than as an inheritance due him as the eldest son. Without his father's estate to rely on, George was forced to take a career: he chose the ministry and became rector of Somersby, though he himself was somewhat of a religious skeptic. To make matters worse, George came of a family whose genes carried both epilepsy and madness, not to mention a propensity for alcoholism and drug addiction to which Alfred's brothers fell prey. This "black blood" of the Tennysons haunted Alfred for most of his life with fears of insanity and epilepsy.

In stark contrast, George's wife, Elizabeth, was a simple, cheerful woman with a strong Christian faith and an un-self-conscious, if somewhat frivolous, approach to life. Though she supplied her children with the love and emotional support they seldom got from their father, she was unable to provide them with either discipline or the necessary social graces. This is not wholly surprising, since she gave birth to twelve children in fourteen years, only the first of whom died young (two boys, Frederick and Charles, followed; Alfred Tennyson was born fourth). Life at Somersby was erratic at best, fluctuating wildly between times of angst and even hatred brought on by the gloomy father and his troubles and times of true familial joy and camaraderie.

As is often the case with large families, the Tennysons could be quite insular and were often the scandal of the neighborhood with their unkempt hair and clothes and their often aloof manner. But their eccentricities also drove them close to one another. One feels sure that, at least when George Tennyson was in a good mood, Christmases must have been delightful at Somersby. In *In Memoriam* #78, which recounts the second Christmas after Hallam's death, we get a brief glimpse of what family life at Somersby must have been at its best:

> As in the winters left behind,
>   Again our ancient games had place,
>   The mimic picture's breathing grace,
> And dance and song and hoodman-blind. (9–12)

Certainly there was joy to be had; indeed, the junior Tennysons often remind us of those other insular children of a humble country parson, the Brontës, who like the Tennyson children were quite adept at amusing themselves with imaginary worlds and feats of poetic and dramatic bravado. In fact, just as the Brontë sisters published together an early, pseudonymous collection of poetry, so did Tennyson and his two older brothers publish a similar work: *Poems by Two Brothers* (1827).

Alfred Tennyson was very much a product of Somersby and of his oddly matched parents. Both his mother's faith and his father's skepticism wrestled continuously within the poet, as did the sentimental optimism of the one and the frustrated melancholy of the other.

There is in Tennyson and his poetry a sense of both the special child gifted by the muse and the disinherited orphan who must struggle in a world he did not make under a fate he did not chose. Like his siblings, Tennyson remained unkempt in appearance even after he became famous: his long, dark, wavy hair setting off his strong, handsome features and his six-foot-plus frame. To add to his personal eccentricities, Tennyson most often dressed in a sombrero and Spanish coat, remnants of an early trip he took in support of Spanish revolutionaries (oddly paralleling Wordsworth's youthful flirtations with revolutionary France; both poets later went conservative!).

Though Tennyson would later move in the highest, most influential circles of society, he remained in many ways an enigmatic figure, lonely, isolated, and insular. He delighted in reading his works aloud in public (he was quite dramatic), but was often awkward in conversation and became moody and depressed when his poetry was criticized. His awkwardness was exacerbated further by his severe nearsightedness, which caused him to look strangely at people and led him often to press his face onto the ground in order to see clearly whatever natural objects he hoped to enshrine later in his poetry.

IMITATOR OF KEATS

As we saw in chapter 7, Tennyson's moodiness and shyness were mitigated somewhat when he enrolled at Trinity College, Cambridge (in 1827), met Arthur Hallam, and joined the Apostles. As noted earlier, Hallam (who I might add here was also an intimate friend of that other great Victorian institution: the future prime minister Gladstone) encouraged Tennyson in his poetry. In fact, when Tennyson published his second volume of poetry, *Poems, Chiefly Lyrical* (1830), Hallam wrote a glowing review of the work for the *Englishman's Magazine*, in which he presented Tennyson as the true successor to Shelley and Keats, a poet "of sensation rather than reflection."[1] In his review, Hallam praises Tennyson's "luxuri-

---

[1] Quoted in *Tennyson's Poetry*, edited by Robert W. Hill, Jr. (New York: W. W. Norton, 1999), 582.

ance of imagination" and his "exquisite modulation of harmonious words." More vitally, he highlights the poet's "vivid, picturesque delineation of objects, and the peculiar skill with which he holds all of them fused . . . in a medium of strong emotion." Though Hallam's review was a bit excessive, much of Tennyson's characteristic genius is displayed in the collection, particularly in what is surely the finest poem of the volume: "Mariana." In this strangely beautiful poem, Tennyson offers an intense, psychological portrait of a dejected woman who has been jilted by her lover and is left to grieve in isolation in a decaying house. Tennyson borrowed the character and the situation from a few lines in Shakespeare's *Measure for Measure*, but the mood and the tone are pure Keats:

> With blackest moss the flower-pots
>   Were thickly crusted, one and all;
> The rusted nails fell from the knots
>   That held the pear to the gable-wall.
> The broken sheds look'd sad and strange;
>   Unlifted was the clinking latch;
>   Weeded and worn the ancient thatch
> Upon the lonely moated grange.
>   She only said, "My life is dreary,
>   He cometh not," she said;
>   She said, "I am aweary, aweary,
>   I would that I were dead!" (1–12)

Almost plotless, the poem (here and in the six stanzas that follow) devolves into a succession of set pieces that capture and freeze the emotions that simmer just beneath the surface. Indeed, although the theme of the poem (dejection) is a wholly abstract one, Tennyson successfully objectifies and concretizes it by embodying Mariana's grief in a series of precisely described objects: the black moss, the thickly crusted pots, the rusted nails, the broken sheds, and so on.

Tennyson, after the manner of the great odes of Keats, succeeds in this task by providing his readers with what the great critic-poet

T. S. Eliot would later term an "objective correlative."[2] According to Eliot, an objective correlative is an external object, situation, or chain of events that parallels an internal emotion. Emotions are stubbornly difficult things to express in language; they cannot be perceived by the senses, and they refuse to be contained by "dictionary definitions." But with the help of carefully chosen external objects, situations, and events, it is possible to render them concrete, to give them (if I may paraphrase Shakespeare) a local habitation and a name. Tennyson does so in "Mariana" not only through the medium of his brooding set pieces (which hang languidly in the mind long after the poem has been put aside), but by incarnating Mariana's dejection in the verbal music of the poem. The stanzas are so written, the syllables so arranged, that the poem cannot be read quickly (thus, in the film version of *My Fair Lady*, Henry Higgins tests Eliza Doolittle's skills at diction by having her read aloud the above quoted stanza with her mouth filled with marbles). The heavy, melancholy four-line refrain that ends the first stanza and that is repeated again and again (with slight modifications) throughout the poem intensifies the mood and allows the reader almost to feel the silent despair and isolation that has gripped the soul of the title character.

Hallam was well aware of Tennyson's unique gift for objectifying emotion and painting with words, and he hoped, I believe, to play Coleridge to Tennyson's Wordsworth: that is, to be the critical voice that would guide Tennyson to the full realization of his poetic genius. He was, however, perhaps too eager to mold Tennyson into a spokesman for the kind of introspective poetry that the Apostles liked; indeed, the Apostles' tendency to view themselves as an elite coterie and their overpraise of Tennyson may have increased the poet's isolation from the greater society. Why was this the case? Perhaps the liberal, progressive views of the Apostles and of their society at large impelled the young collegians to carve out a separate poetic world. Perhaps in the absence of that sacred permanence that

---

[2] "Hamlet and His Problems," *Critical Theory Since Plato* (New York: Harcourt, Brace, Jovanovich, 1992), 766.

those other young collegians at Oxford had found in traditional Anglicanism, the Apostles (especially Hallam) needed to fashion a space with its own liturgy and symbols, its own ritualistic language. In any case, they were sure of one thing: poetry (to quote John Stuart Mill) was not a thing to be heard, but overheard.

In December 1832, Tennyson published a new volume called *Poems* (dated 1833), in which the full flowering of his talents was finally displayed. The volume included "The Lady of Shalott," "The Palace of Art," "The Lotos-Eaters," and "The Hesperides" (all discussed below) as well as other fine pieces. Still, though the poems had great merit, they all had a tendency to focus too exclusively on isolated Romantic figures. Had Tennyson continued to write in this mode (as Hallam and the Apostles would no doubt have encouraged him to do), his talent might very well have dried up. Hallam's sudden death, however, along with the negative, even vicious, reviews his poems received, dealt Tennyson a blow that forced him to remake and reconstruct both himself and his poetry. Tennyson continued to write poetry (both *In Memoriam* and other individual lyrics), but he did not publish another collection until 1842. During this "silent decade," he also spent much time revising and greatly improving upon his earlier poems (it is these revised versions I will analyze below).

FROM KEATS TO VIRGIL

Slowly, painfully, Tennyson matured into one of the greatest poetic craftsmen in the language, showing a facility for numerous (often experimental) poetic forms and a flawless ear for meter and tone. Just as importantly his poetry expanded slightly in range, became less detached and insular. In the year of Hallam's death he wrote both his most controlled evocation of isolation ("Tithonus") and his first celebration of the Victorian spirit of progress ("Ulysses"). "Locksley Hall" soon followed, a poem that, like *In Memoriam* itself, traces the shift in the poet's sensibility from Romantic isolation to Victorian progress (I will discuss all three poems below).

Still, though Tennyson perfected his lyrical gifts, his poems never found the intellectual, philosophical depth they lacked (as noted in the one positive review of his 1833 *Poems* by J. S. Mill!). Only in *In Memoriam* was Tennyson able to find and sustain a unifying idea that would link his separate lyrics into a satisfying and organic intellectual whole; too often his other works, though possessing a lyricism unmatched in English poetry, lack any real point.

At times, Tennyson would fill this intellectual void with an oversentimentality, as in a long poem that was popular when written but is now scorned by modern critics: Enoch Arden. Also lacking in Tennyson's work is any real, physical passion; his poetry (unlike that of Shelley and Keats) is marked by an almost total absence of erotic imagery (oddly, this is also true of that other great nineteenth-century poet to whom the Victorians awarded the laureateship: William Wordsworth). Indeed, one cannot help but discern a link between Tennyson's ludicrously extended betrothal to Emily Sellwood and the absence of a sexual dimension to his poetry. And yet, so overpowering was his poetry that Tennyson was able to overcome these very real flaws in his work to carve himself a permanent place in the pantheon of British (if not world) poetry.

In closing, I cannot help but return to that most decisive moment in the life and career of Alfred Lord Tennyson: the early, sudden death of Arthur Hallam. Not only *In Memoriam*, but the finest section of *Idylls of the King* ("Morte d'Arthur," see chapter 7), the companion pieces, "Tithonus" and "Ulysses," and his best lyrics were directly inspired by Hallam's death and possess an elegiac tone that is as sincerely personal as it is universally accessible. Indeed, the mature Tennyson is often compared to Virgil, the great Roman poet who, in a poetry of the purest lyricism, not only sang (in his *Eclogues*) the death of the pastoral world, but balanced perfectly (in his *Aeneid*) the melancholy sense of loss that accompanies the Fall of Troy and the death of Aeneas's family with the celebration of the mighty Roman Empire to come.

Let me end this chapter, then, by quoting what is surely Tennyson's greatest lyric, one that embodies both the tonal quality and elegiac mood of Virgil, a poem so rich in its sound you will swear that it rhymed (but it doesn't) and so heartfelt in its sorrow that you cannot help but make that sorrow your own:

> Tears, idle tears, I know not what they mean,
> Tears from the depth of some divine despair
> Rise in the heart, and gather to the eyes,
> In looking on the happy autumn-fields,
> And thinking of the days that are no more.
>
> Fresh as the first beam glittering on a sail,
> That brings our friends up from the underworld,
> Sad as the last which reddens over one
> That sinks with all we love below the verge;
> So sad, so fresh, the days that are no more.
>
> Ah, sad and strange as in dark summer dawns
> The earliest pipe of half-awaken'd birds
> To dying ears, when unto dying eyes
> The casement slowly grows a glimmering square;
> So sad, so strange, the days that are no more.
>
> Dear as remember'd kisses after death,
> And sweet as those by hopeless fancy feign'd
> On lips that are for others; deep as love,
> Deep as first love, and wild with all regret;
> O Death in Life, the days that are no more!

Like "Mariana," the poem makes use of a heavy, melancholy refrain, but this time, the poem is suffused with a quieter maturity, a sense of experience suffered and accepted. And the music, too, is richer, more carefully modulated. The poet's first love has been lost and all the freshness has gone, but there reverberates beneath the lines, in a region deeper and more sonorous than rhyme, the faint hope of return. It is enough.

14

THE ISOLATED POET
Tennyson the Romantic I

IN "MARIANA," Tennyson presents his reader with a sensitive, overly self-conscious figure who feels cut off and isolated from her society. To embody that isolation, Tennyson makes use of a series of objective correlatives that render these emotions concrete. So much I suggested in the previous chapter. I would now go on to suggest further that "Mariana" actually makes use of a double layer of objective correlatives. That is to say, while the black moss, thickly crusted pots, and rusted nails of the poem give form to Mariana's grief and dejection, Mariana herself objectifies and concretizes Tennyson's own struggles with grief and isolation. Indeed, throughout his early works, Tennyson seems ever in search of characters and situations that will embody his own inner moods of alienation and quiet despair. Two such poems that achieve this most successfully are "The Lady of Shalott" and "Tithonus."

THE SHADOWS ON THE CAVE WALL

In what is perhaps his most lyrically beautiful and formally challenging poem, "The Lady of Shalott," Tennyson takes up an issue that was deeply felt by the Romantic poets, especially Shelley and Keats. In the poem, Tennyson whisks us away to the legendary realm of Camelot, a place and an age that haunted him throughout his poetic career and that he realized in epic form in his *Idylls of the King*. The protagonist here, however, is not Arthur or Guinevere, not Lancelot or Merlin, but the fabled Lady in the High Tower, a Rapunzel figure cut off from the world and its passions. In the first two stanzas, Tennyson quickly establishes the poem's physical terrain:

> On either side the river lie
> Long fields of barley and of rye,
> That clothe the wold and meet the sky;
> And thro' the field the road runs by
>   To many tower'd Camelot;
> And up and down the people go,
> Gazing where the lilies blow
> Round an island there below,
>   The island of Shalott.
>
> Willows whiten, aspens quiver,
> Little breezes dusk and shiver
> Thro' the wave that runs for ever
> By the island in the river
>   Flowing down to Camelot.
> Four gray walls, and four gray towers,
> Overlook a space of flowers,
> And the silent isle imbowers
>   The Lady of Shalott. (1–18)

Before considering the content of the stanzas, let us pause to consider their poetic form. For his poem, Tennyson chose a grueling rhyme scheme: AAAABCCCB. To make it even more difficult, the B rhymes (with two exceptions) are always Camelot and Shalott. The rhyme scheme (a medieval form used often in the Wakefield Cycle of Mystery Plays) not only demonstrates Tennyson's incredible facility with the language, but lends the poem an incantatory quality that weaves a spell 'round its listener. In fact, the singer Loreena McKennitt (in her album, *The Visit*) has set the poem to an appropriately haunting, medieval melody. To listen to her sing it is to be lifted up on the airy wings of poesy.

Perhaps to complement the intricate rhyme scheme, Tennyson chose for the setting of his poem a simple landscape. Long miles of fertile fields are bisected by a river that flows downward from the silent island of Shalott to the bustling court of Camelot. In the center of the island is a tower in which lives the Lady of Shalott, a fairy figure whose face is never seen, but whose voice is often heard by reapers at dawn. Allegorically speaking, Shalott (and its embowered Lady), as it lies at the head of the river, is the source of the life and vitality that flows down to and is embodied in Camelot; yet, oddly, the Lady seems unable to partake of that life of which she is the source.

In Part II of the poem, we learn why:

> There [in her tower] she weaves by night and day
> A magic web with colors gay.
> She has heard a whisper say,
> A curse is on her if she stay
>   To look down to Camelot.
> She knows not what the curse may be,
> And so she weaveth steadily,
> And little other care hath she,
>   The Lady of Shalott.
>
> And moving thro' a mirror clear
> That hangs before her all the year,
> Shadows of the world appear.
> There she sees the highway near
>   Winding down to Camelot;
> There the river eddy whirls,
> And there the surly village-churls,
> And the red cloaks of market girls,
>   Pass onward from Shalott.
>
> Sometimes a troop of damsels glad,
> An abbot on an ambling pad,

Sometimes a curly shepherd-lad,
Or long-hair'd page in crimson clad,
   Goes by to tower'd Camelot;
And sometimes thro' the mirror blue
The knights come riding two and two:
She hath no loyal knight and true,
   The Lady of Shalott.

But in her web she still delights
To weave the mirror's magic sights,
For often thro' the silent nights
A funeral, with plumes and lights
   And music, went to Camelot;
Or when the moon was overhead,
Came two young lovers lately wed:
"I am half sick of shadows," said
   The Lady of Shalott. (37–72)

The curse that holds the Lady prisoner in the tower forbids her not only to participate in the life around her but even to look directly at that life. Day and night, she sits with her back to the window, her only visual link a mirror that reflects the images of the bustling world that passes by outside her window. With intense longing and yearning, she gazes dreamily into that mirror, and whatever life she sees reflected therein (whether shepherds or knights, abbots or damsels) she weaves into her magic web.

She is, in short, one of the prisoners in Plato's Cave. According to the strange allegory that Plato conjures for us in his *Republic*, the prisoners in the cave are tied down in high-backed chairs that allow them to look only directly in front of them. Behind them a mighty fire roars brightly, and between them and the fire puppeteers parade human figures whose shadows are cast on to the wall. The prisoners (who spend their lives staring at the wall) take these shadows for reality, never realizing that what they are seeing is but the shadow of a shadow, a reflection of a reflection: twice-removed from the real world outside the cave. In *The Republic*, the fate of the prisoners is, finally, that of all people who have not learned the discipline of philosophy; however, the tendency to focus on (and even celebrate) objects that are twice-removed from reality is a fault chiefly found in poets. In fact, as poetry is but an imitation of an imitation of Reality (what Plato calls the Forms), and as the perfect City and its Guardians must be regulated by these Forms, Plato finds it necessary to kick the poets out of his *Republic.* They can have no place in a well-regulated society.

Of course, the England of Tennyson's day was fast becoming indifferent (if not hostile) to poetry, due not to Platonic philosophy but to modern utilitarian theories that privileged progress and efficiency over art and emotion. Tennyson, in his early, Romantic phase, has little to offer in response to this threat. The Lady of Shalott, a thinly disguised metaphor for the Romantic poet, is completely isolated from her world. All she can do is weave the events she dimly sees into her visual poem (her web) as Homer's Helen weaves into a tapestry the battles of the Trojan War she initiated but is unable to influence. Indeed, the poem suggests that her isolation is, in part, the price she must pay for the poem (web) she weaves. We cannot, it seems, possess the world both physically and aesthetically. Like the proverbial prima ballerina she must chose either life or art; she can't have both.

To be enabled to create, to possess the gift, the Lady must forsake actual knowledge of both eros and thanatos, the rites both of love (the newlyweds) and of death (the funeral procession). She lives in a dream world in which she yearns for but can never possess earthly love. Her mournful cry ("I am half sick of shadows") is that of an innocent who desires experience. And yet, as we shall see, her initiation into that world of experience, her rite of passage, will lead not to enlightenment but to darkness, to a consummation not of love but of death. Unlike the Platonic philosopher, her education will lead to destruction, an end to growth.

Her fatal coming-of-age is initiated by the sudden appearance of the great knight of romance:

> A bow-shot from her bower-eaves,
> He rode between the barley-sheaves.
> The sun came dazzling thro' the leaves,
> And flamed upon the brazen greaves
>   Of bold Sir Lancelot. (73–77)

I stop in the middle of the stanzas to emphasize the fact that the word Lancelot here takes the place of the expected "Camelot"; three stanzas later (line 117), it will take the place of "Shalott."

The significance of this is, I think, quite clear: the moment Lancelot appears on the scene his magnificence consumes the whole chivalrous world. He *becomes* Camelot and all it represents.

Then, when the Lady sees the bold knight reflected in her mirror, and her heart goes out to him fully, her self (fragile as it is) is both sucked into and effaced by the glory of Lancelot:

> His broad clear brow in sunlight glow'd;
> On burnish'd hooves his war-horse trode;
> From underneath his helmet flow'd
> His coal-black curls as on he rode,
>   As he rode down to Camelot.
> From the bank and from the river
> He flash'd into the crystal mirror,
> "Tirra lirra," by the river
>   Sang Sir Lancelot.
>
> She left the web, she left the loom,
> She made three paces thro' the room,
> She saw the water-lily bloom,
> She saw the helmet and the plume,
>   She look'd down to Camelot.
> Out flew the web and floated wide;
> The mirror crack'd from side to side;
> "The curse is come upon me," cried
>   The Lady of Shalott. (100–117)

G. K. Chesterton has commented (in *Orthodoxy*) that all fairy-lands (beginning with Eden) are conditional places: all that beauty and wonder is yours, but you mustn't say the word "cow."[1] Like glass, they have strong exteriors, but shatter easily when they are dropped. The Lady of Shalott (like Eve before her) seeks an experience she was not meant to have, and by so doing, brings a curse down upon her. The spell is broken, the mirror cracks, and her web (her poem and her self) comes unraveled. She has tasted the forbidden fruit, which, in the poem, signifies not only physical contact with the world but a loss of sexual innocence. The helmet, the plume, and the blooming water-lily are all clear symbols for sexual awareness and the loss of virginity (as is, of course, the cracked mirror).

In the closing section of the poem, the Lady leaves her tower, descends to the river bank, and, in a boat on which she has inscribed her name *(The Lady of Shalott)* floats down the river toward Camelot. But her actions cannot prevent the curse from taking its dark vengeance. As she glides along the water singing a mournful tune, her blood slowly freezes, and before reaching Camelot, she dies. In describing her death, Tennyson includes lines that allude to at least two tragic female figures: Cassandra, the Trojan prophetess whose predictions always came true but who was never believed; and Ophelia, the sad, jilted lover of Hamlet who goes mad, falls in a brook, and, chanting snatches of old songs, is pulled under the water. The former allusion surfaces in lines 128–30 ("Like some bold seër in a trance, / Seeing all her own mischance— / With a glassy countenance"); the latter in line 152 ("Singing in her song she died"). In both cases, the heroines alluded to are sensitive and even wise, yet their sensitivity and wisdom are ineffectual to save either others or themselves.

In the final two stanzas, the boat washes ashore at Camelot, and the knights and ladies stare in wonder at her dead body. The last words of the poem are put in the mouth of Lancelot, who, though ignorant of the fact that it was he himself who lured her to her death, speaks her epitaph: " 'She has a lovely face; / God in his

---

[1] G. K. Chesterton, *Orthodoxy* (New York: Doubleday, 1990), 55.

mercy lend her grace, / The Lady of Shalott'" (169–71). The ending of the poem, though beautiful in its lyricism, leaves little hope for the artist. Though art may be the power that sustains the world (as Shalott is the source of the river that nourishes Camelot), and though that power may be magical, the poet cannot impact the world directly with his art. He must either choose isolation or risk entry into a world that will stifle (or kill) his gift.

THE GIFT THAT IS ALSO A CURSE

"The Lady of Shalott" offers Tennyson's fullest statement on the isolation of the Romantic poet, but it is by no means his only poem to explore this subject. Let us look briefly, then, at one other poem that takes up a similar theme, but handles it in a slightly different way. The poem is "Tithonus," and in it we hear the voice of a tortured, melancholy anti-Romantic who, like the Lady of Shalott, possesses a gift that he wishes he did not have.

In Greek mythology, Tithonus was a beautiful youth who attracted the loving attention of the Goddess of the Dawn. In a fit of passion, she won for her lover the gift of immortality, but, in her haste, she forgot to ask that he also be awarded the gift of immortal youth. In the opening lines of the poem, the incredibly aged Tithonus (who now lives in the mystical, legendary realm of the dawn) mourns his sad and lonely fate:

> The woods decay, the woods decay and fall,
> The vapors weep their burthen to the ground,
> Man comes and tills the fields and lies beneath,
> And after many a summer dies the swan.
> Me only cruel immortality
> Consumes; I wither slowly in thine arms,
> Here at the quiet limit of the world. (1–7)

Only Tennyson, I believe, could have captured with such pathos the psychological grief and anguish of being eternally old in the presence of eternal youth. Line 5 alone expresses in four painfully elongated words what might have been the fate of Adam and Eve had they, after falling from grace, returned to Eden and eaten of the Tree of Life. And only Tennyson could have understood the full meaning of Tithonus's plight: to have achieved a thing that Romantic poets such as Shelley and Keats longed for (the desire to live in a world of direct sensation, far above all mundane, earthly cares) and then to regret bitterly that achievement.

Too late, Tithonus realizes that to be special, to be chosen by the gods and breathed on by the muses, to be the revolutionary prophet of the new day, is, in a profound sense, to cease to be human. Yes, his divine gift allows him to see things no mortal eye has ever seen. In the poem, for example, he watches with awe as the horses of the dawn

> shake the darkness from their loosened manes,
> And beat the twilight into flakes of fire. (41–42)

Still he cannot thrive or even live in this immortal realm: "Yet hold me not forever in thine East," he begs his bride, "How can my nature longer mix with thine?" (64–65). Like the Byronic hero, Tithonus has tasted of forbidden fruit and found it bitter. In trying to soar to the level of an angel, he has fallen almost to the level of a beast. By stepping outside of the natural cycle of day, month, year, he has stranded himself in a threshold world of utter isolation.

In the end, the "poet," having broken all human limits, wishes only to be human again:

> Let me go; take back thy gift.
> Why should a man desire in any way
> To vary from the kindly race of men,
> Or pass beyond the goal of ordinance
> Where all should pause, as is most meet for all? (27–31)

The sentiment expressed here is not that of a Romantic, but of a man from the eighteenth-century Age of Reason. Indeed, it sounds very much like the neoclassical ethos advocated by Alexander Pope in his theodicy, *An Essay on Man* (see chapter 7). Nothing to excess; everything in moderation. Keep within the classical boundaries of reason and common sense. Do not attempt to rise higher or sink lower than your rung on that Great Chain of Being that stretches from God down to the smallest microbe. Tithonus, like many a Romantic before him, has yearned to step out of his rung. In the poem, he achieves his heart's desire . . . and with it, finds despair.

As before, Tennyson offers little hope for the would-be Romantic poet: either he remains within the social sphere and thus sacrifices the divine vision, or he risks all to achieve it and lives to regret his choice. Either way, the poet, isolated and embowered, has little to offer society. ☜

15

THE DANGERS OF SOLIPSISM
Tennyson the Romantic II

JUST AS TENNYSON OFTEN VISITED the legendary realms of King Arthur in search of poetic subjects and inspiration, so he often turned his poetic eye toward the mythology of ancient Greece. We have already seen in the previous chapter how Tennyson transformed the myth of Tithonus into an exploration of Romantic longing and angst. In the same way, Tennyson, in several of his other works ("The Lotos-Eaters," "The Hesperides," "Ulysses," and so on), scoured the Hellenic past of Europe for characters, events, and symbols by which and through which he could embody his own inner struggles and those of his age.

LET US ALONE

In "The Lotos-Eaters," as in "Tithonus," Tennyson seizes hold of an ancient legend of which little is actually told (Homer, in *Odyssey* IX, devotes less than a hundred lines to the tale) and invests that legend with a weight of psychological analysis. Here, in brief, is what Homer tells us: Odysseus and his crew, during their long journey from Troy to Ithaca, land on an island where the friendly natives feast them on lotos. Unfortunately, those who taste of this honey-sweet plant lose all desire to return home or to take risks or to do anything but sit around all day and eat lotos. Like

proto-hippies, Odysseus's men quickly throw off all their responsibilities and elect to stay forever on the island, but Odysseus, who
has not tasted of the fruit, herds them forcefully back onto the
ship. Out of this sketchy raw material, Tennyson fashions a poem
that is both a lyrical tour de force and a profound statement of
what happens to the artist who forsakes his social role.

The poem is broken into two parts: a five-stanza, third-person
prologue that establishes the setting, and an eight-stanza, first-
person choric song that expresses the sailors' desire to stay on the
island. The opening stanzas are written in a slow, stately, complex,
traditional form known as the Spenserian stanza after Edmund
Spenser, who used the form for his epic *Faerie Queene* (the difficult rhyme scheme is ABABBCBCC). The stanzas of the choric
song, on the other hand, are free-flowing, incantatory, and
chaotic, with no set rhyme scheme or line length. Tennyson's purpose for using this hybrid form is, I think, quite clear: When the
men taste of the lotos and cast off all their social cares and duties,
the traditional strictures of society (represented by the Spenserian
stanzas) break down and a kind of aesthetic anarchy takes over.
Indeed, in another poem (written in the same year) that also
explores the seductive power of art, "The Hesperides," Tennyson
employs a similar device, beginning the poem with a stately Mil-
tonic blank verse, then breaking into a burst of lyricism even
more chaotic than the choric song of "The Lotos-Eaters."

In the opening Spenserian stanza of "The Lotos-Eaters," Tennyson quickly sets a mood of lazy indolence:

> "Courage!" he [Odysseus] said, and pointed toward the land,
> "This mounting wave will roll us shoreward soon."
> In the afternoon they came into a land
> In which it seemed always afternoon.
> All round the coast the languid air did swoon,
> Breathing like one that hath a weary dream.
> Full-faced above the valley stood the moon;
> And, like a downward smoke, the slender stream
> Along the cliff to fall and pause and fall did seem. (1–9)

Unlike England, which is even now gearing up for the full flowering of her Industrial Revolution, the isle of the Lotos Eaters is a place of perpetual stasis that seems ever to hang in suspension. It is, Tennyson tells us: "A land where all things always seem'd the same" (24). Odysseus's men quickly fall under the island's slothful spell:

> They sat them down upon the yellow sand,
> Between the sun and moon upon the shore;
> And sweet it was to dream of Fatherland,
> Of child, and wife, and slave; but evermore
> Most weary seem'd the sea, weary the oar,
> Weary the wandering fields of barren foam.
> Then some one said, "We will return no more;"
> And all at once they sang, "Our island home
> Is far beyond the wave; we will no longer roam." (37–45)

And with that, they throw away any hope of future progress or discovery. Like the Romantics at their most melancholy, they relish their memories but lose the will to regain their past. They give in to that Byronic kind of overemotionalism and intense self-pity that John Stuart Mill almost succumbs to during his crisis and that the Tennyson of *In Memoriam* #27 is also tempted to embrace. Or again, like Hamlet, that great proto-Romantic, they allow their "native hue of resolution" to become "sicklied o'er with the pale cast of thought." They have had enough of progress, of responsibility, of order. With line 45, the Spenserian stanzas end, and the sailors throw themselves (languidly) into the choric song.

"There is sweet music here" (46), they sing, in this place where all is gentle, cool, wet, and soporific. Then, in a fit of solipsistic ennui and self-satisfaction, they complain:

> Why are we weigh'd upon with heaviness,
> And utterly consumed with sharp distress,
> While all things else have rest from weariness?
> All things have rest: why should we toil alone,
> We only toil, who are the first of things,

And make perpetual moan . . .
Why should we only toil, the roof and crown of things?
   (57–62, 69)

Their complaint (line 62 of which directly echoes a line from Keats) possesses a kind of logic, but it is a dangerous logic that, if indulged in by all members of society, would cause progress to grind to a halt. The argument, which is perhaps a parody of England's traditional aristocratic ethos (an ethos the rising Victorian middle class sought to change), is that those who are the best and most fit, those who stand at the top of the food chain, owe it to themselves to take it easy and enjoy their prerogatives. This is, of course, the very opposite of the Victorian call-to-arms that Tennyson would later go on to sound in the latter sections of *In Memoriam* (see chapters 12 and 16): namely, that it is the duty of man (the crown of nature) to continue to evolve and perfect himself (to let the "ape and tiger die"). Indeed, in the epilogue to *In Memoriam*, it is the "crowning race" (of whom Hallam was a "noble type") who will conquer nature and create utopia. Here, in contrast, those who are "the roof and crown of things" desire nothing more than to escape toil and indulge their sloth.

Instead of engaging society and vexing it forward, the sullen sailors cry out:

Let us alone. Time driveth onward fast,
And in a little while our lips are dumb.
Let us alone. What is it that will last?
All things are taken from us, and become
Portions and parcels of the dreadful past.
Let us alone. What pleasure can we have
To war with evil? Is there any peace
In ever climbing up the climbing wave?
All things have rest, and ripen toward the grave
In silence—ripen, fall, and cease:
Give us long rest or death, dark death, or dreamful ease.
   (88–98)

In John 21, Jesus commissions Peter three times to "Feed my sheep"; here, the men abdicate, three times, their responsibility to care for anything or anyone. What is the point, they cry, of ever pushing onward. Unlike the heroic ethos of the *Iliad* (which says that since death is coming and cannot be avoided, we might as well seek glory), they adopt an over-self-conscious, melancholy Romanticism that, like the speaker of Keats's "Ode to a Nightingale" is "half in love with easeful Death." Rather than rise above nature, they seem content to join in a natural cycle that moves from ripeness, to rot and decay, to death; rather than fight against entropy and disorder they give in to it:

> Let what is broken so remain.
> The Gods are hard to reconcile;
> 'Tis hard to settle order once again. (125–27)

There is in these sailors none of that Victorian earnestness that sought to make order out of chaos, none of their commitment to carrying the blessings of civilization to the greater world.

Though the link between the sailors and the artist is perhaps not as clear as it is in "The Lady of Shalott" or "Tithonus," when "The Lotos-Eaters" is read in the context of Tennyson's other work, it is clear that in this poem too Tennyson is musing, in part, on the social role (or lack thereof) of the poet. However, here, Tennyson is more concerned with those forces (mostly psychological) that tempt the artist to remain in isolation rather than risk reentry into society. More than that, Tennyson pierces down to that solipsistic attitude that often allows the artist to rationalize in his own mind his decision to withdraw from all social duties and responsibilities.

In the final stanza of the poem, the sailors take the following oath:

> We have had enough of action, and of motion we,
> Roll'd to starboard, roll'd to larboard, when the surge was
>   seething free,
> Where the wallowing monsters sprouted his foam-fountains
>   in the sea.

> Let us swear an oath, and keep it with an equal mind,
> In the hollow Lotos-land to live and lie reclined
> On the hills like Gods together, careless of mankind,
> For they lie beside the nectar, and the bolts are hurl'd
> Far below them in the valleys, and the clouds are lightly curl'd
> Round their golden houses, girdled with the gleaming world;
> Where they smile in secret, looking over wasted lands,
> Blight and famine, plague and earthquake, roaring deeps
>   and fiery sands,
> Clanging fights, and flaming towns, and sinking ships, and
>   praying hands.
> But they smile, they find a music centered in a doleful song
> Steaming up, a lamentation and an ancient tale of wrong,
> Like a tale of little meaning tho' the words are strong.
>   (150–64)

The gods the sailors refer to are the Stoic, arbitrary gods that Lucretius writes of in his *On the Nature of Things*: gods, that is, who look down with complete indifference on the woes of man. To these gods, mortal men, with all their hopes and dreams, are so many playthings to be interfered with or ignored at will. Both our joys and our pains mean nothing to them. Like these uncaring, self-absorbed deities, the sailors would remove themselves from petty human cares, content to eat their honeyed lotos like mini-gods feasting on nectar and ambrosia. The sailors just cannot be bothered with mundane concerns. They prefer to live in their isolated aesthetic world where each of them is a monarch and a kingdom unto himself.

Though the modern reader may see immediately the danger inherent in this attitude, it was one that the young Tennyson struggled with often, one that took him many years to shake off. Indeed, as we saw in chapter 13, the Apostles were not above fancying themselves a sort of elitist coterie of young literati, with Tennyson as their poetic voice. Apart from the death of Hallam, Tennyson might well have remained forever on the island of the Lotos-Eaters: eternally making his eternal complaint, and only wishing to be left alone.

A Room of One's Own

But let us turn now to a second poem from Tennyson's Romantic period that embodies even more fully than "The Lotos-Eaters" the dangers of aesthetic isolation and the arrogance that accompanies it. The poem is called "The Palace of Art," and it is written in the first person. The speaker of the poem is never directly identified as Tennyson, but the young poet cannot fool us: The poem is strongly autobiographical and deals directly with the poet's own struggles to break free from his youthful flirtations with solipsism.

The poem begins abruptly with a stanza that is unmistakably Tennysonian:

> I built my soul a lordly pleasure-house,
>   Wherein at ease for aye to dwell.
> I said, "O Soul, make merry and carouse,
>   Dear soul, for all is well." (1–4)

What we have here is solipsism at its most extreme: The desire to construct a microcosm for one's soul and to dwell alone in that little world. Indeed, Tennyson goes on to make this clear:

> My soul would live alone unto herself
>   In her high palace there.
> And "while the world runs round and round," I said,
>   "Reign thou apart, a quiet king." (11–14)

Seldom has a poet been so direct in admitting to this temptation to seclude oneself in a personal kingdom and then crown oneself as the sole monarch of that kingdom. But Tennyson does, and then goes one step further: For the next two hundred lines, he describes in detail exactly what every room of his palace of art will look like. That is to say, most of the poem devolves into a succession of tableaux, a catalogue of aesthetic set pieces that are at times extraneous but are more often exquisite in their precise word-painting.

As you can well imagine, the poem lacks the unity of "The Lady of Shalott," "Tithonus," and "The Lotos-Eaters," but what it lacks in tightness, it repays in a rich luxuriance of sound and color. My own favorite "room" depicts the abduction of Europa by Zeus (in the form of a bull):

> Or sweet Europa's mantle blew unclasp'd,
> From off her shoulder backward borne;
> From one hand droop'd a crocus; one hand grasp'd
> The mild bull's golden horn. (117–20)

Another favorite takes us to the side of the sleeping King Arthur (the son of Uther Pendragon) where he rests on the fairy isle of Avalon:

> Or mythic Uther's deeply-wounded son
> In some fair space of sloping greens
> Lay, dozing in the vale of Avalon,
> And watch'd by weeping queens. (105–8)

As these stanzas suggest, the rooms of the palace form a sort of museum of Western culture, a sophisticated, aesthetic world of beauty untrammeled by physical time or space. It marks the embodiment of a sensuous rather than sensual male fantasy: the desire to possess beauty without having to engage oneself in any "messy" personal relationships; the yearning for a magical realm of process in stasis that resembles the Grecian urn that Keats longs to enter and meld with.

But there is a dark side to this Romantic solipsistic dream. In addition to freezing the poet in an adolescent, almost prepubescent state, the dream eventually breeds arrogance and even defiance. Having completed his palace of art, the speaker exclaims boldly:

> O all things fair to sate my various eyes!
> O shapes and hues that please me well!
> O silent faces of the Great and Wise,
> My Gods, with whom I dwell!
>
> O Godlike isolation which art mine,
> I can but count thee perfect gain,

What time I watch the darkening droves of swine
   That range on yonder plain. (193–200)

Like the sailors in "The Lotos-Eaters," the speaker of the poem, in cutting himself off from human contact, comes to feel only scorn and condescension for his fellow men. Like the wicked kings condemned in the Old Testament, his attitude becomes: "I am and there is no other beside me." The only god he now worships is the idol he has made:

I take possession of man's mind and deed.
   I care not what the sects may bawl.
I sit as God holding no form of creed,
   But contemplating all. (209–12)

With the pride of the builders of the Tower of Babel, the speaker declares himself above all petty religions and systems: a declaration that is, finally, the natural fruit of his solipsistic isolation.

Well, as in the story of Babel, God hears his boast and tears down his arrogance. The speaker is humbled and realizes that his self-enclosed fairy world is a sick and stagnant one. In the end, after a long period of contrition, the speaker is restored, and there is even a slight suggestion of hope that the palace can be redeemed as well. Its beauty need not be lost. Still, the poem holds out little hope for the artist who seeks beauty merely as an end in itself. The upshot of the poem is that the poet must find something other than himself and his art to serve.

Eventually, Tennyson found this "something" in that spirit of progress that was slowly building in the England of the early 1830s and that would soon pull the poet into its vortex. In the next two chapters, we shall explore how Tennyson embodied that spirit in verse.

16

PRESSING FORWARD
Tennyson and the Victorian
Spirit of Progress I

THOUGH WE COMPLETED our "official" look at *In Memoriam* in chapter 12, I would like to pause here for a backward glance at one last section of *In Memoriam* that fully embodies the Victorian ethos. Already we have discussed in some detail those sections of the poem in which Tennyson resolves his doubts and fears about religion, about the immortality of the soul, and about the implications of the new science; what remains is to consider how the poet found an equal resolution for the challenge issued him by the third traveler who accosts the weeping poet in #27. That is to say, we have yet to analyze the section in which Tennyson was able to embrace fully the Victorian desire to press forward and leave the past behind. That section is #106, and in it Tennyson celebrates the utilitarian dream: to found a utopia in which poverty, crime, and ignorance have been abolished and virtue, law, and unity are triumphant.

THE POSTMILLENNIAL KINGDOM

The occasion for section 106 of *In Memoriam* is the third New Year's Eve after the death of Hallam. As Tennyson celebrates the passing of the old year and the coming of the new, he widens his vision to take in not only the start of a new year but the promise of new life and hope for both him and his age. To catch fully the powerful movement of this triumphant section, one must read it straight through without pause or interruption. As such, I will first include the poem in full, and then return to analyze the details of the vision.

> Ring out, wild bells, to the wild sky,
> > The flying cloud, the frosty light:
> > The year is dying in the night;
> Ring out, wild bells, and let him die.
>
> Ring out the old, ring in the new,
> > Ring happy bells, across the snow:
> > The year is going, let him go;
> Ring out the false, ring in the true.
>
> Ring out the grief that saps the mind,
> > For those that here we see no more;
> > Ring out the feud of rich and poor,
> Ring in redress to all mankind.
>
> Ring out a slowly dying cause,
> > And ancient forms of party strife;
> > Ring in the nobler modes of life,
> With sweeter manners, purer laws.
>
> Ring out the want, the care, the sin,
> > The faithless coldness of the times:
> > Ring out, ring out my mournful rhymes,
> But ring the fuller minstrel in.
>
> Ring out false pride in place and blood,
> > The civic slander and the spite;
> > Ring in the love of truth and right,
> Ring in the common love of good.
>
> Ring out old shapes of foul disease;
> > Ring out the narrowing lust of gold;

Ring out the thousand wars of old,
Ring in the thousand years of peace.

Ring in the valiant man and free,
    The larger heart, the kindlier hand;
    Ring out the darkness of the land,
Ring in the Christ that is to be.

The best way to describe this vision is to call it a mature, even practical, version of what John Lennon (in a more adolescent, idealistic fashion) celebrates in his famous and moving song "Imagine." It is a vision of a world of total equality (where wealth and poverty alike have been abolished) that is yet filled with wonder and beauty; a world where a fallen aristocracy has given way not to a lowest common denominator world, but to one where all men have been raised up to a nobler mode of existence.

And how is this utopia to be achieved? It is to come about through the twin "ministries" of education and social planning; through an internal change in man's psyche and an external change in his political and economic institutions. This is the world envisioned in the optimistic, utopian works of the ultra-Victorian H. G. Wells: a world of sanitized, shimmering glass buildings ruled by enlightened leaders for the good of all. Needless to say, this utopic dream was dashed by the horrors of the First World War and completely put to death by the dreadful unleashing of the atom bomb at the end of the Second. We moderns can no longer naively trust in the benefits of science and technology, but for those, like Tennyson, who lived at the bright dawn of the Industrial Age, everything seemed possible.

Science promised all things to those happy children of the Enlightenment; there was no problem that human ingenuity could not fix. Still, despite the thrilling advances in technology, it was not science alone that allowed for visions such as the one Tennyson expresses so powerfully in his poem. Such hopes rested too on another kind of change: a radical shift in the moral, ethical understanding of man. According to the Christian view, the chief problem with man, the great obstacle holding him back from glory, is sin. In contrast, the modern, liberal view (which was born out of the Enlightenment and the French Revolution and came of age during the Victorian period) held that the problem with man was neither sin nor pride nor disobedience, but ignorance and poverty. In the conservative (Judeo-Christian, Greco-Roman) view, where sin is the problem, any true utopia is, of course, impossible, since no matter how much he progresses technologically, man will yet remain a sinner. Even if we were to kill off all the thieves, murderers, exploiters, and tyrants, we would still be left with the evil that lurks in the breast of every human being. No, according to the conservative view, the best a government or church can do is to try to stem the excesses of pride through legal and moral laws.

However, if the liberal view, which was first fully indulged in Victorian England, is true, then something *can* be done. Through proper education, human ignorance can be remedied. That great Victorian institution Charles Dickens says as much in *A Christmas Carol.* Near the end of his "interview" with the Ghost of Christmas Present, Scrooge notices something rustling beneath the robes of the jolly man. Father Christmas, for that is who he is, lifts his robes to reveal two ugly, disheveled urchins. Scrooge asks whose children they are and is told that they belong to man: The name of the boy, is Ignorance and the name of the girl is Want. Scrooge is told to beware the children, most of all the boy, for unless society can eradicate them, it will never be able to prosper.[1]

All that is a long way around to say that the leading Victorians, with the exception (though not the total exception) of Newman, believed that man was perfectible and that a society could be created where, as in Arthur's Camelot, might would be used only for right. In the seventh stanza of #106, Tennyson proclaims the coming of that utopia of wisdom and plenty, calling it the "thousand years of peace." The proclamation is purely Victorian, but

---

[1] Charles Dickens, *The Christmas Books,* volume 1 (London: Penguin Classics, 1971), 108.

the metaphor in which it is cloaked is biblical. Tennyson's "thousand years of peace" alludes directly to Revelation 20, where John (exiled and imprisoned on the island of Patmos) prophesies the coming of a thousand-year reign of peace, known, traditionally, as the millennium (from the Latin for "one thousand"). The passage is a famous one and has brought hope and consolation to countless generations of Christians; nevertheless, theologians since John have differed quite widely in their interpretation of Revelation 20.

The most popular interpretation today (enshrined in the widely successful Left Behind series) goes by the name of premillennialism; it argues that the millennial kingdom will be established and ruled over by Christ himself, who will return to earth just before (pre-) it begins. Amillennialism, on the other hand (the more traditional view), argues that the Church Age is itself the millennium (that is to say, we are living in it now; it is led by the Spirit that indwells the Church). The Victorians, buoyed up by optimism and a faith in the unlimited potential of man, adopted a third view, one that is, I believe, hard to reconcile with Scripture. Though Revelation is, admittedly, a difficult book to interpret, it seems to suggest quite clearly that things will get much worse before they get better. The Victorians, heady with positivistic dreams, overlooked this fact and adopted instead a belief that as the end draws near, things will get better and better. Indeed, they believed, through the benefits of technology, social planning, the free market, and universal education, man would propel *himself* into the millennium. This position (shared by many of the early Puritans in America) is called postmillennialism, for it teaches that Christ will not return to earth until after (post-) the millennium is over. This Victorian postmillennial faith was so strong it even infected non-religious thinkers such as Marx, who believed that history was moving unstoppably toward a millennium of pure communism. It proved strong enough to pull even Tennyson out of his Romantic isolation.

TO SAIL BEYOND THE SUNSET

But let us now shift our focus away from the monumental *In Memoriam* to look at a brief, isolated poem that captures just as strongly the Victorian spirit of progress: "Ulysses."

The poem, written shortly after Hallam's death (1833), tells the story of the last voyage of Ulysses (the Latin name of Homer's Odysseus) from the point-of-view of Ulysses himself. However, the Ulysses of Tennyson is quite different from the Odysseus of Homer. True, like the hero of *The Odyssey*, Ulysses is the warrior king of the island of Ithaca, who spends ten years fighting in the Trojan War and an additional ten years fighting his way home; true as well Ulysses, like Odysseus, visits many strange lands during his decade of wandering. His naval adventures allow him to see sights and learn mysteries that few mortals have ever seen or known. But here the similarity ends.

Despite the lure of exotic isles, and even more exotic women, Homer's Odysseus remains a focused man with but one goal in mind: to get home. Tennyson's Ulysses, on the other hand, burns with an unquenchable wanderlust. He is the ultimate explorer, a Greek Sinbad the Sailor with a desire to see and to experience all that the world has to offer. He is, in short, not a heroic Greek of the late second millennium B.C., but a heroic Brit of the middle nineteenth century A.D. Both Odysseus and Ulysses would never be tempted to stay with the Lotos Eaters, but for radically different reasons. Odysseus has a home to return to; Ulysses has more undiscovered lands to conquer and to explore.

The setting of the poem is Ithaca; the time, three years ("three suns") after his return. Ulysses, alone and disconsolate, muses on his boring, cloistered life:

> It little profits that an idle king,
> By this still hearth, among these barren crags,
> Match'd with an aged wife, I mete and dole
> Unequal laws unto a savage race,
> That hoard, and sleep, and feed, and know not me.

I cannot rest from travel; I will drink
Life to the lees. All times I have enjoy'd
Greatly, have suffer'd greatly, both with those
That loved me, and alone; on shore, and when
Thro' scudding drifts the rainy Hyades
Vext the dim sea. (1–11)

Despite his love for his family and his people, Ulysses can no longer remain on Ithaca. His travels have made him unfit for life on his provincial, backwater island. He has grown past his subjects (*and* his family), who seem to him almost barbaric in their narrow, unsophisticated pursuit of subsistence. Both his wife and his kingly duties have ceased to charm; his thoughts now are on the sea, on the life of adventure to which he yearns to return. In his mind, he surveys his heroic past and asserts his desire to move on, to stay true to the quest no matter where it leads him. Like a good Victorian, he must ever press onward and upward.

After a pause, he turns, in his mind, to his son, Telemachus, to whom he bequeaths Ithaca:

This is my son, mine own Telemachus,
To whom I leave the sceptre and the isle—
Well-loved of me, discerning to fulfill
This labor, by slow prudence to make mild
A rugged people, and thro' soft degrees
Subdue them to the useful and the good.
Most blameless is he, centred in the sphere
Of common duties, decent not to fail
In offices of tenderness, and pay
Meet adoration to my household gods,
When I am gone. He works his work, I mine. (33–43)

Telemachus does not share his father's need to travel. In the poem (the ethos of which we must remember is Victorian rather than Hellenic), Telemachus plays the role of the good nineteenth-century wife; he will remain behind to care for the home, the domestic sphere, so that Ulysses may indulge his passion to explore. He will watch over the "household gods," over all those traditions and duties and societal mores that are as much a part of the Victorian world as are the explorers and empire builders. He will be the fixed foot of the compass that allows the other foot to travel wide, to encircle the globe, without ever losing its balance or its center.

After a second pause, Ulysses, having freed himself (or so he imagines) from any guilt or responsibility toward his family or his country, moves, physically and mentally, to the port of Ithaca, where his ship lies ready to embark on one final adventure of discovery. He calls on his old friends to join him on his journey, promising them either death or glory as their reward. Yes, they are old and feeble (as is he), but they are men and capable of one last victory:

> There lies the port; the vessel puffs her sail;
> There gloom the dark, broad seas. My mariners,
> Souls that have toil'd, and wrought, and thought with me—
> That ever with a frolic welcome took
> The thunder and the sunshine, and opposed
> Free hearts, free foreheads—you and I are old;
> Old age hath yet his honor and his toil.
> Death closes all; but something ere the end,
> Some work of noble note, may yet be done,
> Not unbecoming men that strove with Gods.
> The lights begin to twinkle from the rocks;
> The long day wanes; the slow moon climbs; the deep
> Moans round with many voices. Come, my friends.
> 'Tis not too late to seek a newer world.
> Push off, and sitting well in order smite
> The sounding furrows; for my purpose holds
> To sail beyond the sunset, and the baths
> Of all the western stars, until I die.
> It may be that the gulfs will wash us down;
> It may be we shall touch the Happy Isles,
> And see the great Achilles, whom we knew.
> Tho' much is taken, much abides; and tho'
> We are not now that strength which in old days

Moved earth and heaven, that which we are, we are—
One equal temper of heroic hearts,
Made weak by time and fate, but strong in will
To strive, to seek, to find, and not to yield. (44–70)

I find it impossible to read these lines without being profoundly moved by their spirit and their force. To read them aloud (and this poem *must* be read aloud) is to hear the sound of the sea, of the waves crashing against the shore, and of the restless spirit that longs to conquer that sea and ride those waves. If the reader can but feel in his heart and along his veins the power of that forward thrust, he will have come a long way toward understanding the Victorian spirit of progress. Hidden in these majestic lines is all the urgency, all the insistence to travel and to grow that impelled the Victorians to remake themselves and their world.

And yet, if we read the entire poem closely, we will find, also hidden behind its indomitable spirit, a critique (whether conscious or unconscious on the part of Tennyson) of one of the downsides of Victorian positivism. In the first half of the poem, Ulysses, after recounting his past adventures, has this to say of himself:

I am a part of all that I have met;
Yet all experience is an arch wherethrough
Gleams that untravell'd world whose margin fades
For ever and for ever when I move. (18–21)

In this brief but vital passage, Ulysses, perhaps unwittingly, sets himself up for a kind of life and purpose that will never be satisfied or consummated. For if every time he approaches the arch it recedes into the distance, then, truly, will he never reach that world he seeks. He is like a modern business major whose life goal is to make a million before reaching his twenty-fifth birthday, but who, when he reaches twenty-five, decides he will not be satisfied unless he makes ten million before his thirtieth. And so on, and so on. Spurred on by his insatiable desire for adventure and discovery, Ulysses will never truly reach a place of rest.

That, in a nutshell, is the dark side of Victorianism, a temptation that marks the reverse of the Romantic dark side of sloth, isolation, and overindulgent self-pity. Toward the end of his life, Tennyson would find himself struggling with it as well, but for now, at this stage in his life, he can see only the waves crashing ahead of him, beckoning with the promise of unlimited, endless potential.

17

RESISTING TEMPTATION
*Tennyson and the Victorian
Spirit of Progress II*

"LOCKSLEY HALL" offers, in a shorter, concentrated form, both the grand movement from Romantic melancholy to Victorian positivism that we saw in *In Memoriam,* and the shift from isolated, self-pitying artist to prophet of the coming millennium of progress that we have traced in the preceding three chapters. Though difficult to read at times, on account of the excessive emotional angst and bitterness felt by the protagonist and inflicted on the captivated reader, the poem deserves its high reputation, both for its lyrical range and power and for its success at embodying the conflicting emotions of its speaker (and poet). Indeed, in order to achieve both of these goals, Tennyson (as he did for *In Memoriam*) chose carefully a poetic form that could adequately capture this lyrical and emotional range. The technical name for the form he chose is trochaic octameter couplets: in layman's terms, rhyming lines that consist of fifteen syllables, with all the accents falling on the odd-number syllables. The poem, that is to say, is written in (and can be sung to) the same meter as Beethoven's "Ode to Joy." Tennyson's reason for selecting this particular form is, I think, quite clear. Depending on the way they are read, trochaic octameter couplets can sound soothing and romantic (lines 19–20), petty and spiteful (41–42), or energetic and thundering (117–18).

As you come to each of these couplets, all of which are quoted below, I would invite you to read them aloud with the appropriate mood and passion.

PARADISE GAINED AND LOST

"Locksley Hall" is told in the first person from the point of view of an unnamed young man who has been jilted by his beloved. (Although the speaker is not Tennyson, autobiographical elements can be discerned in the poem, and the "black blood" of the Tennysons ever hovers in the background.) As the poem opens, the young man is preparing to leave for war, but he pauses for a moment to reflect nostalgically (like a Romantic) on his more innocent past. He thinks of his younger days, when all seemed possible: when the past was full of goodness, the present full of promise, and the future full of unbounded hopes and dreams. And then he thinks of that spring when he courted and won the love of his cousin, Amy:

> In the spring a fuller crimson comes upon the robin's breast;
> In the spring the wanton lapwing gets himself another crest;
>
> In the spring a livelier iris changes on the burnished dove;
> In the spring a young man's fancy lightly turns to thoughts
>   of love. (17–20)

Tennyson has long been celebrated as one of the great craftsmen of English verse, as a poet who knew intimately the tonal value and quality of every word in the language. The above four lines bear testimony to his lyrical gift. The fourfold repetition of "in the spring," which, in a lesser poet, would have rung hollow and even monotonous on the ear, works together magically with the "a" and "o" vowel sounds to swell the music from a single chord to a rolling arpeggio. Indeed, so lush and sweeping is the music that it works in spite of the fact that we have all heard that fourth line a hundred times in a hundred hackneyed forms.

But it is not only the reader who is caught up in the strains of Tennyson's music. The poet too seems to be swept away by it, drawn irresistibly back into the Romanticism of Shelley and Keats. Not surprisingly then, the opening section of the poem crescendos with four splendid lines that celebrate love in purely Romantic terms:

> Love took up the glass of Time, and turned it in his glowing
> hands;
> Every moment, lightly shaken, ran itself in golden sands.
> Love took up the harp of Life, and smote on all the chords
> with might;
> Smote the chord of Self, that, trembling, passed in music out
> of sight. (31–34)

What better or more lovely image can there be of the Romantic desire to restore Eden, to return to an innocent pastoral world where time stands still and lovers can become a world unto themselves? It is the ideal that Tennyson almost achieved through his friendship with Hallam. Love empowers the speaker to leave behind the world with all its duties and distractions; however, unlike the speaker of "The Palace of Art," his withdrawal from the social sphere does not cast him into the abyss of Romantic solipsism. The lovers have moved beyond their individual selves and are thus in no danger of prideful self-absorption.

The Romantic paean continues for two more breathless couplets, and then is squelched forever. In the distinctly un-Romantic world in which they live, neither their love nor their joy can last. Whereas Amy is the daughter of an aristocrat, the speaker is from a family that has fallen in class. Love, it seems, is not strong enough to stand against social hypocrisy. The Romantic dream is dashed, and the speaker's intense love for Amy turns into an even more intense hatred:

> O my cousin, shallow-hearted! O my Amy, mine no more!
> O the dreary, dreary moorland! O the barren, barren shore!

Falser than all fancy fathoms, falser than all songs have sung,
Puppet to a father's threat, and servile to a shrewish tongue!
(39–42)

As so often happens to the overly Romantic, the speaker swings
from one extreme to the other: His idealism turns to bitterness,
his joy to rage, his selfless love to egocentric ranting. And believe
me, his ranting goes on and on. He curses not only Amy and her
family but every social institution of his day. At one point in his
diatribe (lines 59–62), he even indulges in a reverse beatitude,
beginning four successive lines, not with "In the spring," but with
"Cursed be." At his lowest, most spiteful point, the one-time
lover actually prays that Amy's new husband will be a boor and a
brute and that she will eventually sink to his level:

As the husband is, the wife is; thou art mated with a clown,
And the grossness of his nature will have weight to drag
thee down.

He will hold thee, when his passion shall have spent
its novel force,
Something better than his dog, a little dearer than his horse.
(47–50)

No one but the speaker has the capacity to appreciate Amy's
unique qualities. To her new aristocratic husband she will be
merely another possession: a thing, perhaps, to be doted on, as he
dotes on his dog or horse, but certainly not to be known and
loved. Such thoughts fill and obsess the speaker's mind, and he
comes almost to relish the thought of Amy's abasement.

All that is as much to say that the speaker of "Locksley Hall" succumbs to one of the great Romantic temptations, a temptation we
have seen before in this series: the tendency to indulge in Byronic
self-pity and over-self-consciousness. Mill felt this temptation during his crisis, and Tennyson felt it throughout the early stages of his
grief for Hallam; even Newman was tempted to indulge a persecu-

tion complex. Indeed, most of the great Victorian sages were, in some sense, converted Romantics who rechanneled their individual angst and shattered idealism into the greater social dreams of Victorian England. Our speaker too will embrace this rechanneling, but for now, he plays the role of that great proto-Romantic, Hamlet: he who is jilted by a lover (Ophelia) who takes her father's politic counsel. In anger and rage, the speaker forsakes all society and becomes an isolated figure who haunts the margins of civilized and domestic life: a sort of mix of Dracula and Heathcliff. He is trapped, imprisoned within his own tortured psyche, and the previous generation can offer no way of escape.

THINGS TO COME

Then, as we approach the middle of the poem, an unexpected shift occurs that severs it completely from its roots in the Romantic poetry of Byron, Shelley, and Keats. Suddenly, without warning, the speaker snaps out of his bitter reverie and decides that the only remedy is both to link himself to and to lose himself in some greater cause. He thinks back to his youthful, pre-Amy optimism, and, with renewed vigor, cries out:

> Can I but relive in sadness? I will turn that earlier page.
> Hide me from my deep emotion, O thou wondrous
>   Mother-Age! (107–8)

As all Victorians must, he swiftly and decisively crushes his inner Byron and adopts a new progressive spirit that links him to the wider movements of his age:

> Make me feel the wild pulsation that I felt before the strife,
> When I heard my days before me, and the tumult of my life;
>
> Yearning for the large excitement that the coming years
>   would yield,
> Eager-hearted as a boy when first he leaves his father's field,

And at night along the dusky highway near and nearer drawn,
Sees in heaven the light of London flaring like a dreary dawn;

And his spirit leaps within him to be gone before him then,
Underneath the light he looks at, in among the throngs
of men;

Men, my brothers, men the workers, ever reaping
something new;
That which they have done but earnest of the things that they
shall do. (109–18)

In his celebration of London, we can see the speaker has forsaken his Romantic pastoral ethos for one that sees the city not as a cold, atomized prison of hypocrisy and artificiality (as Blake and Wordsworth often saw it) but as a thriving, vital center of excitement, adventure, and boundless opportunities. The answers and the consolation lie not in a lost, irretrievable past, but in a bright future that shimmers before the physical and spiritual eye of the speaker. The sight and promise of London do call back the speaker's youth, but only that part that sought for excitement in the tomorrows that lay ahead. He becomes again like a boy whose first love is not nature and romance, but science, speed, and skyscrapers. The gadget-loving boy within is revived, and he is drawn to the city with its flaring lights and its vast throngs of men. Indeed, what finally allows the speaker to separate himself from his grief is his newfound ability and desire to identify instead with the workers, builders, and shapers of the future.

In the couplets that follow, the speaker, on wings of soaring poetry, goes on to celebrate the brave new world that these workers will build:

For I dipped into the future, far as human eye could see,
Saw the Vision of the world, and all the wonder that
would be;

Saw the heavens fill with commerce, argosies of magic sails,
Pilots of the purple twilight, dropping down with costly bales;

Heard the heavens fill with shouting, and there rained a
    ghastly dew
From the nations' airy navies grappling in the central blue;
    (119–24)

Here we have the high Victorian millennial dream: a world where science and technology have bent nature to their will, and the glories of commerce and the free market have taken to the air. Yes, at first, these new inventions will be used to wage war (prophetically, Tennyson pictures a battle in the sky), but this will last only a short while; the peace of utopia will follow:

Till the war drum throbbed no longer, and the battle flags
    were furled
In the Parliament of man, the Federation of the world.

There the common sense of most shall hold a fretful realm
    in awe,
And the kindly earth shall slumber, lapped in universal law.
    (127–30)

Not since the glory days of the Roman Empire had Europe indulged in such a vision: not just world conquest, but the victory of law, order, and civilization over nature, division, and barbarism. The Virgilian Tennyson surely has in mind Jupiter's prophecy (*Aeneid* I) of the coming Roman Empire, and his promise that for Rome he will "set no limits, world or time, / But [will] make the gift of empire without end" (lines 374–75; Fitzgerald translation). Here, now, in England rather than Italy, the great Roman roads would be rebuilt and global commerce would once again flourish. This time, however, utilitarian efficiency would ensure that all, not just the wealthy few, would share in the benefits of trade and that these benefits would truly endure for all time to come, world without end. In his utopic novel, *Things to Come,* H. G. Wells pictures a millennial city of glass run not by politicians but by engineers; Tennyson's vision comes close to this in its celebration of technology. No more will kingdoms shudder at the arbitrary will of tyrants; here in this ivory tower of science triumphant, reason alone shall be king.

By such a grand and glorious vision does the speaker pull himself out of the Byronic temptation to overindulge in despair and self-pity. Unfortunately, near the end of the poem, as he thinks on Amy again, he falls prey, for a moment, to a second temptation that the speaker, Tennyson, and every other would-be Victorian must overcome if he is to mature past his Romantic youth. It is a temptation that persists even today (especially in its Hollywood incarnation) and that owes its origin not to Byron but to Rousseau.

THE LURE OF THE NOBLE SAVAGE

As the speaker remembers his love for Amy, he thinks not of her betrayal of that love but of the possibility that his love for her was too pure to exist within the rigid social structures of Britain. No, the only solution is to throw off the restraints of society and find a barbaric place where middle-class morality, with all its puritanical repressions and phony propriety, does not hold sway. Were he an American, he might, perhaps, run off and become a cowboy; instead, as a citizen of Victorian England, he dreams of finding a primitive island on the outskirts of the Empire:

> There methinks would be enjoyment more than in this march
>   of mind,
> In the steamships, in the railways, in the thoughts that
>   shake mankind.
>
> There the passions cramped no longer shall have scope and
>   breathing place;
> I will take some savage woman, she shall rear my dusky race,
>
> Iron-jointed, supple-sinewed, they shall dive, and they
>   shall run,

Catch the wild goat by the hair, and hurl their lances at
    the sun; (165–70)

In this wonderful, exotic "male fantasy," the speaker is tempted to forsake not just the customs and mores of Victorian society, but all duty and responsibility to any cause outside himself. He desires, to refer back to chapter 15, to abandon England for a lustful version of the isle of the Lotos Eaters. It is a dangerous, powerful temptation (well expressed in both the musical *South Pacific* and the three film versions of *Mutiny on the Bounty*), one that threatens the utopian, postmillennial dream. More than that, it threatens the evolution of man into the Crowning Race, threatens to permanently stifle man's development and leave him stranded in primitive stagnation.

However, as the Victorian spirit of progress pulls him out of his first temptation, so does it release him from the second; in a fit of self-disgust, the speaker suddenly cries out:

Fool, again the dream, the fancy! but I know my words
    are wild,
But I count the gray barbarian lower than the Christian child.

I, to herd with narrow foreheads, vacant of our glorious gains,
Like a beast with lower pleasures, like a beast with
    lower pains!

Mated with a squalid savage—what to me were sun or clime?
I the heir of all the ages, in the foremost files of time—

I that rather held it better men should perish one by one,
Than that earth should stand at gaze like Joshua's moon
    at Ajalon!

Not in vain the distance beacons. Forward, forward let
    us range,
Let the great world spin forever down the ringing grooves
    of change.

Through the shadow of the globe we sweep into the
  younger day;
Better fifty years of Europe than a cycle of Cathay [China].
  (173–84)

You may sense in these lines a strong touch of ethnocentrism and
even of racism; this is true, but it is a prejudice founded less on
color than on civilization, progress, and culture. What the Victorians meant by the "white-man's burden" was not so much the
right of the British to enslave colored natives (though it often
degraded into that) but the responsibility of the British to spread
both their social institutions and technological advances to the
farthest reaches of the globe. In many ways, the "white man's burden" is equivalent to American "manifest destiny"; people in both
countries felt that they had come up with moral, political, and
economic systems that worked, and they were eager to share the
blessings of their accomplishments with less advanced nations and
peoples. Indeed, though one cannot deny a strong jingoist sentiment in the speaker's words, it is also true that his final vision is
less about British hegemony than the progress of the human race.
The speaker does not so much drive progress as he is driven by it.
He has rejected all Romantic inaction, melancholy, and self-pity
and desires only to be part of the greater Victorian vision. Only
one direction is left to him: forward!

18

CARLYLE'S SARTOR RESARTUS
Spiritual Critiques of Progress

THOMAS CARLYLE, the eldest literary son of the Victorian Age, was born in Scotland in 1795 and was raised by poor parents who both espoused a strict Calvinist creed. Though he always maintained a strong Protestant work ethic and a sense of religious awe in the face of the universe, Carlyle soon shed his Calvinist beliefs to become a devotee of German philosophy. Indeed, just as Coleridge had served his countrymen in the role of interpreter of German thought throughout the first half of the nineteenth century, so Carlyle took up the mantle of Teutonic sage for the second half. However, whereas Coleridge moved closer to orthodox Christianity as he matured, Carlyle, like Blake before him, soon abandoned orthodoxy for a vigorous and creative creed of his own. Once established, this new creed energized Carlyle's work and thought, but in the interim, his loss of traditional faith caused him much anguish and despair. It occasioned in him, that is to say, a true Victorian crisis of faith that, like that of John Stuart Mill left him devoid of all hope and, like that of Tennyson, left him feeling stranded in a hostile and indifferent universe.

RESISTING THE STEAM ENGINE

Carlyle's crisis of faith was among the darkest of the nineteenth century, and it is therefore not surprising that his emergence from and resolution of that crisis remained one of the defining moments in his life. So vital was it, in fact, that he eventually enshrined his emotional and spiritual victory in a fictional auto-biography that he patterned on the German *bildungsroman* ("novel of education"), a genre that attempts to trace the struggle and growth of a representative mind. (Other examples of a *bildungsroman* include Goethe's *Wilhelm Meister,* Dickens's *David Copperfield,* and Joyce's *A Portrait of the Artist as a Young Man;* Tennyson's *In Memoriam* might also, arguably, be considered a "novel of education.") The work, *Sartor Resartus,* purports to tell the inner wrestlings of a German professor as they are related in a series of random journal entries discovered and pieced together by a fictional editor. The professor (whose journals mimic not the physical but the intellectual events of Carlyle's life) is named Diogenes Teufelsdröckh, which means "God-born devil's-dung." This ironic, paradoxical name gives us our first clue to Carlyle's conception of man as a creature caught between God and the devil, between our divine origin and our bestial urges. Like that great proto-Romantic, Hamlet, Carlyle struggled heroically to reconcile (intellectually, spiritually, and aesthetically) how we can be, at once, "noble in reason . . . infinite in faculty" and a weak, even pathetic "quintessence of dust."

Though this hybrid view of man is, on the surface, consistent with the Calvinist doctrines of his parents (man was made in God's image but is, on account of original sin, totally depraved), the "religion" of *Sartor Resartus* is heterodox at best and comes closest in spirit to American Transcendentalism. Carlyle, that is to say, shared Ralph Waldo Emerson's distrust of scientific rationalism and sought a more intuitive understanding of the universe, able to discern in nature a greater spiritual unity. In fact, though *Sartor Resartus* was not well received when it was published serially in England in 1833–34, it was a huge success when, under the auspices of Emerson, it was published in America (1836). *Sartor Resartus* is an extremely complex and arcane work that would take many chapters to unpack; in this single chapter, I will focus only on those aspects that have direct bearing on this book. Our focus will be the two central chapters in which Diogenes suffers and resolves his crisis.

In Book II, chapter 7, of *Sartor Resartus* ("The Everlasting No"), Carlyle recounts the chief factors that led to his crisis. (In terms of the work itself, the "his" here refers, of course, to Diogenes; however, since Carlyle is writing in his most autobiographical mode, I will, from this point on, substitute Carlyle for Diogenes.) First and foremost among these factors is the painful loss of his religious faith: that horrible moment when doubt crosses over into unbelief, and the world grows dark, cold, and uncaring. Like the Tennyson of *In Memoriam*, Carlyle fears that life has lost its purpose, that the dreams of man are but empty illusions, that hope, virtue, and duty are but names: "To me," writes Carlyle,

> the Universe was all void of Life, of Purpose, of Volition, even of Hostility: it was one huge, dead, immeasurable Steam-engine, rolling on, in its dead indifference, to grind me limb from limb.

God, if he exists, seems to be only an "absentee-God," the watchmaker God of the rationalist-deists of the eighteenth century who set the world in motion and then abandoned it. He is, in many ways, closer to the arbitrary, inscrutable deity that would come, several decades later, to haunt the novels of the naturalists (Zola, Hardy, Norris, Dreiser, and so on) than to the loving, personal God of the Methodists or even the somewhat sterner yet still personal God of the Calvinists. If only God would speak in the darkness and give him a command, he would be willing to leap into the fire, but his cry is answered only with silence (see *In Memoriam* #54).

To make it worse, his society seems unconcerned with his inner struggles. Wrapped up in their utilitarian view of happiness as the greatest good for the greatest number, they deny the needs of the soul. "If what thou namest Happiness be our true aim," rages Carlyle in his poetic prose, "then are we all astray. With Stupidity and sound Digestion man may front much." With the passion of a prophet, Carlyle takes his society to task for reducing mankind and his true purpose to simple creature comforts; indeed, Carlyle claims, he has "discovered, in contradiction to much Profit-and-loss Philosophy, speculative and practical, that Soul is not synonymous with Stomach." Carlyle, in short, will not jump on the utilitarian bandwagon. He realizes, as Mill did in his crisis, that were Utopia to be achieved, that in itself would not be enough to satisfy our deeper yearnings. He refuses to accept a mechanistic view of society or of man that would put its faith in laissez-faire capitalism and enlightened self-interest. There are just some things that cannot be tabulated and calculated on a graph, things that cannot be fixed or answered through technology and social reform.

In lonely, solitary agony, Carlyle cries out but is greeted only with what he calls "the Everlasting No," a cosmic, existential despair that would crush both his volition and his purpose.

In response, Carlyle rises up in indignation and asserts his divine origin and his freedom. In doing so, he comes close to paraphrasing that climactic moment in *In Memoriam* #124 when Tennyson stands up "like a man in wrath" and answers "I have felt." But there is one vital difference. Whereas Tennyson then backs off and says "no," he was more "like a child in doubt and fear," Carlyle remains resolute and defiant to the end. Along with Blake (who shared not only his refusal to accept a mechanistic or utilitarian ethos for himself or his society but also his propensity for fashioning esoteric systems of thought as well), Carlyle is one of the many proto-Nietzscheans to rise up out of the Romantic Age. Most of Carlyle's work, from *Sartor Resartus*, to *The French Revolution*, to *On Heroes, Hero-worship, and the Heroic in History*, calls out for charismatic leadership and for the need for great men to assert their will-to-power and thus propel society out of its stagnation, hypocrisy, and materialism.

THE EVERLASTING YEA

Carlyle's proto-Nietzschean act of defiance leads, in chapter 9 ("The Everlasting Yea"), to a series of three resolutions by which he hopes to free himself from his crisis of faith. First, to combat the Romantic over-self-consciousness that led in part to the emotional anguish of his crisis, Carlyle adopts what he terms "the first preliminary moral Act, Annihilation of Self." Like John Stuart Mill, Carlyle discovers that as long as he tries to make his own individual happiness his direct aim, the happiness slips away. Only when he forgets himself and his own personal needs and focuses on some other object outside of himself does he find true contentment. In fact, in his *Autobiography*, Mill says that though he had not yet read Carlyle at the time, he was in fact learning what he calls "the anti-self-consciousness theory of Carlyle."

Here is that theory in Carlyle's own twisted, perversely beautiful prose:

> What is this that, ever since earliest years, thou hast been fretting and fuming, and lamenting and self-tormenting, on account of? Say it in a word: is it not because thou are not HAPPY? Because the THOU (sweet gentleman) is not sufficiently honoured, nourished, soft-bedded, and lovingly cared for? Foolish soul! What Act of Legislature was there that *thou* shouldst be Happy? A little while ago thou hadst no right to *be* at all. What if thou wert born and predestined not to be Happy, but to be Unhappy! Art thou nothing other than a Vulture, then, that fliest through the Universe seeking after somewhat to eat; and shrieking dolefully because carrion enough is not given thee? Close thy *Byron*; open thy *Goethe*.

As both Mill and Tennyson had to learn in their crises, the self-absorbed, egocentric pity and isolation of Lord Byron had to be discarded: the time for Romantic self-indulgence was over.

Instead, Carlyle holds up the great German writer Goethe as his model: a playwright, novelist, and poet who developed from the leader of the emotional *Sturm und Drang* ("Storm and Stress") movement (during which he wrote an overwrought account of a young, lovesick man who commits suicide: *The Sorrows of Young Werther*) to an advocate of classical balance, restraint, and resignation. Oddly, Carlyle's attack here on the self offers *both* a critique of the individualistic greed latent in a free-market economy and an embodiment of the Victorian shift from the individual to society. Yet, this paradox is not so odd, for the same Victorians whom Carlyle (and his fellow sages) attacked as Philistines, dutifully bought, read, and even absorbed these attacks. Likewise, though middle-class morality privileges the accumulation of wealth, it also preaches restraint and social service. Carlyle stands at the center of this paradox, even as he, though he called for annihilation of self, was (along with his role model, the equally esoteric Blake) an intensely self-indulgent artist.

Carlyle's second resolution to his crisis springs out of a sudden awareness that man's unhappiness is actually the key to his happiness: that his unrest proves he was made for greater things. In another overt attack on the utilitarian theories of his day, Carlyle asserts:

> Man's Unhappiness, as I construe, comes of his Greatness; it is because there is an Infinite in him, which with all his cunning he cannot quite bury under the Finite. Will the whole Finance Ministers and Upholsterers and Confectioners of modern Europe undertake, in joint stock company, to make one Shoe-black HAPPY? They cannot accomplish it, above an hour or two; for the Shoeblack also has a Soul quite other than his Stomach.

Carlyle believed strongly that all men possess a sense of the infinite and that nothing on this earth can fully satisfy the yearning to know and share in that higher divinity. In this sense he breaks company somewhat with Mill, who, despite his crisis, still championed utilitarian causes and still harbored positivistic dreams of a future utopia on earth. Likewise, it never allowed him to share fully Tennyson's enthusiasm for the Victorian spirit of progress. Carlyle (like Blake and the Transcendentalists) believed real change came from an internal perceptual shift that would allow us to pierce through the facade of nature to see the indwelling spirit. To quote Blake's *Marriage of Heaven and Hell*: "If the doors of perception were cleansed every thing would appear to man as it is, infinite."

Only spiritual, intuitive wisdom can supply us with real knowledge of the universe. Indeed, in a later chapter ("Natural Supernaturalism") Carlyle parodies astronomers who think that because they have come up with a name for a stellar phenomenon they therefore understand the nature and purpose of the stars: Such pretension is merely witchcraft, a superstitious faith in the "potency of names." In a wonderful, characteristic sentence, Carlyle states that for all the nicknaming of asylum doctors, madness remains "a mysterious-terrific, altogether *infernal* boiling-up of the Nether Chaotic Deep, through this fair-painted Vision of Creation, which swims thereon, which we name the Real." Of course, in privileging intuitive knowledge over scientific rationalism, Carlyle allies himself with the Romantics (not only Blake, but Coleridge and Shelley as well), but only partially. For Carlyle, intuitive knowledge and our innate sense of the infinite must lead not to Byronic over-self-consciousness and isolation but to a more Victorian engagement with wider social and philosophical concerns.

SECULAR SPIRITUALITY AND THE RELIGION OF WORK

Carlyle's third resolution involves the fashioning of a new spiritual ethic and ethos. Though Carlyle agreed with French Enlightenment thinker Voltaire that the "mythus" of Christianity was no longer viable or believable in the modern age, he felt that Voltaire's skepticism was finally a dead end since it made no attempt to build a new mythus to take the place of the old discarded one. Skeptics such as T. H. Huxley could not help spiritual-minded thinkers like Carlyle, for they tended to deny that supernatural realm that Carlyle felt was finally our true home; yet, as we just saw, Carlyle (like many of his contemporary intellectuals) rejected the creeds of orthodox Christianity. He could not follow Newman into Anglo-Catholicism, nor could he adopt the pure agnosticism of Mill or the rather feeble, half-agnostic/half-Christian compromise of Tennyson. (Oddly, the irascible, fiery Carlyle and the moody Tennyson were lifelong friends.)

No, the only solution for Carlyle was to forge a new spirituality, a specifically *secular* spirituality that would not rely on creeds or rituals or ancient traditions and that could coexist with the new theories of science and biblical scholarship. Of course that spirituality would have to adopt and even create a new kind of language and vocabulary to express its mysteries (hence Carlyle's cryptic phrases and tortured syntax), and yet, strangely (or not so strangely) the ethic it would go on to embody would not be so far removed from Victorianism. For, odd as it may sound, the mystical Carlyle advocated a religion of work (there's that Calvinist work ethic), and championed Goethe's mandate to "Do the duty which liest nearest thee." "Here," he writes, "in this poor, miserable, hampered, despicable Actual, wherein thou even now standest, here or nowhere is thy Ideal: work it out therefrom; and working, believe, live, be free."

With a spiritual fervor that is not all that different from the Victorian spirit of progress, Carlyle lays it down as man's destiny to spread that divine Light that alone can bring order out of chaos. The major difference, however, is that whereas thinkers such as Mill and Tennyson (along with most Victorians) saw the goal of civilizing the world as a group project to be accomplished through technological progress and educational reform, Carlyle saw it as being initiated by a strong, charismatic leader with an apocalyptic vision (here again, we see Carlyle's link to the later Nietzsche.) Carlyle had little patience with the moderation advocated by Mill, Tennyson, and Huxley; like Newman, he held a more extreme position with the courage to follow out its convic-

tions to the end. That is, as with Newman his Victorian earnestness and searching intellect led him to adopt a position that
finally contradicted the Protestant bourgeois ethos of his day.

And yet, as we have seen, the very bourgeois they attacked
eagerly bought their books and subscribed to journals that published their numerous essays. Too often, we moderns view Victorians as monolithic and self-satisfied. That the iconoclastic
theories of Newman and Carlyle were bred (and read) by those
very Victorians they so colorfully and vehemently took to task
gives that view the lie.

19

RUSKIN'S "THE NATURE OF THE GOTHIC"
Aesthetic Critique of Progress

OF ALL THE VICTORIANS, John Ruskin may have had the most rich and fertile mind: a mind that could encompass both critiques of art and society and, more importantly, perceive the links between the two. In the heyday of his popularity, which lasted for decades, Ruskin's was the last word on aesthetic style and taste, and his reflections on social justice, no matter how extreme, were eagerly read by the very people who would have been most hurt had they actually been put into practice.

ART AS RELIGION

Ruskin was born in 1819 to parents who, like Carlyle's, were devout, pious Christians but who, unlike Carlyle's, were quite well off financially. Much of that money they used for European travel and the purchase of fine art, both of which helped Ruskin to develop sophisticated, cosmopolitan tastes and a love (nay, worship) of art. Indeed, when Ruskin (like Carlyle) eventually (one almost says inevitably) pulled away from his Christian faith, he adopted not a secular spirituality but a religion of art and beauty. However, as Carlyle's new faith retained the Protestant work ethic of his Calvinist parents, so Ruskin threw himself into the criticism of art with an intensity both aesthetic and moral.

Few critics, I believe, have ever achieved the depth of Ruskin's insight into the soul of art; even fewer have understood and felt so strongly the spiritual and ethical impact of art on society. In every meaning of the word, Ruskin became a true Victorian sage: His pronouncements on art not only held sway for half a century but actually set the aesthetic standards and tastes of his age. When one reads Ruskin's essays, one feels that art is the most important thing in the world, that it matters intensely, that it demands of us the same seriousness we ascribe to religion. Indeed, art, in all its purity and power, was a kind religion to Ruskin, an aspect of his character that may account in part for the great "scandal" of his life. In 1846, he married young, pretty Effie Gray; six years later the marriage was annulled because it had *never* been consummated! (Effie later married Pre-Raphaelite painter John Everett Millais.) Apparently, though Ruskin found Effie pretty, he was repelled by her naked body, perhaps because it could not measure up to the classical purity of the nude female statues he loved.

But let us turn our focus now to a single essay, taken from volume 2, chapter 6, of *The Stones of Venice* (1851–53), that not only proved to be vastly influential in Ruskin's day but also offers a unique, aesthetic critique of the Victorian spirit of progress. In "The Nature of the Gothic" Ruskin not only advocates a return to Gothic architecture but argues (seriously) that England, in adopting a utilitarian ethos for both its architecture and its mass-produced, societal arts, had impoverished and enslaved the souls of the British. As he does in all his critical work, Ruskin begins his argument by defining terms and laying down historical and aesthetic categories; here, he distinguishes between three kinds of architectural ornamentation: the servile, the revolutionary, and the constitutional.

In servile ornamentation (Greek, Assyrian, Egyptian), writes Ruskin, "the execution or power of the inferior workman is entirely subjected to the intellect of the higher." In other words, in ancient pagan societies, where temples are built by slave labor, the drudge workers who are responsible for the numerous architectural details that go to make up the temple are allowed no individual creativity; rather, the master craftsman gives them simple, rigid instructions that they must obey. The watchword of this architectural style (and arrangement) is absolute precision and symmetrical uniformity. The orders (and aesthetic taste) of the master are supreme and unquestioned. In revolutionary (Renaissance) ornamentation, on the other hand, every artisan is his own master; no higher authority operates, and, in the absence of proper restraint, the worker's "original power is overwhelmed." In either case, the soul of the worker is not afforded true human dignity; it is either crushed by dull uniformity and artistic suppression or frittered away in chaos and exhibitionism.

The proper compromise is found in constitutional ornamentation (Gothic/Middle Ages) "in which the executive inferior power is, to a certain point, emancipated and independent, having a will of its own, yet confessing its inferiority and rendering obedience to higher powers." This style, argues Ruskin, is distinctly Christian in that it acknowledges man's hybrid status as made in God's image yet fallen (as for Carlyle, the Christian view of man was deeply ingrained in Ruskin's psyche and remained with him even after he abandoned orthodoxy). Only a master craftsman (and a society) that understands and accepts both the "individual value of every soul" and the imperfections native to it will be able to appreciate and fashion the Gothic, a style Ruskin defines as embodying a love both of variety and richness and of the rude grandeur of nature. The Gothic cathedral, like the Egyptian pyramid, possesses power and rigidity, but it is an elastic, often nonsymmetrical rigidity, alive with aesthetic tension and a touch of the grotesque. It has the feminine playfulness of a Renaissance cathedral, yet retains its masculine fixedness and strength.

A DEGRADING LOVE OF ORDER

Ruskin clearly prefers the Gothic, *both* as an architectural style and as a method for creating art. Unfortunately, the England of his day shared neither his taste nor the ethos and ethic behind it.

Like the ancient Greeks, Ruskin complains, the English seek "in all things, the utmost completion or perfection compatible with their nature"; worse yet, they "prefer the perfectness of the lower nature to the imperfection of the higher." That is to say, the Victorian taste in art, much to Ruskin's dismay, was gravitating more and more toward a kind of assembly-line perfection, in which every object made had the same uniform finish and gloss. Indeed, so low had their taste sunk that most of them preferred to possess smooth, perfectly rounded, machine-made glasses rather than the flawed, inconsistent, yet aesthetically priceless goblets of Venice.

As did all the Victorian sages in one way or another, Ruskin desired to set and define the tastes of his fellow Englishman. In "The Nature of the Gothic," he begins this process by exposing and ridiculing (with a view to altering) their slavish love of order:

> . . . that Love of Order which makes us desire that our house windows should pair like our carriage horses, and allows us to yield our faith unhesitatingly to architectural theories which fix a form for everything.

Now, Ruskin does admit that the British love of order is useful in some ways ("it helps us in our commerce and in all purely practical matters; and it is in many cases one of the foundation stones of morality"), but, he asserts adamantly, the love of order must not be confused with the love of art. Art for Ruskin must always retain within it the pattern of nature, and as nature is ever changing and vibrant, so art must mimic both this vitality and this irregularity. But alas, the British will have their standardized buildings and manufactured glass beads. They simply will not learn that imperfection, to quote Ruskin, is the very "sign of life in a mortal body, that is to say, of a state of progress and change."

But Ruskin does not stop here. Art and aesthetic taste do not exist or operate in a vacuum. The narrowing and vulgarizing of British taste, Ruskin warns, cannot help but have repercussions, both architectural and spiritual. Their love of order has blinded the British public to one of the most essential truths of humanity, namely, that

> All things are literally better, lovelier, and more beloved for the imperfections which have been divinely appointed, that the law of human life may be Effort, and the law of human judgment, Mercy.

To love only perfection is finally to reject not only the natural but the human as well; it is to privilege an impersonal progress and efficiency over a personal sympathy with and celebration of both man's hard-won victories and his all-too-human failures. Many bioethicists in our own day have warned that our modern desire (temptation?) to so manipulate advances in genetic research as to produce perfect, "made to order" offspring may result in a cheapening of human life and even a "culture of death." Ruskin, living a full century before such genetic manipulation seemed even remotely possible, already saw this danger writ large in the growing demand for aesthetic perfection.

However, the artistic and the spiritual are not the only aspects of human life disrupted and even perverted by Britain's utilitarian ethos: the social sphere suffers as well. For England can have the mass-produced precision she desires only by transforming her blue-collar artisans and industrial laborers into machines, what Dickens (in *Hard Times*) calls "hands":

> You must either make a tool of the [worker], or a man of him. You cannot make both. Men were not intended to work with the accuracy of tools, to be precise and perfect in all their actions. If you will have that precision out of them, and make their fingers measure degrees like cog-wheels, and their arms strike curves like compasses, you must unhumanize them.

England must choose, and Ruskin, as Victorian sage, will force them to be at least cognizant *of* that choice. You can't have *both* a free, dignified, and human work force *and* "engine-tuned precision"; one or the other *must* be sacrificed. To put this in modern terms: you can't have the designer shoes without the sweat shops. Ruskin, writing at the dawn of the industrial age when free-market capitalism was just coming into its own, saw with the vision of a prophet the human cost of a consumer society, and he expresses that cost in words that still ring true today (as you read, replace England with America):

> And now, reader, look round this English room of yours, about which you have been proud so often, because the work of it was so good and strong, and the ornaments of it so finished. Examine again all those accurate mouldings, and perfect polishings, and unerring adjustments of the seasoned wood and tempered steel. Many a time you have exulted over them, and thought how great England was, because her slightest work was done so thoroughly. Alas! if read rightly, these perfectnesses are signs of a slavery in our England a thousand times more bitter and more degrading than that of the scourged African or helot Greek. Men may be beaten, chained, tormented, yoked like cattle, slaughtered like summer flies, and yet remain, in one sense, and the best sense, free. But to smother their souls within them, . . . to make the flesh and skin . . . into leathern thongs to yoke machinery with, —this is to be slave-masters indeed.

If you hear in this impassioned tirade intimations of Marxism, you are right, for Ruskin agreed with Marx that to divide the worker from the products of his labor is to dehumanize him. Indeed, later in life, Ruskin turned to outright social criticism, in which he called on factory owners to treat their workers with dignity and humanity and called for fairness in wages.

Ruskin's Christian upbringing, however, and his devotion to individual freedom kept him from ever becoming anything like a doctrinaire Marxist. There was, as well, an elitist side to him (as there was to Carlyle) that prevented him from ever really sympathizing with the needs and tastes of the worker. There may be much truth to Ruskin's shocking claim that "every young lady . . .

who buys glass beads is engaged in the slave trade"; yet, it is equally true that utilitarianism and the free market were allowing the underclasses of England to be able to afford luxuries they never could before. (Think of the countless American teens who perform drudge labor in order to purchase unnecessary designer clothes!) Still, whether we agree with him or not, Ruskin forces us (as he did the Victorians) to acknowledge both the cost of our creature comforts and the social price of our taste for precision and finery. Many an American politician has gotten on his soapbox to expose the exploitation of third-world labor, or the relocation of factories to Mexico, or the wars fought and compromises made to ensure a continual flow of cheap oil and other raw materials into our country. But how many of these same politicians have had the courage to state clearly that to end such things we must as a nation be willing to sacrifice high-quality yet inexpensive VCR and DVD players, affordable produce twelve months a year, and a host of consumer outlets from Wal-Mart to the local $1 store? Were Ruskin living in America today, he would not have shied away from making such uncomfortable connections.

THE GOTHIC SPIRIT

Like Carlyle, then, Ruskin attacked with great relish the dangers of utilitarianism, and yet, again like Carlyle, at moments in his essay he embodies fully some of the key aspects of Victorianism. Thus, despite his critique of the excesses and ramifications of the Victorian spirit of progress, Ruskin goes on to argue that part of the problem with precision is precisely that it leaves no room for growth. In a sublimely beautiful passage he hails

> . . . that strange *disquietude* of the Gothic spirit . . . that restlessness of the dreaming mind, that wanders hither and thither among the niches [of a Gothic cathedral], and flickers feverishly around the pinnacles, and frets and fades in labyrinthine knots and shadows along wall and roof, and yet is not satisfied, nor shall be satisfied.

In other words, the Gothic embodies that very restless spirit of progress that is celebrated in Tennyson's "Ulysses" and that drove the great Victorian explorers to traverse the globe. It is a spirit of perpetual dissatisfaction that is best summed up in two lines from Browning's "Andrea del Sarto" that capture fully the Victorian ethos: "Ah, but a man's reach should exceed his grasp, / Or what's a heaven for?"

Indeed, toward the end of "The Nature of the Gothic," Ruskin presents the characteristics of the Gothic style as specifically Northern traits and contrasts them with the artistic and national traits of the South: a passage that comes close to expressing the same ethnocentric pride in the superior culture and ethos of England that we encountered at the close of Tennyson's "Locksley Hall." Hence, in the Northern mentality, Ruskin discerns "strength of will, independence of character, resoluteness of purpose, impatience of undue control, and [a] general tendency to set the individual reason against authority, and the individual deed against destiny"; in the South, on the other hand, he encounters "languid submission . . . of thought to tradition, and purpose to fatality." It is clear which mentality Ruskin prefers, and clear which mentality is destined to define the world: not the "listless repose" of the (Catholic) South but "the Protestant spirit of self-dependence and inquiry." Reading such a passage on this side of Hitler and his Arian dream is distinctly unsettling, but if we remember that it was the possession of this spirit in England (and America) that allowed her to resist Nazism when so many other more "listless" nations fell, the aftertaste is not so bitter.

Yes, for all his criticism of utilitarianism, Ruskin shared much of the Victorian spirit of progress; indeed, he celebrates again and again those very qualities of the English character that Cardinal Newman fled from!

20

TENNYSON'S ANGRY YOUNG MAN
Maud and the Dark Side of Progress

SIMULTANEOUSLY WITH ROBERT BROWNING, Tennyson was responsible for inventing a new genre of poetry that is still used by many poets today: the dramatic monologue. Dramatic monologues feature first-person speakers who are *not* to be confused with the poet. The speakers may be taken from literature, myth, or history, or they may be wholly the invention of the poet; whatever the case, the speakers tend to be warped in some way. Though not necessarily evil, they are usually marginal figures cut off from their society. This is obviously true of Tithonus and of the speaker of "Locksley Hall," but it is also the case with Ulysses, who appears unable to fit back into the dull, everyday world of Ithaca. For the reader, the dramatic monologue poses two challenges: (1) We must play detective and fill in the narrative gaps that the speaker leaves unstated; and (2) we must play psychotherapist and try to figure out what motivates these often perverse speakers to do the things they do and say the things they say.

Though "Ulysses" is a great poem, it was Browning, finally, who most excelled in the genre, for he was able to separate himself from, and thus study, his speakers in a way Tennyson could not. Browning's poems are almost wholly detached from their age; one need know nothing of Victorianism to understand them. Nearly all of Tennyson's dramatic monologues, on the other hand, embody autobiographical elements: a fact that makes it difficult to study his poetry apart from the Victorian Age. Both "Tithonus" and "Ulysses," for example, express the contrary emotions inspired in the poet by the death of Hallam (grief and isolation in the one; the need to move on in the other). And this tendency to explore his own inner conflicts through the mediation of speakers continued on even after he became poet laureate in 1850. Indeed, five years later, Tennyson published a long, brooding dramatic monologue *(Maud)* that offers us a direct if disturbing look into the doubts, passions, and fears that still raged in the poet's breast.

HAMLET ON STEROIDS

In *Maud*, Tennyson plays (as he did also in "Locksley Hall") on the tortured history of his family: most notably, his grasping, controlling grandfather; his moody, disinherited father; his rich, ostentatious uncle; and (above all) the "black blood" of the Tennysons (madness, epilepsy, addiction). The plot (what little there is) of this complex, thirty-page poem concerns a sensitive, unnamed young man whose father has recently committed suicide after a speculative capitalist venture blew up in his face. As a result, the rich father of the speaker's fiancée (Maud) calls off the engagement. Maud (like Amy in "Locksley Hall") obeys her father and, egged on by her snobbish libertine brother, breaks all contact with the speaker. Later, however, they meet in a garden, where the brother surprises them and pushes the speaker into a duel. The brother is killed in the duel and, out of sorrow and remorse, Maud dies. The distraught speaker slowly goes insane, and at one point is even committed to an asylum. In the end, the speaker exorcises his ghosts by joining up to fight in the Crimean War.

The plot, of course, bears much in common with that of "Locksley Hall" (jilted lover rages against society, then joins war effort); it also parallels *Hamlet*, not only in the morbid introspection of the hero, but in the triangular link between Maud-Father-

Brother and Ophelia-Polonius-Laertes. However, the poem lacks the unity of "Locksley Hall" and of *Hamlet*, and by the middle of the poem, most readers tire of being locked up in the brain of its crazed, unstable speaker. Indeed, piecing together a plot out of his ravings is quite difficult, as is deciding (1) what the context of his various speeches is, (2) whether or not we can trust him, and (3) whether or not he is a mouthpiece for Tennyson. All this is rendered even more difficult by the odd organization of the poem. It devolves itself into a series of separate lyrics of varying length and focus, the links between which are often obscure. It is a true grab bag, which holds together in a tenuous balance bitter, anti-progressivist ravings against society, love songs of exquisite beauty, self-deprecating accusations of guilt, evocations of past innocence, fragmented memories of the asylum, and jingoistic, apocalyptic celebrations of war. And amidst this lyrical anarchy, the only real unifying force is the madness of the speaker (and behind that, perhaps, Tennyson's own anxiety over inheriting the "black blood" of his ancestors).

As you might imagine, the poem, though it sold well, was not popular with the public.

They found it too confusing and morbid and felt, perhaps, that their poet laureate was losing touch with his public and their Victorian values and tastes. Tennyson was upset by the criticism and became a full-time apologist for his poem, often subjecting his friends and admirers to frequent recitations of the *entire* poem (a two- to three-hour ordeal!). Ironically, though Tennyson's more sentimental pieces have fallen out of favor today, *Maud* has gained in reputation, partly because the poem anticipates many modern literary developments. First, the poem is extremely experimental both in its meter (at times it borders on free verse) and in its disturbing technique of allowing the mind of the speaker to wander aimlessly and make its own personal associations (Joyce, Faulkner, and Virginia Woolf would call this stream of consciousness). Second, it anticipates the "unreliable narrator" of much postmodern fiction. Third, its intense psychological insight into a tortured mind has greater appeal in a post-Freudian world that scours literature for such things as neuroses, repressed emotions, and sublimation. Fourth, in the speaker we have an early portrait of those angry, disaffected young men whose disgust with and alienation from bourgeois society would later draw them to Marxism or Fascism. Indeed, when I read the poem, I cannot help but recall the grotesque yet oddly compelling antiheroic narrator of Dostoevsky's *Notes from Underground*: he who begins his journal with the words "I am a sick man. . . . I am a spiteful man. I am an unattractive man. I believe my liver is diseased."

Though it was written in 1855 at the height of Victorian optimism, there is in *Maud* a sense of the malaise, the pessimism, the sickness of soul that would infect the Victorian spirit at the century's end. Much nearer that end, in 1886, Tennyson would, in fact, write yet another variation on the jilted speaker of "Locksley Hall" that would express that very mood in a bitterness bordering on hysteria. In the poem, "Locksley Hall Sixty Years After," the aged speaker of the early work shares with his grandson, who has himself been jilted by a rich fiancée, his disaffection with the modern world. He has lost the optimistic faith in progress expressed at the close of the earlier poem; he has, in fact, come to see evolution in a new light, as a process that lunges forward only to revert back. He surveys the historical past of England and sees not growth toward a future utopia but unending cycles of hatred, warfare, and intolerance: no brave new world looms on the horizon. Even the city, which the Victorian Tennyson once celebrated as the center of growth and progress, becomes a ghastly place where technology has failed to eliminate either ignorance or poverty:

> Is it well that while we range with Science glorying in
> the Time,
> City children soak and blacken soul and sense in city slime?

> There among the glooming alleys Progress halts on
> palsied feet,

Crime and hunger cast our maidens by the thousand on
   the street. (217–20)

The tone is not far removed from that of Blake's "London." In his
antimodernist tirade, the speaker even attacks democracy (the
masses are to be feared), the novels of Zola (they are decadent),
and ugly architecture (he prefers Ruskin's Gothic). The speaker, it
appears, has lost his ability to adapt and grow with his society, as
perhaps the seventy-seven-year-old Tennyson has as well; where
he once saw unity of purpose, he now sees only fragmentation. It
is a dark vision, one that shows that Tennyson, as the poet of his
age, was aware of both the achievements and the failures of Victorianism, and perhaps felt a calling to embody both in his verse.

SAD ASTROLOGY

But let us now return to *Maud* and consider carefully some specific passages from the work that illuminate the conflicts that
troubled and obsessed the aging poet laureate. In the opening section, Tennyson treats us to the dark side of financial and mercantile progress. A worm has burrowed into, and a cancer grown in,
the promised utopia of peace and plenty:

Why do they prate of the blessings of peace? we have made
   them a curse,
Pickpockets, each hand lusting for all that is not its own;
And lust of gain, in the spirit of Cain, is it better or worse
Than the heart of the citizen hissing in war on his own
   hearthstone?

Peace sitting under her olive, and slurring the days gone by,
When the poor are hovell'd and hustled together, each sex,
   like swine,
When only the ledger lives and when only not all men lie;
Peace in her vineyard—yes!—but a company forges the wine.
   (I.21–24, 33–36)

Yes, cries the speaker, we have gained our peace, but at what cost? Prosperity has not made England better or nobler, only fatter, greedier, more self-satisfied. The vitality has gone out of her as it has out of Maud, whom the speaker describes as "Faultily fault-less, icily regular, splendidly null"; her "Cold and clear-cut face" is "passionless" (I.82, 88). She embodies, we might say, that same love of perfection but loss of humanity that Ruskin rages against in "The Stones of Venice." And that love and loss have resulted in the very corruption, the very "commodification," of society against which Ruskin warned.

But this is not the worst of it. As Maud and her society have grown cold and distant and less than human, so have the stars lost their brilliance, their sympathetic link with we who dwell on earth. Except the redeeming love of Maud shine down on him, it would "be better to be born"

> To labor and the mattock-harden'd hand
> Than nursed at ease and brought to understand
> A sad astrology, the boundless plan
> That makes you tyrants in your iron skies,
> Innumerable, pitiless, passionless eyes,
> Cold fires, yet with power to burn and brand
> His nothingness into man. (I.632–38)

The new advances in astrology have not illuminated the heavens but extinguished them; the astrology is sad for it no longer speaks of higher purpose but of a cold, existential emptiness. In one sense, what Tennyson (or at least the speaker) expresses in the passage is similar to the early sections of *In Memoriam* and the early lines of "Locksley Hall," but here the mood is far less hopeful, for the Victorian spirit of progress lies not ahead of but behind the speaker's despair.

Indeed, the speaker ends up cut off both from Romantic nostalgia, with its promise of a restored pastoral world, and Victorian positivism, with its forward thrust toward the crowning race. The abandonment of the latter occurs early in the poem as the speaker comes to see himself and others as puppets in the hands of an arbitrary force, an unseen hand that, like the invisible hand of laissez-faire capitalism, moves its chessmen at will, now lifting them up, now brushing them off the board. Then, in a stunning reversal of the epilogue of *In Memoriam*, he states:

> A monstrous eft was of old the lord and master of earth,
> For him did his high sun flame, and his river billowing ran,
> And he felt himself in his force to be Nature's crowning race.
> As nine months go to the shaping an infant ripe for his birth,
> So many a million of ages have gone to the making of man:
> He now is first, but is he the last? is he not too base?
> (I.1323–27)

Perhaps Hallam is not a foretaste of the crowning race; perhaps we will, after all, end up as fossils sealed in the iron hills (*In Memoriam* #56): evolution offers patterns for both futures. Perhaps we are "infants crying in the night," and the Victorian faith is just as false as the Romantic faith it replaced. After all, the speaker goes on to assert:

> . . . the drift of the Maker is dark, an Isis hid by the veil,
> Who knows the ways of the world, how God will bring
> them about?
> Our planet is one, the suns are many, the world is wide.
> Shall I weep if a Poland fall? shall I shriek if a Hungary fail?
> Or an infant civilization be ruled with rod or with knout?
> I have not made the world, and He that made it will guide.
> (I.144–49)

The statement and the ethos behind it are defiantly anti-Victorian. The speaker refuses to engage himself in the struggles of his day or even to acknowledge them as worthy of consideration. He would rather withdraw into himself, as his Romantic forebears did before him.

A TROUBLED RESOLUTION

But the nostalgic turn inward will no longer work. Divorced from any Romantic sense of the richness of the interior life and the communion of nature, his withdrawal will only increase his isolation and angst. Indeed, the Romantic way is knowingly rejected in the poem, a rejection made even more profound by its contrast to the celebration of the pastoral world that occurs midway through the poem, as the poet recalls, in language reminiscent of the Song of Solomon, the love he and Maud might have shared. The central love lyric, set in an edenic garden, begins with a breathless invitation:

> Come into the garden, Maud,
> For the black bat, night, has flown,
> Come into the garden, Maud,
> I am here at the gate alone;
> And the woodbine spices are wafted abroad,
> And the musk of the rose is blown. (I.850–55)

The lyric continues for fourteen stanzas, each of which brings the natural world more and more to life, and each of which builds on the almost messianic expectation of Maud's arrival. The concluding stanza, one of the most perfect in the language, shimmers with rapture:

> She is coming, my own, my sweet;
> Were it ever so airy a tread,
> My heart would hear her and beat,
> Were it earth in an earthy bed;
> My dust would hear her and beat,
> Had I lain for a century dead,
> Would start and tremble under her feet,
> And blossom in purple and red. (I.916–23)

For a brilliant, heady moment, it seems that love can redeem the grave, that love, as Solomon sings, is stronger than death, that its power is the power of Resurrection in Nature and in Man.

But alas, Maud's faithlessness, the corruption of society, and that "black blood" which drives the speaker's father to suicide all conspire to kill the possibilities of a return to the pastoral world: indeed, kill it from the very beginning of the poem, whose first stanza is a virulent anti-Romantic tirade:

> I hate the dreadful hollow behind the little wood;
> Its lips in the field above are dabbled with blood-red heath,
> The red-ribb'd ledges drip with a silent horror of blood,
> And Echo there, whatever is ask'd her, answers "Death."
> (I.1–4)

There is no hope of a redemptive word springing forth out of the natural world: All is sickness and disease and madness. It is as if all of nature has taken its cue from two despairing lines from Hamlet's first soliloquy: " 'tis an unweeded garden, / That grows to seed; things rank and gross in nature / Possess it merely" (I.ii.135–37). Eden has fallen, and no manmade utopia can take its place. Solace is to be found in neither the memories of the past nor the promises of the future.

Truly the speaker is cut off from all sources of restoration, and yet, as noted above, he does find partial resolution, as does the speaker of "Locksley Hall," in joining himself to a higher cause. As he stands, in the final section of the poem, on board a mighty warship heading to the Crimea, his sanity is restored. From his perch atop the rolling deck, he watches the tormenting phantom of Maud flit away and exults:

> Let it go or stay, so I wake to the higher aims
> Of a land that has lost for a little her lust of gold,
> And love of a peace that was full of wrongs and shames,
> Horrible, hateful, monstrous, not to be told;
> And hail once more to the banner of battle unroll'd.
> (III.38–42)

In his apocalyptic view of events, the speaker sees the Crimean War as a divine crucible that will purify the evils of British materialism and rebaptize England with the passion she has lost. It offers a fiery end to selfishness and the unchecked acquisition of wealth, and the hope of a new vision, a new and higher aim to strive for. And yet, as most critics have argued, the ending does not work: the Crimean War was hardly noble or just; it was neither a war-to-end-all-wars nor a harbinger of the postmillennial kingdom. Of course, we must be reminded that this is not Tennyson's resolution, but that of a mentally unstable speaker newly released from the asylum; still, the ending remains problematic. And, because it is problematic, it casts in a somewhat darker light Tennyson's earlier faith in the Victorian spirit of progress as a force and an ethos that can sweep away past errors and griefs.

Is the poem, then, a masterpiece or a failure? It certainly lacks the cohesion most great poetry demands, yet its very fragmentation and tenuousness strengthen Tennyson's critique of his own Victorian ideals and present the poet laureate as a man capable of seeing his age from every angle.

21

TAMING THE BEAST
Tennyson's Idylls of the King *I*

It is surely no exaggeration to say that the tales of King Arthur and his Round Table have played as vital and decisive a role in the aesthetic history of Western Europe as the tales surrounding the Trojan War did in the belles lettres of ancient Greece. From the early incarnations of these tales in the works of Geoffrey of Monmouth, Chrétien de Troyes, Wolfram Von Eschenbach, the anonymous author of *Sir Gawain and the Green Knight*, and Sir Thomas Malory, to their later handling by writers as diverse as Mark Twain, William Morris, T. S. Eliot, and T. H. White, to the more recent explosion of Arthurian-inspired fantasy novels, the legends of Arthur, Merlin, Lancelot, Guinevere, Galahad, Percivale, and a host of other characters have continued to exert an almost hypnotic hold on the consciousness of the Western world. Whatever the age (Medieval, Renaissance, Enlightenment, Romantic) and whatever the artistic medium (painting, poetry, prose, opera, film), the chivalric world of Arthur and his knights has proven remarkably resilient as an ever contemporaneous arena for intellectual, emotional, spiritual, and aesthetic wrestling. It is no wonder, then, that Victorian England's greatest poet should eventually come to wrestle (both for himself and on behalf of his age) with the whole vast corpus of Arthurian legends.

THE EVOLUTION OF AN EPIC

True to the dominant metaphor of his age, Tennyson's Arthurian epic *(Idylls of the King)* was, like *In Memoriam*, more a product of evolution than of creation. Indeed, whereas *In Memoriam* took seventeen years to complete, *Idylls of the King* was composed over a period of nearly fifty-five years. Ironically, the first part of the epic to be written actually stands at the very end, the elegiac "Morte d'Arthur" that Tennyson composed in 1833, shortly after the death of Arthur Hallam. (We might compare this with the equally ironic fact that the Prologue of *In Memoriam*, though it appears first, was actually written last.) As discussed in chapter 7, "Morte d'Arthur" recounts the last moments of Arthur's life as he commands Sir Bedivere to cast Excalibur back into the lake from which it came. Tennyson's use of the Arthurian material (his closely followed source is Malory) is both fresh and bold, and it serves as a fit companion to his other great treatment of the Age of Camelot, the lovely and fragile poem "The Lady of Shallot," written a year earlier, in 1832.

Tennyson was inspired by his success with these two poems (along with several other more minor pieces), and the idea of eventually composing an epic based on the Arthurian tales as told by Malory remained with him for the next two decades. He did not, however, return to this project until after the success of *In Memoriam* (1850). Perhaps buoyed up by the critical and popular praise of his epic-length meditation on the grieving process, Tennyson soon took up again the long-dormant project. In 1859, he published four separate and disconnected *Idylls* dealing with Vivien's seduction of Merlin, Guinevere's betrayal, the tragic death of Elaine, and the tale of Geraint and Enid. About ten years later, four more *Idylls* appeared: " The Coming of Arthur" and "The Passing of Arthur" (which eventually served as the first and last *Idylls* of the complete epic, the latter being an expansion of the earlier "Morte d'Arthur"), "The Holy Grail," and "Pelleas and Ettarre." In the early 1870s, Tennyson composed most of the three remaining

Idylls, but he continued to tinker with them and eventually (in 1888) divided the earlier "Geraint and Enid" into two Idylls.

When finally published as a complete work, the epic consisted of twelve Idylls that fall into three equal parts of four Idylls each: the first covers the rise of Camelot and the heyday of the chivalric code; the second recounts the erosion of the initial ideal; the third chronicles the decay and fall of Camelot. However, despite this tripartite arrangement (and a parallel seasonal shift from spring to summer to autumn to winter) the epic hardly holds together as a unified work. Though not as fragmented perhaps as *Maud*, it lacks the cohesion of *In Memoriam* and tends to break into its constituent parts. This disunity is due partly to the poem's helter-skelter method of composition and to the difficulty of assimilating such diverse material into an organic whole (Sir Thomas Malory himself, in his fifteenth-century chronicle of the legends of Arthur and the Round Table, *Le Morte d'Arthur*, was unable to do so); however, it is also a function of Tennyson's lifelong struggle with the intellectual side of poetry. As stated several times before, Tennyson's true skill was in his lyrical power and his precise observations of the natural world, and the Idylls are perhaps more famous for their verbal and visual gems than for their narrative power and thematic richness.

Still, this is not to say the *Idylls of the King* is devoid of an intellectual or moral purpose.

Tennyson *did* have something to say, and some of it does come across in the poem: a tribute to the long and frustrating hours he spent editing and reshaping the poems. Most vitally, he wanted to show the need for the physical and the spiritual to be united. When the one is divided from the other, the *Idylls* warn us, only grief and ultimate ruin can come of it. Thus, while Tennyson's Arthur represents (especially in "The Coming of Arthur") an older Christian ideal with the power to combat the corrosive forces of materialism and naturalism (all that is bestial in man), Tennyson also imbues his Arthur (in "The Holy Grail") with an understanding that the pursuit of pure spirituality (the angel in man) unconnected to our earthly duties is likewise disastrous.

Though Tennyson never really became an orthodox Christian (as many critics have noted, Tennyson's only firm and consistent Christian belief was in the immortality of the soul: a belief he felt necessary if he was to continue living!), he was a strong opponent of the growing materialism of his age. Indeed, in a late dramatic monologue, "Lucretius" (1865), Tennyson exposes the final despair that comes of a too strict naturalist viewpoint: in the absence of God, duty becomes meaningless, and even sensual pleasure (whether Epicurean or hedonistic) offers little peace and no hope of real immortality. This note is sounded in many of Tennyson's late poems and helps to account for the growing bitterness Tennyson felt toward his age and its slow abandonment of faith in the spiritual. In fact, Tennyson's eventual disillusionment with the utilitarian ethos of his age (see chapter 20, on *Maud*) was predicated less on a sense of social injustice (as in Mill or Ruskin) than on the spiritual emptiness of this ethos and its single-minded focus on earthly, if not sensual, pleasures. In the same way, Tennyson's disgust at the sexual sins of Guinevere and Vivien (an aspect of the Idylls that does not sit well with modern audiences) should be interpreted not simply as an expression of Victorian prudishness, but as evidence of Tennyson's distrust of passions that are indulged in apart from any higher code or ethic.

But let us turn our focus now to the first of the Idylls, "The Coming of Arthur," and study up close how Tennyson was able to embody poetically his own struggles with the excesses of Victorian materialism and utilitarianism.

THE MARRIAGE OF PHYSICAL AND SPIRITUAL

Tennyson does not begin his epic with the birth of Arthur, but leaps in *in medias res* ("in the middle of things"), at the moment of Arthur's ascendancy to power and kingship. The opening lines of the poem are unforgettable in their slow, stately grandeur:

For many a petty king ere Arthur came
Ruled in this isle and, ever-waging war
Each upon other, wasted all the land;
And still from time to time the heathen host
Swarm'd over-seas and harried what was left.
And so there grew great tracts of wilderness,
Wherein the beast was ever more and more,
But man was less and less, till Arthur came.
For first Aurelius lived and fought and died,
And after him King Uther fought and died,
But either fail'd to make the kingdom one.
And after him King Arthur for a space,
And thro' the puissance of his Table Round,
Drew all their petty princedoms under him,
Their king and head, and made a realm and reign'd. (5–19)

Arthur, as presented here and throughout the *Idylls*, is a bringer of unity. The unity he brings, however, is not just external and political; it is internal and spiritual as well. Like the Hercules of classical mythology, Arthur is the beast slayer, but the beast he slays lies more in the heart of man than in a labyrinth or cave.

In the final lines of *In Memoriam* #118, Tennyson issues the evolutionary mandate: "Move upward, working out the beast / And let the ape and tiger die." By these words he meant that man, if he is to enter the postmillennial kingdom, must rid himself of the savage, bestial side of his nature. Before Arthur came, Tennyson suggests, England was ruled more by passion and civil strife than law and order; worse yet, overindulgence in that passion was deteriorating their very humanity. Before Arthur, "the land of Cameliard was waste, / Thick with wet woods, and many a beast therein, / And none or few to scare or chase the beast" (20–22); and the men who fought these beasts were no better themselves: "wolf-like men," Tennyson calls them, "Worse than the wolves" (32–33). But then Arthur came and "drave"

The heathen; after, slew the beast, and fell'd
The forest, letting in the sun, and made
Broad pathways for the hunter and the knight. (58–61)

In the first Idyll, Arthur is very much a messianic figure: both the
Forerunner who makes straight the paths of the Lord and the
long-awaited Christ who brings light into a world of darkness and
sin. Nevertheless, the legendary King is, in and of himself, too
spiritual a figure to effect a full reconciliation and to establish a
kingdom. His vision needs to be brought to earth, to incarnate
itself into the physical now.

In the opening Idylls, this is accomplished through marriage
and the swearing of vows. When Arthur first looks on Guinevere,
he feels desire arise within him and exclaims:

I seem as nothing in this mighty world,
And cannot will my will nor work my work
Wholly, nor make myself in mine own realm
Victor and lord. But were I join'd with her,
Then might we live together as one life,
And reigning with one will in everything
Have power on this dark land to lighten it,
And power on this dead world to make it live. (86–93)

In the wider allegory of *Idylls of the King*, the marriage of Arthur
and Guinevere is like that of Christ and the Church, a fusion of
spirit and flesh, soul and body, that ushers in the New Jerusalem.
In and through the flesh of Guinevere, Arthur will stamp his more
spiritual image on the land; the joining of the two into one will
bear fruit in the social and political realm as well as in the moral.
Later in the Idyll, Tennyson compares Arthur to the "sun of May"
and Guinevere to the "earth's beauty" (462): the first breathes life
on the second; the second transforms that life into fecundity.

But the mere physical joining is not enough; the marriage
must be both predicated on and creative of vows of duty and
oaths of loyalty. Indeed, in "The Coming of Arthur," the King

makes special vows with both Guinevere and Lancelot, the very two whose later breaking of their vows (through adultery) will bring down the Table. To Guinevere, Arthur vows:

> Behold thy doom is mine.
> Let chance what will, I love thee to the death. (466–67)

Completely (and, as it turns out, tragically) Arthur links his own fate to hers. To Lancelot, he makes a similar irrevocable vow:

> Man's word is God in man;
> Let chance what will, I trust thee to the death. (132–33)

As love will bond him to Guinevere, so the act of vowing will link him to Lancelot. And that act of vowing is more than just a verbal exchange; it is itself a kind of marriage, a joining of two into one: or, in the case of the Knights of the Round Table, of many into one. Indeed, in a powerfully mystical scene, an onlooker describes the communal vow of the knights:

> Then the King in low deep tones,
> And simple words of great authority,
> Bound them by so strait vows to his own self
> That when they rose, knighted from kneeling, some
> Were pale as at the passing of a ghost,
> Some flush'd, and others dazed, as one who wakes
> Half-blinded at the coming of a light.
>
> But when he spake, and cheer'd his Table Round
> With large, divine, and comfortable words,
> Beyond my tongue to tell thee—I beheld
> From eye to eye thro' all their Order flash
> A momentary likeness of the King. (259–70)

Vows are indeed sacred things, both for Arthur and, it seems, for Tennyson. In fact, the vow is itself a nexus between physical action (praxis) and spiritual word (logos), between doing and being. The vow at its highest is a type of Eucharist, by which all the knights share almost literally in the body and blood of their Lord; as long as this mystical bond remains in place, Camelot is strong.

This physical/spiritual joining of oneself to some greater cause or purpose or unity is certainly what Tennyson was trying to suggest at the close of both "Locksley Hall" and *Maud.*

Here, however, the image is more effective, partly because it is shrouded in the mystery of England's legendary past, but also because the chivalric ideal is both an external and internal discipline. Chivalry is not just something one does; it is something one is. The knights are linked not merely by some physical cause but by an immaterial spirit that imbues them with a higher purpose. The materialistic philosophies and utilitarian ethics of Tennyson's day rendered such vows illusory at best; in the absence of God and the supernatural, the vow loses both its power and reality.

It is not enough, Tennyson knew, for the masses to rally to some political cause (as they would later do in Russia and Germany); rather, the spirit of God (and his earthly regent) must illuminate those around him. For when it does, then will the millennium arrive; so sing they at the wedding of Arthur:

> Blow trumpet, for the world is white with May!
> Blow trumpet, the long night hath roll'd away!
> Blow thro' the living world—"Let the King reign!"
>
> Blow trumpet! he will lift us from the dust.
> Blow trumpet! live the strength, and die the lust!
> Clang battle-axe, and clash brand! Let the King reign!
> (481–83, 490–92)

In this victory cry of the new order, with its chorus of "blow trumpet," Tennyson offers an Arthurian equivalent to the "Ring out the old, ring in the new" of *In Memoriam* #103. And when this victorious union is achieved, then nothing will be impossible, as the officials of the declining Roman Empire, come for the annual tribute, learn to their chagrin:

There at the banquet those great lords from Rome,
The slowly-fading mistress of the world,
Strode in and claim'd their tribute as of yore.
But Arthur spake: "Behold, for these have sworn
To wage my wars, and worship me their King;
The old order changeth, yielding place to new,
And we that fight for our fair father Christ,
Seeing that ye be grown too weak and old
To drive the heathen from your Roman wall,
No tribute will we pay." So those great lords
Drew back in wrath, and Arthur strove with Rome.

And Arthur and his kingdom for a space
Were all one will, and thro' that strength the King
Drew in the petty princedoms under him,
Fought, and in twelve great battles overcame
The heathen hordes, and made a realm and reign'd. (503–18)

Finally, Arthur rules not on the basis of mere strength alone, but on the basis of a moral power that can hold back and even tame the beast. This new kind of power, based on a Christian unity that binds physical and spiritual, external and internal, vassal and lord, enables Arthur not only to defeat the declining empire of Rome but to draw together the scattered princedoms of England into a single Kingdom of Light.

It was this spirit, I believe, that Tennyson saw in the Victorian Age when it was most worthy of itself, and it was to this ideal (rather than to material progress) that he pledged his poetry. Britain must not be merely another tyrant; she must become and remain the great Christian Kingdom foreshadowed at Camelot. She must represent a new order ruled by a higher vision of a community united both spiritually and ethically. Unfortunately, as he aged, Tennyson saw less and less of this spirit in his country, and thus grew more and more embittered and isolated from the material and scientific progress of the Victorian Age. Indeed, in the opening

scene of the last Idyll ("The Passing of Arthur"), the King expresses
a pessimism that the elder Tennyson seems to have shared:

> I found Him [God] in the shining of the stars,
> I mark'd Him in the flowering of His fields,
> But in His ways with men I find Him not. (9–11)

In *In Memoriam* #124 (chapter 11), Tennyson's "testimony," the
poet claims that he found God not in nature but in his heart.
Here, at the close of his second, later epic, nature seems the only
place where God shines forth, for the heart of man has grown
dark. The only hope offered at the end of *Idylls of the King* is the
image of the rising sun; the prophecy that Arthur ("the Once and
Future King") will someday return is hazy at best.

But how can it be otherwise? Man has so changed, has so sacrificed his spiritual powers and his faith, that neither the lyrical poetry
of Tennyson nor the epic form can bring back the Golden Age.

22

THE ROLE OF THE SACRED
Tennyson's Idylls of the King II

For centuries, artists in every genre have been fascinated by the legend of the Holy Grail, the belief that the cup from which Christ served the wine of the Last Supper and into which Jesus' own blood (from the spear wound in his side) was poured still exists and possesses mystical powers of healing. The legend, meaningful to all the countries of Western Europe, possessed especial significance to the British, for legend held that Joseph of Arimathea had brought the sacred chalice to England. In most accounts, the quest for the Grail is a holy and righteous one that tests to the full the bravery and purity of the knights, but for Tennyson it signified something far different.

DIVINE CONTAGION

Right from the start of the eighth Idyll ("The Holy Grail"), we can tell that Tennyson's version of the Grail Legend will be darker, less hopeful, and more fragmented than earlier accounts of that chivalric quest for the unattainable. The tale is told in flashback from the point of view of Sir Percivale, who relates the quest to a monk in the monastery that he has joined; worse yet, line 7 tells us Sir Percivale died shortly after telling the tale. Our first image, that is to say, is one not of devotion and high adventure, but of death and isolation. True, in Malory's version of the quest, most of the knights end up in monasteries, but in Tennyson's version, as we shall see, the retreat to monastic life is depicted finally as a life- and flesh-denying withdrawal from society and their duties to it.

The vision of the Grail, according to Percivale, came first to his sister, a devout nun, who then passed on that vision, and the desire to find it, to the chaste and pure knight, Sir Galahad:

> And this Galahad, when he heard
> My sister's vision, fill'd me with amaze;
> His eyes became so like her own, they seem'd
> Hers, and himself her brother more than I. (139–42)

The image is reminiscent of "The Coming of Arthur," when Arthur's knights take on the imprint of their lord; however, here the passing of the spirit seems more a contagion, a kind of madness. Rather than draw together Percivale and his sister, the vision disrupts and divides their natural sibling relationship, replacing it with an illusory marriage that is not really a marriage. Indeed, to ensure this point will be clear, Tennyson has Galahad and the nun go through a parody of Arthur and Guinevere's marriage ceremony, a joining of souls that denies the need for flesh. With these words (almost a spell), the nun binds Galahad to herself:

> "My knight, my love, my knight of heaven,
> O thou, my love, whose love is one with mine,
> I, maiden, round thee, maiden, bind my belt.
> Go forth, for thou shalt see what I have seen,
> And break thro' all, till one will crown thee king
> Far in the spiritual city;" and as she spake
> She sent the deathless passion in her eyes
> Thro' him, and made him hers, and laid her mind
> On him, and he believed in her belief. (157–65)

What Tennyson describes here is a perversion of that medieval courtly love in which the knight performs deeds in the name of a

lovely and inaccessible lady. The image Tennyson conjures for us
is more like a possession, one that hypnotizes Galahad and robs
him of his free initiative: one, we might argue, that de-masculin-
izes and even emasculates him.

Worse yet, it represents a new kind of oath that abrogates the
greater unity of the oath made to Arthur in the first Idyll; and
that abrogation leads to a second and greater one. As the knights
are gathered in the hall, Galahad enters and sits in the mysterious
Siege Perilous. As soon as he does, thunder is heard overhead, and
the image of the Grail floats into the room. Though none but
Galahad actually sees the Grail, all the knights hastily and impulsively swear a sacred vow that they will go on a quest to find it.
Shortly after, Arthur arrives at court and scolds his knights for
making their vows and thus depriving him of their presence and
their strength. He insists that had he been there he would have
prevented the knights from swearing, but Percivale says had he
been there he would have sworn. The fact that Tennyson
chooses to have Arthur absent from court when the vows are
made (in Malory, the King is there), emphasizes Tennyson's view
that the vow to seek the Grail is finally destructive of the initial
vow to serve Arthur and the Round Table.

More importantly, Tennyson goes beyond his source material
(Malory) to have Arthur offer a deeper explanation as to why the
vow of Percivale and his fellow knights is foolish:

> "Ah, Galahad, Galahad," said the King, "for such
> As thou art is the vision, not for these."

It is not that the sacred quest is, in and of itself, wrong, but it is
meant to be undertaken only by a chosen few. In anger, the King
goes on to question his knights and to prophecy their doom:

> "What are ye? Galahads? . . .
>   . . . nay," said he, "but men
> With strength and will to right the wrong'd, of power
> To lay the sudden heads of violence flat . . .

But one hath seen, and all the blind will see.
Go, since your vows are sacred, being made.
Yet—for ye know the cries of all my realm
Pass thro' this hall—how often, O my knights,
Your places being vacant at my side,
This chance of noble deeds will come and go
Unchallenged, while ye follow wandering fires
Lost in the quagmire! Many of you, yea most,
Return no more." (306–20)

These knights have no business devoting themselves to a wholly spiritual cause; their proper role is in the physical world, using their martial skill to bring order and peace to the realm. Unlike their proper vow to Arthur, which unites them, their vow to seek the Grail leads to disunity and fragmentation, as each knight goes off on his own foolish, finally futile quest.

THE QUEST IS NOT FOR ME

Though we learn bits and pieces of these various quests, the focus rests on Percivale's, a twelve-month journey that quickly devolves into a nightmare, an existential dark night of the soul. In some of his eeriest and most richly psychological verse, Tennyson takes his knight through a wasted landscape that is more internal than external, a world where nothing is what it seems. No sooner does Percivale arrive at a place or meet a person, but they crumble into dust. Guilt and despair pursue him wherever he goes, incessant reminders that the quest is not for him.

But there is one ray of hope. Midway in his quest, he comes upon a real castle, where the people immediately hail him as a Knight of the Round Table and, on bended knee, beg him thus:

"We have heard of thee; thou art our greatest knight,
Our Lady says it, and we well believe.
Wed thou our Lady, and rule over us,
And thou shalt be as Arthur in our land." (602–5)

Percivale here is offered a chance to fulfill, in a righteous and wholly proper manner, his calling as a knight and to bring to the outer realms of Camelot the peace and order of Arthur . . . but it is not to be. At night, the vision of the Grail burns in Percivale's heart, and he flees the castle.

Viewed in the context of the entire Idyll (if not the entire epic), Percivale's choice to abandon kingship and marriage for the sake of a holy quest is the wrong one. It represents not noble self-sacrifice or Christian piety but an ascetic rejection of the flesh and a shirking of our earthly duties. In terms of Tennyson's own age, I might add, it also marks a rejection of the Victorian spirit of progress and that strong emphasis on duty and the social gospel that Tennyson honored. Even the cloistered, celibate monk to whom Percivale tells his tale is saddened by his choice:

> O the pity
> To find thine own first love once more—to hold,
> Hold her a wealthy bride within thine arms,
> Or all but hold, and then—cast her aside,
> Foregoing all her sweetness, like a weed! (618–22)

As noted in the previous chapter, Tennyson believed that the rejection of the physical was finally as destructive as a narrow-minded materialism that denies the soul. Indeed, in an early dramatic monologue ("Saint Simeon Stylites," one of his best) Tennyson parodies a historical early Church ascetic who felt he could gain holiness and win God's favor by living his life atop a narrow pillar. However, as Tennyson's poem reveals, Simeon's savage mortification of his flesh, far from making him spiritual-minded, causes him to focus exclusively (and self-righteously) *on* his flesh.

Tennyson very subtly drives this point home in the scene when the Grail appears to the knights at court by eliminating a vital and memorable detail from Malory's account of the episode. In *Le Morte d'Arthur* (Book XIII, ch. 8), when the Grail floats into the room, the hall is filled "with good odours, and every knight ha[s] such meats and drinks as he best loved in this world." Had he wanted to, Tennyson could have made wonderful poetic fare out of this detail, but he chose instead to drop it from his version, while otherwise modeling his syntax at this point very closely on Malory's. To my mind, there can be only one explanation for this decision to leave out such a memorable detail. In keeping with his belief that pure spirituality divorced from the physical is as ultimately damaging as pure materialism divorced from the spiritual, Tennyson wanted to limit his presentation of the Grail to a wholly other-worldly object incapable of enriching the physical world. To have granted to the Grail the power to enhance the physical appetites would have been to suggest that the quest for it could equally enhance the earthbound sociopolitical realities of Arthur's England.

Thus, though Galahad *does* find the Grail in the end, his discovery does not enrich the King or his court in any way. As soon as Galahad finds the chalice, both he and the Grail are translated directly into heaven. The quest *has* fulfilled Galahad's spiritual desires, but Camelot has gained nothing. The futility of the quest becomes even more clear in the closing scene, when the knights regather at the Round Table to relate their adventures to Arthur: Galahad attained it, but then was taken away; Sir Bors saw it, but cannot speak of it; Percivale saw it, but abandons court for the monastery; Lancelot saw it, but it was veiled. In all four cases, neither society (Camelot) nor its leaders (Arthur) are strengthened (nay, they are made weaker). The knowledge the knights gained is for themselves alone; the world has not been changed.

Still, this is not to deny that some are called by God to undertake spiritual quests. Indeed, when Gawain, who makes the mistake of going from one extreme to the other, swears that from now on he will be deaf to "holy virgins in their ecstasies," Arthur responds:

> Deafer . . .
> Gawain, and blinder unto holy things,
> Hope not to make thyself by idle vows,
> Being too blind to have desire to see.

> But if indeed there came a sign from heaven,
> Blessed are Bors, Lancelot, and Percivale.
> For these have seen according to their sight. (865–71)

The answer is not to reject the sacred but to confine it to its proper role and place. Tennyson was no Huxley; he knew that both spiritual language and supernatural visions were essential parts of the human psyche that could not simply be dismissed or denied. They are, rather, gifts to be practiced and disseminated by those to whom the gift was given. They should not take the place of science or politics or business, but they should also not be eclipsed by those more pragmatic, earthbound pursuits.

In the closing lines, Arthur, as moral anchor of the Idyll, voices the central message:

> And some among you held that if the King
> Had seen the sight he would have sworn the vow.
> Not easily, seeing that the King must guard
> That which he rules, and is but as the hind
> To whom a space of land is given to plow,
> Who may not wander from the allotted field
> Before his work is done . . . (899–905)

Again, the Victorian keynote of duty is sounded. The spiritual is not bad, but unless there are those willing to incarnate that spirituality into practical earthly forms, there will be chaos and death. However—and here Tennyson rises to the very height of his poetic powers—Arthur makes it clear that once one's duty is performed, he may open his soul to receive. Arthur thus continues:

> . . . but, being done,
> Let visions of the night or of the day
> Come as they will; and many a time they come,
> Until this earth he walks on seems not earth,
> This light that strikes his eyeball is not light,
> This air that smites his forehead is not air

> But vision—yea, his very hand and foot—
> In moments when he feels he cannot die,
> And knows himself no vision to himself,
> Nor the high God a vision, nor that One
> Who rose again. (905–14)

Man *does* have a spiritual side that must be fed, that must be assured of its own immortality, and in that spiritual side is to be found our true self. No, Arthur does not refuse to seek the Grail because he lacks spiritual insight; rather (like the Tennyson of *In Memoriam*), he finds the true assurance of God's reality and power not in natural, external objects, or even in the saying of vows, but in moments of mystical insight.

THE FINAL VOYAGE

Tennyson the man (as opposed to Tennyson the poet) was rarely able to achieve Arthur's assurance of the Resurrection of Christ; yet surely he desired it, for in the epitaph he wrote for himself (a poem that he requested be always placed at the end of all future collections of his poetry), he receives that certainty which he and his doubting age so sorely lacked. The poem, "Crossing the Bar," is one of Tennyson's finest and best-loved lyrics, and it employs a metaphor that Tennyson returned to again and again in his poetry: that of water. In the first Idyll, for example, Arthur is said to have been born out of water, carried to shore on the ninth wave; in the final Idyll, his body is carried over water to the mystical isle of Avalon. Water too flows freely through *In Memoriam*, most notably, in a section we did not discuss (#103), in which the dreaming Tennyson is taken by boat to meet the glorified Arthur Hallam.

Here, in a poetic and mystical treatment of his own death, Tennyson imagines himself on board a boat whose once shadowy pilot is finally revealed to him:

> Sunset and evening star,
>   And one clear call for me!

And may there be no moaning of the bar,
    When I put out to sea,

But such a tide as moving seems asleep,
    Too full for sound and foam,
When that which drew from out the boundless deep
    Turns again home.

Twilight and evening bell,
    And after that the dark!
And may there be no sadness of farewell,
    When I embark;

For tho' from out our bourne of Time and Place
    The flood may bear me far,
I hope to see my Pilot face to face
    When I have crost the bar.

In the epilogue to *In Memoriam* (Lecture 12), Tennyson speaks of a soul being drawn from out the vast and moved through various phases till it rises up a man. Here, that soul, buffeted and blown by the winds of fate, and "dipped in baths of hissing fears" (#118), finally returns home.

The poet asks for "one clear call," and we can only pray that when he reached that other shore, when the last veil was ripped away and what was once seen but dimly in a mirror came forth in perfect clarity, that he finally knew, with absolute certainty, the voice and the face of his Savior.

23

MATTHEW ARNOLD:
Failed Romantic Poet

It IS NO EASY THING to be raised in an Age of Transition. Born too late to feel fully a part of the previous era, but born too early to embrace unconsciously the era to come, the child of transition is often left stranded on the fence, unsure of which side to fall on. "Should I hold on to what has come before and seek to preserve it," he asks himself, "or should I forsake the past and lose myself in the swift (*too* swift?) forward-moving tide." Whichever way he finally chooses to go, he will have to sacrifice something. For such a one, there can be no easy answers; he may, in fact, have to carve out his own niche in time. Such a man was Matthew Arnold, Victorian England's greatest sage.

THE GROWTH OF A SAGE'S MIND

Matthew Arnold was born on Christmas Eve 1822, the eldest son of Thomas Arnold, legendary headmaster of Rugby School and one of the "Eminent Victorians" Lytton Strachey parodies in his collective biography. Thomas Arnold (or Dr. Arnold as he is often called) was, in his earlier years, a close friend of John Keble, who would initiate the Oxford Movement in 1833. Dr. Arnold, however, broke company with him when Keble began to advocate publicly a return to conservative church polity and dogma.

Instead, Dr. Arnold chose the liberal path, and became a spokesman for a less credal Christianity whose focus would be social and moral rather than theological. In direct contrast to that other leader of the Oxford Movement (Cardinal Newman), Dr. Arnold believed that Christianity must adapt itself to the modern world and become "useful." As headmaster at Rugby, Dr. Arnold, in almost military fashion, trained his young men in a vigorous, rational, ethical Christianity whose greatest call was duty to the state. To the decadent, early-modern Strachey, Dr. Arnold's goals and methods (like those of Florence Nightingale, whose biography also appears in his book) bordered on the neurotic and paranoid. For Dr. Arnold himself, they represented order, sanity, and a higher duty. The supernatural elements of Christ's teachings might be set aside for the sake of the new science, but his ethical teachings were to be carefully instilled in England's youth.

Matthew would eventually absorb and champion his father's liberal Christianity and would himself become committed to education; however, during his school years, much to his father's chagrin, Matthew delighted in playing the role of Epicurean dandy (he even sported white kid gloves!). Rejecting the Victorian earnestness of his father, Arnold identified himself with a group of young men who, though a bit too cynical and refined to return to the simple ideals and passions of the Romantics, were unable to find either beauty or depth or sincerity in their own increasingly utilitarian Age. Like Tennyson amongst the Apostles, Arnold struggled to find his own poetic voice; unlike Tennyson, he never truly found it, settling instead for a style that imitated the angst and over-self-consciousness of the Romantics. Imagine what Tennyson might have been had Hallam never died and he had continued to write poems like "Mariana" and "The Palace of Art," and you can catch a glimpse of Arnold the poet.

In 1849, Arnold published his first collection of poems *(The Strayed Reveller, and Other Poems)* and, in 1852, his second *(Empedocles on Etna, and Other Poems)*. Both collections were indifferently received by public and critics alike, who saw them as too remote and distant from the concerns of the day. Arnold was mulling over problems and dilemmas that were no longer relevant to the changes and developments in society. He was behind the times. The critics, we might say, treated Arnold in a manner similar to the three travelers who scorn and even rebuke the weeping Tennyson when they see him mourning by the grave of Hallam in *In Memoriam* #21. They want Arnold to "get over it," to move on, to stop gazing back longingly and with pain on what has passed away. Ironically, it is precisely this melancholy quality of Arnold's poetry that has caused it to be remembered and that has given it a fixed place in the Western canon. Every survey course in the literary history of Britain must (if it is worth its salt) include several poems by Arnold, for Arnold captures better than any other poet what it meant to live, to struggle, and to *feel* in one of the key transitional moments in the history of England (and of Europe).

True, the critical consensus of the last century and a half has been that Arnold's poetry is flawed (both in form and in content) and that, as a poet, he is not in the same class as Keats or Tennyson or Browning. Nevertheless, one cannot deny the sincerity and directness of the emotional anguish and despair his poetry embodies. Indeed, the overarching problem with Arnold's poetry is that most are variations and reexpressions of the same basic anguish and despair: the grief of one who was born in an age of transition and thus feels stranded between a past ethos he can no longer embrace and a future one he feels cut off from. Of these angst-ridden poems, the best known is surely "Dover Beach," but the one that most fully charts the heights and depths of Arnold's anguish and despair is "Stanzas from the Grand Chartreuse."

WANDERING BETWEEN TWO WORLDS

In "Stanzas from the Grand Chartreuse" (1855), Arnold journeys to a Carthusian monastery built on the dizzying slopes of the French Alps. The purpose of his poem, however, is not to describe the monastery or the mountainous landscape that surrounds it, but to use it as an occasion for dealing with an inner emotional and spiritual struggle. As Arnold stands before the monastery (which represents the traditional Christian faith of Europe that was disrupted by the Enlightenment), he thinks back on his own rationalistic, utilitarian education and wonders guiltily what his teachers would say if they could see him standing there:

> For rigorous teachers seized my youth,
> And purged its faith, and trimmed its fire,
> Showed me the high, white star of Truth,
> There bade me gaze, and there aspire.
> Even now their whispers pierce the gloom:
> What dost thou in this living tomb? (67–72)

In stark contrast to the strict Calvinist upbringing of Carlyle, Arnold was raised (by his father and others) to be a skeptic in all matters supernatural, and to seek answers in the material world.

Above all he was taught to reject anything that smacked of superstition or of rigid, antirational, unscientific dogma, whether that surfaced in Catholicism (the direct reference in the poem) or in the resurgent dogmatism of the Anglo-Catholic Oxford Movement (its more indirect reference).

Indeed, in the poem, Arnold presents himself (as does Mill in his *Autobiography*) as a product of a more materialistic, utilitarian educational program meant to purge his mind of all sloppy, emotional thinking: a sort of dogmatically undogmatic training in the secular religion of the nineteenth century. His teachers were harsh, demanding ones, ready to weed out all heresy, and Arnold (like a schoolboy about to be flogged) shakes nervously as he begs their forgiveness and understanding:

> Forgive me, masters of the mind!
> At whose behest I long ago
> So much unlearnt, so much resign'd—
> I come not here to be your foe!

> I seek these anchorites, not in ruth,
> To curse and to deny your truth;
>
> Not as their friend, or child, I speak!
> But as, on some far northern strand,
> Thinking of his own Gods, a Greek
> In pity and mournful awe might stand
> Before some fallen Runic stone—
> For both were faiths, and both are gone. (73–84)

Fear not, he reassures that sternest of taskmasters, Dr. Arnold, I come not here, like Cardinal Newman, to convert to Catholicism; rather, I come as a spectator, as one who can mourn for a glory and a faith that has passed. Just as a sophisticated, cynical ancient Greek who has grown beyond the gods of his ancestors, might, in the presence of another country's dying religion, think nostalgically of his own, so Arnold cannot help but mourn the loss of a faith that at one time united and inspired all Europe.

Then, with this as preface, Arnold offers what is perhaps his most representative stanza:

> Wandering between two worlds, one dead,
> The other powerless to be born,
> With nowhere yet to rest my head,
> Like these, on earth I wait forlorn.
> Their faith, my tears, the world deride—
> I come to shed them at their side. (85–90)

In these unforgettable lines, Arnold captures precisely and succinctly the dilemma faced by all those unlucky enough to be born in an Age of Transition. And that dilemma, expressed throughout Arnold's poetry but nowhere better and clearer than here, is that Arnold feels stranded between an old world that cannot be revived and a new one not yet fully born. Like so many of his generation (for whom Arnold acts as spokesman), the speaker feels powerless to move on and embrace fully the new ethos. In that special sense, though Arnold does not share the faith of the monks, he does share their isolation: Neither of them has found a secure place in the modern world. Both the faith of the monks (and the followers of the Oxford Movement) and Arnold's melancholy are considered passé by Victorian society, for that society has cast off not only religious dogma but that Byronic self-pity and over-self-consciousness rejected by Mill, Carlyle, and Tennyson.

Like the "Victorian businessman" of *In Memoriam* #21 who rebukes the grieving Tennyson for indulging in personal sorrow when society is on the move, the silent critics who accuse the speaker of the poem (like the real critics who accused Arnold the poet) see no use or purpose in his tears. To the contrary, they deride him as foolish and self-indulgent. Such melancholy (note the messianic persecution complex Arnold betrays when he claims he has nowhere to rest his head) is "a passed mode, an outworn theme." Very well, answers Arnold:

> . . . if it *be* passed, take away,
> At least, the restlessness, the pain;
> Be man henceforth no more a prey
> To these out-dated stings again!
> The nobleness of grief is gone—
> Ah, leave us not the fret alone!
>
> But—If you cannot give us ease—
> Last of the race of them who grieve
> Here leave us to die out with these
> Last of the people who believe! (103–12)

Though Arnold would go on to be one of the great modern advocates of a naturalized and even secularized Christianity, here he voices what is actually a powerful apologetic for Christianity!

Why, he says, if our age has purged the need for religious "crutches," do I still feel within a spiritual and emotional void? Must the "disease" remain even after the remedy is removed?

And, if you cannot answer these questions, he pleads, then at least leave me here to weep with people who understand my grief, even if they do not share my beliefs and ideals.

As the mind of the poet continues to move and shift throughout the poem, Arnold next thinks back on all those Romantic revolutionaries who fought and died for an ideal that his contemporaries now scorn:

> For what availed it, all the noise
> And outcry of the former men?
> Say, have their sons achieved more joys,
> Say, is life lighter now than then?
> The sufferers died, they left their pain—
> The pangs which tortured them remain.
>
> What helps it now that Byron bore,
> With haughty scorn which mocked the smart,
> Through Europe to the Aetolian shore
> The pageant of his bleeding heart?
> That thousands counted every groan,
> And Europe made his woe her own? (127–38)

Literary critic Harold Bloom has written that all those poets who lived (and still live) after the Romantic Age suffer from a sense of belatedness, of having missed out on that explosion of vitality and creativity.[1] Arnold here struggles with that belatedness, a struggle made worse by the fact that, as far as he can tell, the massive exertions of the Romantics have borne no real fruit. Byron, for all his angst and self-pity, for all his short-lived fame as the passionate heart of Europe, for all his suffering in the War of Greek Independence, has left no lasting legacy. The Romantics gave of themselves, suffered like Prometheus to bring us the fire, yet we, their heirs, are neither happier nor more at ease; we have inherited not their joy but only their pain (one might say the same thing of the

---

[1] See, for example, *Bloom's Anxiety of Influence* (Oxford: Oxford University Press, 1973) and *The Western Canon* (New York: Harcourt Brace, 1994).

cultural and sexual revolutions of the 1960s and '70s). Was it all worth it? Why all that fuss and fury if England is to abandon the spiritual and emotional richness of the Romantic Age in favor of a dry, joyless, overly rational utilitarian ethos?

LEFT BEHIND

In the closing movement of the poem, Arnold (like Tennyson) lifts his vision to contemplate a future, postmillennial kingdom; unlike Tennyson, however, he feels unable finally to participate in it. Arnold builds his image and his argument slowly, gracefully, and powerfully:

> Years hence, perhaps, may dawn an age,
> More fortunate, alas! than we,
> Which without hardness will be sage,
> And gay without frivolity.
> Sons of the world, oh, speed those years;
> But, while we wait, allow our tears!
>
> Allow them! We admire with awe
> The exulting thunder of your race;
> You give the universe your laws,
> You triumph over time and space!
> Your pride of life, your tireless powers,
> We laud them, but they are not ours. (157–68)

As does Tennyson in the closing sections of *In Memoriam*, Arnold here conceives of a future crowning race that will conquer nature and impose the rule of law and order on the universe. The glorious leaders of that brave new world will be wise but not cynical (159), joyous but not frivolous (160). That is to say, though they "shall look / On knowledge," they shall not weary of it, and though "the ape and tiger" shall die, they shall not therefore lose their higher passions. Arnold hails their coming (though, as in Tennyson, it is "far off"), but has lost the faith, the hope, and the will to join them in their great lunge forward. No, he muses, I cannot be part of your kingdom, nor can I join in your "secular rapture" (as I like to call it), but since I cannot, at least leave me hear to weep in the interim. Like Moses (or Martin Luther King, Jr.), though Arnold has the vision to glimpse the coming Promised Land, he knows he will not himself enter that land, but will die in the wilderness.

To help express the dichotomy between himself and those of the crowning race, Arnold then fashions a metaphor that I consider one of the best realized in his poetry:

> We are like children reared in shade
> Beneath some old-world abbey wall,
> Forgotten in a forest glade,
> And secret from the eyes of all.
> Deep, deep the greenwood round them waves,
> Their abbey, and its close of graves!
>
> But, where the road runs near the stream,
> Oft through the trees they catch a glance
> Of passing troops in the sun's beam—
> Pennon, and plume, and flashing lance.
> Forth to the world those soldiers fare,
> To life, to cities, and to war! (169–80)

As the melancholy Arnold, along with those who still cling to the faith of old Europe, sits huddled in his cloistered, parochial world, he watches with awe the march of Victorian progress. He is overwhelmed by the perfection and beauty of these millennium-builders, but lacks the spirit to join; indeed, even when the marchers invite the cloistered children to join, they can only reply:

> Action and pleasure, will ye roam
> Through these secluded dells to cry
> And call us?—but too late ye come!
> Too late for us your call ye blow,
> Whose bent was taken long ago. . . .

> Fenced early in this cloistral round
> Of reverie, of shade, of prayer,
> How should we grow in other ground?
> How can we flower in foreign air?
> —Pass, banners, pass, and bugles, cease;
> And leave our desert to its peace! (194–98; 205–10)

Had Arnold been born a decade earlier, he might have been able to give himself totally to the causes for which Shelley and Byron fought and died. Had he been born a decade later, he might have been able to join their march. As it is, he is caught, suspended between two worlds.

I find these stanzas to be terribly sad. They remind me of that sad, sad last chapter of *Peter Pan*, when Peter comes back to get Wendy, but she has now grown too old to return to Never Land. Neither Arnold nor the monks can be transplanted into the new soil of that secular millennium; they lack that last gasp of vigor that Tennyson's Ulysses musters:

> . . . you and I are old;
> Old age hath yet his honor and his toil.
> Death closes all; but something ere the end,
> Some work of noble note, may yet be done,
> Not unbecoming men that strove with Gods.

24

MATTHEW ARNOLD:
Victorian Prophet and Sage

IN THE PREVIOUS CHAPTER, I offered an image of Arnold the poet as a man stranded between two worlds, who lacked the initiative and the will to move forward and join in the Victorian spirit of progress. Though this portrait is based, admittedly, on only a single poem, it is not too much of an exaggeration to say that in none of his other poetry was Arnold able to move beyond this image of himself. If Arnold is finally a failed poet, the reason lies not so much in technical flaws or even in imprecise imagery but in his inability to move, through his poetry, out of isolation and despair. Indeed, his poetry seemed to act in him more as a drug increasing his melancholy than as a remedy for his internal crises and his philosophical and theological questionings. Arnold badly needed an emotional exorcism, a spiritual enema, but his poetry failed him.

ROMANTIC TO VICTORIAN

Things began to take a turn in 1850, when he finally was able to release himself from a passionate, intensely Romantic, and probably unrequited love that he harbored for a girl he met in Switzerland. To this coldest and most passionless of femme fatales, Arnold gave the name Marguerite; she appears frequently in a series of despairing, angst-ridden lyrics (most notably, "To Marguerite—Continued," "The Buried Life," and "Dover Beach") that betray the dejected melancholy and over-self-consciousness of Shelley and Keats. Luckily for Arnold's mental and emotional state and for the aesthetic history of nineteenth-century England, relief came in 1850 when the tortured poet fell in love with the respectable daughter of a judge. The following year, he was appointed inspector of schools, thus gaining an income and position that satisfied the judge and led him to give his approval (previously withheld) to their marriage. The real change, however, came in 1853, when Arnold published his collected *Poems*, but chose to leave out his *Empedocles on Etna*, a long poem that fairly shimmers with Byronic self-pity. In his own preface to the collection, Arnold explains his exclusion by arguing that true poetry, even when tragic, must give pleasure. His *Empedocles* does not, for it dramatizes a situation "in which the suffering finds no vent in action; in which a continuous state of mental distress is prolonged, unrelieved by incident, hope, or resistance; in which there is everything to be endured, nothing to be done."

This is an amazing statement coming from Arnold, since a large percentage of his poetry fits this description; certainly "Stanzas from the Grand Chartreuse" depicts "a continuous state of mental distress" that is quite lengthily prolonged and that is "unrelieved by incident, hope, or resistance." And yet make the statement he does, signaling both to himself and to his public his desire to shed himself of his Byronic side and move forward into a new ethos and style. As with Newman's conversion to Catholicism, the change in Arnold was as sudden as it was irrevocable. In one fell blow, Arnold turned his back on a decade of internal struggle and creative expression; almost overnight, he matured from an isolated, Romantic outsider into one of the sharpest and most influential critics of his day. Though he would continue to write poetry intermittently, from this point on, Arnold would devote himself fully to prose and would even take on that most public of Victorian roles: professor of poetry at Oxford. By so doing, he would prove (contra Strachey and his ilk) that Victorian sages, far from being repressed, insular reactionaries, were brave and free-minded souls who, like Tennyson's Ulysses, were unafraid "To follow knowledge like a sinking star, / Beyond the utmost bound of human thought." Arnold took to his new role with great passion and industry, and, in no time at all, his aesthetic pronouncements, like those of Ruskin, came to guide and shape public opinion.

Though his poetry seemed unconscious of a wider audience (it seemed, to quote a phrase from John Stuart Mill, more "overheard" than heard), his prose relied on and even demanded such an audience. Indeed, Arnold was the first professor of poetry to deliver his lectures in English rather than Latin! At times Arnold praised the advances of the Victorian Age; more often, he criticized them. But whichever he did, the Victorian middle class (whom he dubbed "Philistines" for their vulgar tastes and their privileging of creature comforts over true art and beauty) bought his works and read them. Arnold's glory is that, like Socrates, he became a gadfly on the state, stinging it into self-awareness; the glory of the Victorian Age is that they did not swat their gadflies, but enshrined them. The more Arnold criticized, the more he was read; the higher his audience rose up to meet his expectations, the higher Arnold lifted the bar.

Arnold was a prolific writer; his collected essays fill many volumes, and most are still worth reading and meditating on today. As I did in the previous chapter, however, I shall confine myself to a single, representative work, an essay that not only embodies Arnold's characteristic genius but may serve as well as a fitting finale to our tour of the Victorian Age

POET TO CRITIC

"The Function of Criticism at the Present Time," the opening essay of Arnold's *Essays in Criticism* (1864), immediately betrays its Victorian origins by highlighting the word "function" and by linking that function to the "present day." For all the aesthetic polish of Arnold's style and for all its classical rhetorical power, the essay is both strongly pragmatic and grounded in the here and now. It is to be taken as "seriously" as the political writings of Mill or the scientific treatises of Huxley. Arnold's goal is not merely to entertain, but to teach; his message is one that must be heard and heeded if England is to maintain her status as the cultural center of the civilized world. The critic/sage (as much as the industrialist or the politician) has his function in society, and that function is a central one: to foster both great literature and a thriving culture. In his earlier, Romantic phase, Arnold would have assigned this function to poets such as Wordsworth or Shelley or Tennyson; here, he takes a far different stance: namely, that Victorian England *needs* her sages and prose prophets as much as she does her poets.

True, he admits at the outset of his essay, the creative faculty is finally superior to the critical, but that does not mean that the latter is not worthwhile and even necessary to society.

Arnold offers two reasons for this, the first of which is individual, the second social. On a personal level, people have the need to exercise what Arnold dubs "free creative activity," a sort of mental play that, Arnold argues, constitutes man's greatest joy. Unfortunately, only a limited number of people are granted the gifts to exercise their free creative activity through the production of literature. For many, the critical (rather than the creative) faculty must serve as their main outlet of free creative activity.

But what exactly *is* the critical faculty, and how is it distinguished from the creative? In answering this question, Arnold helped to shift the aesthetic and intellectual focus of his age from the personal, internalized poetry of the Romantics to a more public, externalized prose. Put simply, the difference between the two faculties is that whereas the creative is emotional and subjective, the critical is intellectual and objective. The main function of the creative faculty is to feel in its bones the thrill of fresh ideas and to synthesize those ideas into a new whole. The function of the critical is to create those fresh ideas through analysis and discovery, by seeing objects *as they are in themselves* (not as they are perceived by a poet). So far, so good, but then Arnold, in a typically Victorian move, expands this distinction onto a wider, social level, offering a unique, aesthetic view of history that distinguishes between two epochs (or ages) in the "life cycle" of a culture.

In epochs of expansion, a culture is rich with new and fresh ideas. During such epochs, poets (such as Tennyson) are needed to harness this intellectual energy and convert it into great works of art. Such epochs are rare; Arnold identifies only two: Periclean Athens (the age of Sophocles) and Elizabethan England (the age of Shakespeare). In epochs of concentration, on the other hand, ideas are stagnant, if not wholly stifled. As poets are needed to harness the energy of epochs of expansion, so critics are needed during epochs of concentration to help create and foster a fresh flow of ideas that will initiate a new epoch of expansion. As such, the poet and the critic are interdependent; one cannot function without the other. For Arnold, great literature is the product of a creative fusion between a great poet ("the man") and an epoch of expansion ("the moment"). It is not enough to be a gifted poet; without the fresh ideas available in such epochs, the poet will lack the necessary raw material for great art.

At this point in the argument, the reader expects Arnold to dub the Romantic Age an epoch of expansion, but he does not. To the contrary, he considers the age he grew up in (born of the French Revolution) to be an epoch of concentration. "This is why," argues Arnold, "Byron's poetry had so little endurance in it, and Goethe's so much; both Byron and Goethe had a great productive power, but Goethe's was nourished by a great critical effort [in Germany] providing the true materials for it, and Byron's was not." We have encountered this pairing of Byron and Goethe before in Carlyle's *Sartor Resartus*: There Carlyle exhorted his readers to close their Byron and open their Goethe, to flee from solipsism, self-indulgence, and morbid introspection and embrace instead an ethos of balance, restraint, and resignation. The advice is strongly Victorian, and yet, we might say, the critic "doth protest too much." By most cultural and aesthetic markers, the Romantic Age matches perfectly Arnold's description of an epoch of expansion.

Why then does Arnold's perceptive critical eye miss the enduring power of Romantic poetry? Could it not be that, unconsciously at least, Arnold needed an "excuse" for his own poetic failure? Indeed, the "Function of Criticism" may be read in part as an aesthetic apology, in which Arnold ascribes his lack of success as a poet to the simple fact that the time was not ripe for great poetry. Glance back at the previous chapter: Is not "Stanzas from the Grand Chartreuse" a poetic meditation on what it means to be stranded in an epoch of concentration? Perhaps the reason Arnold was unable to offer any solutions or even hope in his poetry is that the raw material for such a hope was just not there; certainly on a personal level at least, Arnold was unable to find or express this hope until he switched to both prose and the critical faculty.

THE DISINTERESTED CRITIC

But let us shift our own focus now back to Arnold's definition of the critical faculty, for Arnold clearly felt that it was this faculty above all that his age most needed. Arnold, in a famous and influential phrase, defines criticism as "a disinterested endeavor to learn and propagate the best that is known and thought in the world." Disinterested, as Arnold defines it, is to be distinguished from uninterested; it signifies not an apathetic attitude, but a critical approach that is removed, objective, and free from all political agendas: one that keeps aloof from "the practical view of things." It constitutes a higher kind of curiosity, a "free play of mind" that follows the flow of ideas wherever that flow may lead: even if, to paraphrase Arnold's example, it leads a conservative Tory statesman like Edmund Burke to prophesy that those who oppose progress may one day be opposing God!

It was this kind of criticism that Arnold felt England most needed if she was to propel herself into a new age of expansion, but it was, alas, this very kind of thinking that England most lacked. Indeed, Arnold argues, far from being disinterested, the critics (and the journals) of his day were strongly partisan; they engaged in only as much free play of mind as their party platform (whether Whig, Tory, or Dissenter) allowed. To make matters worse, the British had a negative view of curiosity, saw it as a quality of children that had no practical social value (on the Continent, Arnold argues in a later essay, this is not the case). For Arnold, criticism has a value that transcends not only pragmatism but narrow national boundaries to interest itself in the culture and traditions of all Europe. Thus, in addition to propagating new ideas to inspire poets, the job of the critic also includes identifying "the best that is known and thought," whether that be found in England, France, or Germany.

By "the best," Arnold refers to what is today known as the canon: the Great Books of the Western world (Homer, Dante, Shakespeare, and so on) that have traditionally formed the core of humanistic studies. In contrast to many critics today who view the canon as a product of sociopolitical forces that determine what is and is not acceptable, Arnold firmly believed that such works were aesthetically superior and that they could be shown to be so by objective, disinterested criticism. Arnold, as critic of his age, feared that his countrymen, due to their overly practical view of life and their utilitarian focus on material goods, would never achieve this disinterested view. Like most of his fellow sages, he saw in England much unnecessary ugliness and an "exuberant self-satisfaction" in creature comforts and negative security that was deadly to true culture. Throughout the essay, one hears echoes of Mill's critique of the dearth of imagination in utilitarian thinking, of Carlyle's stinging denunciation of his age's equating of soul with stomach, of Ruskin's frustration at the loss of the restless Gothic spirit he so admired, and of Tennyson's fear that a crude, heartless materialism would kill his country's soul.

And yet, when all is said and done, Arnold (like Mill and Carlyle, Ruskin and Tennyson) remains a Victorian. For all the attacks he levels in his essay against the negative pragmatism and parochialism of England, it is clear nonetheless that the reigning spirit of progress has left on him its indelible mark. Consider this remarkable statement that appears midway through "The Function of Criticism":

> [I]n spite of all that is said about the absorbing and brutalising influence of our passionate material progress, it seems to me indisputable that this progress is likely, though not certain, to lead in the end to an apparition of intellectual life; and that man, after he has made himself perfectly comfortable and has now to determine what to do with himself next, may begin to remember that he has a mind, and that the mind may be made the source of great pleasure. I grant it is mainly the privilege of faith, at present, to discern this end to our railways, our businesses, and our fortune-making; but we shall see if, here as elsewhere, faith is not in the end the true prophet.

All the optimism of his age, with all its heady faith in a brighter future to come, lies latent in this statement. Arnold can attack the middle classes and praise France and Germany over Britain, but at the end of the day, he is an Englishman living in the Age of Victoria, and he cannot help but rejoice.

In the previous chapter, I compared Arnold to Moses, who saw but could not enter the Promised Land; in the final, elegant sentence of his essay, Arnold himself makes the comparison.

He sees the Promised Land of a new epoch of expansion glowing in the distance and knows he will not live to see it. Here, however (in his prose essay), a thought that would have brought only melancholy to the Romantic poet brings a mingled sense of pride and acceptance to the Victorian sage:

> That promised land it will not be ours to enter, and we shall die in the wilderness; but to have desired to enter it, to have saluted it from afar, is already, perhaps, the best distinction among contemporaries; it will certainly be the best title to esteem with posterity.

Finally, whatever their faith, all the Victorians kept their eyes firmly focused ahead, straining with all their heart, all their, soul, all their mind, and all their strength to catch a glimpse of that "one far-off divine event, / To which the whole creation moves." It was given to Tennyson to sound, with all the lyrical power at his command, that coming consummation, but he was joined in his apocalyptic song, as by a chorus, by the no less prophetic voices of the great Victorian sages.

APPENDICES

TIMELINE

1776	*The Wealth of Nations* (Adam Smith)
1795	Birth of Thomas Carlyle
1801	Birth of Cardinal Newman
1806	Birth of John Stuart Mill
1809	Birth of Alfred, Lord Tennyson
1812	Birth of Robert Browning
1819	Birth of John Ruskin
1822	Birth of Matthew Arnold
1825	Birth of T. H. Huxley
1826–27	Mill suffers crisis
1830	*Poems, Chiefly Lyrical* (Tennyson: inc. "Mariana")
1830–33	*Principles of Geology* (Charles Lyell)
1832	First Reform Bill
1832–33	*Poems* (Tennyson: "Lady of Shallot," "Lotos Eaters")
1833	Death of Arthur Henry Hallam
1833	Tennyson: "Ulysses," "Tithonus," "Morte d'Arthur"
1833–34	*Sartor Resartus* (Carlyle)
1837	Beginning of Queen Victoria's Reign
1842	*Poems* (Tennyson)
1842	"Locksley Hall" published
1845	Newman joins Roman Catholic Church
1846	Corn Laws Repealed

1848   *Communist Manifesto* (Marx and Engels)

1849   *The Strayed Reveller, and Other Poems* (Arnold)

1850   *In Memoriam* pub.; Tennyson named Poet Laureate

1851   Great Exhibition (Crystal Palace)

1851–53   *The Stones of Venice* (Ruskin)

1852   *Empedocles on Etna, and Other Poems* (Arnold)

1855   Tennyson completes "Maud"

1855   "Stanzas from the Grand Chartreuse" (Arnold)

1859   First four *Idylls of the King* published

1859   *On Liberty* (Mill)

1859   *Origin of Species* (Charles Darwin)

1861   Death of Prince Albert

1864   *Apologia Pro Vita Sua* (Newman)

1864   "The Function of Criticism at the Present Time" (Arnold)

1867   Second Reform Bill

1868   "On the Physical Basis of Life" (T. H. Huxley)

1869   *Culture and Anarchy* (Arnold)

1869   "Coming of Arthur," "The Holy Grail" *(Idylls of the King)*

1873   Death of John Stuart Mill; *Autobiography*

1881   Death of Thomas Carlyle

1884   Tennyson made a baron; enters the House of Lords

1888   Death of Matthew Arnold

1889   Death of Robert Browning

1890   Death of Cardinal Newman

1892   Death of Alfred, Lord Tennyson

1895   Death of T. H. Huxley

1900   Death of John Ruskin

1900   *The Interpretation of Dreams* (Freud)

1901   Death of Queen Victoria

GLOSSARY

Agnosticism: A philosophical position that states that nothing rational can be known about God or the supernatural world, and that, as a result, such issues are best left unexplored. Huxley is responsible for popularizing the word and (though he denied it) was considered a spokesman for the position. Greek for "doesn't know."

The Apostles: A Cambridge group led by Arthur Hallam of which Tennyson was an active member. The Apostles considered in their meetings the major philosophical and theological issues of their day; in contrast to the founders of the Oxford Movement, they tended to adopt liberal views.

Corn Laws: A trade restriction imposed by Parliament in 1815 that disallowed the import of corn (the British word for wheat) until the price of domestic corn reached a certain price. The repeal of these laws in 1846 marked a major victory for the Whig liberals and helped promote a free-market, laissez-faire economy.

Crystal Palace: *See* Great Exhibition

Dramatic Monologue: A genre of poetry that was simultaneously "invented" by Tennyson and Robert Browning, although it was Browning who most fully realized the potential of the genre. Dramatic monologues feature a first-person speaker (who is not to be confused with the poet) who bares his soul to us in a way reminiscent of the Shakespearean soliloquy. In most cases, the speaker is warped in some way and attempts to garner our sympathy. Tennyson's best dramatic monologues are "Ulysses" and "Tithonus"; among the hundreds of dramatic monologues composed by Browning, some of the best include "My Last Duchess," "The Bishop Orders His Tomb," "Fra Lippo Lippi," and "Andrea del Sarto."

Epoch of Concentration: *See* Epoch of Expansion

Epoch of Expansion: In "The Function of Criticism at the Present Time," Matthew Arnold makes a famous distinction between two epochs (or ages) in the "life cycle" of a culture. In epochs of expansion, a culture is rich with new and fresh ideas; during such epochs, poets are needed to harness this intellectual energy and convert it into great works of art. Such epochs are rare; Arnold identifies two: Periclean Athens (the age of Sophocles) and Elizabethan England (the age of Shakespeare). Oddly, Arnold did not consider the Romantic Age (born of the French Revolution) to be an epoch of expansion. Rather, he considered his own time period to be an epoch of concentration, an age in which ideas are stagnant and the free exchange of ideas is stifled in some way. Just as Arnold believed that great poets were needed to harness the energy of the epoch of expansion, so he believed that critics were needed during epochs of concentration to help create and foster a free flow of ideas that would, in time, catapult their culture into a new epoch of expansion. For Arnold, the crowning works of the canon are the products of a creative fusion between a great poet and an epoch of expansion (between "the man" and "the moment"). It is not enough to be a gifted poet; without the fresh ideas available in such an epoch, the poet will lack the necessary raw material on which to exert his creative gifts.

First Reform Bill: A vital piece of legislation passed by Parliament in 1832. The bill extended the suffrage to the middle class and eliminated an old form of political gerrymandering (what were called the "rotten boroughs," districts with no actual population, which the aristocracy used to maintain electoral power). The bill marked a major victory for the Whig liberals and helped shift power to the middle class. A second reform bill followed in 1867 that extended the suffrage even further.

Great Exhibition: A sort of World's Fair (its full title was the "Great Exhibition of the Works and Industries of All Nations") that was strongly supported by Prince Albert and that provided a showcase for the material prosperity and technological ingenuity of England at the height of the Victorian Age. The Exhibition (which "aired" in 1851) was held under a monumental glass dome called the "Crystal Palace." The dome alone was an architectural hymn to Victorian progress.

Laissez-Faire: A key political and philosophical principle of Victorian liberals that favored a free-market capitalist system guided not by government regulation but by invisible, utilitarian, economic laws (the "guiding hand" of Adam Smith's *Wealth of Nations*). The phrase is French for "let do."

Liberalism: A political, theological, philosophical, and economic school of thought that tended to dominate the 19th century. Liberals (who actually share many opinions with modern-day American conservatives) believed in the benefits of a free-market and sought through social planning, education, and general reform to propel England into a utopic state free from ignorance and poverty. Theologically speaking liberals tended to take a non-supernatural approach to Scripture and to emphasize Jesus the teacher and social reformer over Jesus the Incarnate Son of God. Newman defined himself in opposition to liberalism, as did the Oxford Movement in general. In the realm of politics, the Whigs (who tended to hail from the rising middle class and to favor liquid wealth) were the main proponents of liberalism; their opponents were the Tories, most of whom were aristocrats of a more reactionary, religious bent who favored land-based wealth.

The Noetics: A liberal-minded student group at Oxford that claimed the young Newman as one of its members; Newman, however, soon abandoned the Noetics for a more orthodox approach.

Oxford Movement: A conservative religious movement led by several young men who had attended Oxford and who saw a great need to stem the rising tide of liberalism in England and to promote a return to tradition. Though the mantel of leadership quickly fell to Newman, the movement was initiated by a sermon preached by John Keble in 1833 in response to an attempt by the Whig Parliament to encroach on the authority of the Anglican Church of England. The objectives of the movement (expressed in a series of tracts that won the group the nickname of Tractarians) were to restore the doctrines of the Anglican Church to their original purity, to revive the traditional, "High-Church" aspects of the faith (such as liturgical rituals, the sacraments, and monasticism), and to counteract the rationalism and scientism of the liberals with mysticism and piety. Many of the Tractarians, most notably Newman, eventually joined the Catholic Church. Other famous Tractarians were Hurrell Froude and Edward Pusey.

Poet Laureate: The official court poet of England, appointed by the king (or queen) to compose poetry in honor of royal birthdays and other such state occasions. Though Chaucer and Spenser both served as unofficial court poets, the official designation began with Ben Jonson, who served from 1619 to 1637. Other famous poet laureates include John Dryden, William Wordsworth, and Tennyson. The traditional pay for the laureate was 200 pounds per year plus a butt of sack!

Positivism: A belief system prevalent in the 19th century that held that rationalism, progress, and technology would usher in a new age of happiness; this faith in progress is perhaps best captured in the poetry of Tennyson. In the more doctrinaire positivism of Auguste Comte, a new religion of humanism was announced that would be run by an elite "clergy" of sociologists and philosophers. Though John Stuart Mill was at first an advocate of Comtean positivism, he was later disturbed by Comte's growing totalitarian tone.

Skepticism: In its modern sense, as popularized by David Hume and defended by T. H. Huxley (most notably in his lecture, "On the Physical Basis of Life"), a skeptic is one who refuses to concern himself with issues about which nothing rational or scientific can be known and concerning which no empirical, experimental evidence can be gathered. The skeptical position rejects all metaphysical, theological first principles as unsubstantiated and finally unprovable.

Tory: *See* Liberalism

Tractarians: *See* Oxford Movement

Utilitarianism: A 19th-century school of thought that sought to refound all branches of knowledge (from philosophy to ethics, politics to sociology) on a single, all-encompassing framework: utility. Institutions and moral systems were to be judged not by metaphysical standards of good and evil, but by whether or not they brought the greatest good to the greatest number. The two great founders of utilitarianism are Jeremy Bentham and James Mill; the school was further honed and somewhat humanized by James's son, John Stuart Mill. Though all the Victorian sages felt the need to defend their ideas along the lines of utility, most were horrified at the passionless, amoral nature of utilitarianism and by its tendency to privilege creature comforts over spiritual and aesthetic growth and refinement.

Utopian Socialism: A movement that sought to establish ideal communities in which all labor would be shared and complete equality would be the rule. Many utopian socialists actually put their theories into practice and established communities (some in America). The leading figures of the movement are Charles Fourier, Robert Owen, and Saint-Simon.

Whig: *See* Liberalism

Who's Who

Albert, Prince *(1819–61) See* Victoria (below) and Great Exhibition (*See* Glossary).

Arnold, Matthew *(1822–88)* British poet, essayist, and critic who progressed from a failed Romantic poet to a Victorian sage of the highest order. He was responsible in great part for setting the aesthetic tastes of his nation and for popularizing the word "Philistine" to connote an unrefined money-grubber.

Bentham, Jeremy *(1748–1832)* English philosopher and utilitarian who sought to apply utilitarian methods to all areas of English thought, politics, and institutions. A great influence on both James and John Stuart Mill.

Browning, Robert *(1812–89)* Victorian poet who perfected the dramatic monologue, a genre of poetry that he "co-invented" with Tennyson. His wife, Elizabeth Barrett Browning, was a celebrated poet as well.

Byron, George Gordon, Lord *(1788–1824)* British Romantic poet whose emotional excesses and over-self-consciousness were two key aspects of Romanticism that most Victorian writers rejected. Indeed, Mill, Ruskin, and Arnold all counseled themselves and their fellow Victorians to "close thy Byron."

Carlyle, Thomas *(1795–1881)* Victorian sage who delighted and bewildered Victorian England with his tortured, Germanic prose and his attempts to fashion a new, secular-yet-apocalyptic form of spirituality that would replace the decaying creeds of Christendom and combat the materialism of utilitarian thought. He was a strong influence on Ralph Waldo Emerson, and his ideas influenced American Transcendentalism.

Coleridge, Samuel Taylor *(1772–1834)* British poet, essayist, and literary theorist; a major figure of British Romanticism who helped to anglicize German philosophy. In a set of influential essays, John Stuart Mill discerned two strains of English thought in the conservative, Tory writings of Coleridge and the liberal, Whig writings of Bentham. In terms of this book, Mill's distinction between Coleridge and Bentham can be applied as well to Newman and Huxley.

Comte, Auguste *(1798–1857)* French philosopher who was most responsible for formulating the ideals of positivism. Along with the Saint-Simonians, he developed a theory of history that greatly influenced John Stuart Mill.

Darwin, Charles *(1809–92)* British scientist of the Victorian Age whose book *Origin of Species* (1859) established evolution as a theory to be reckoned with. Though he was one of the key founders of modernism, Darwin's theories reached the public less through his own efforts than through the popularizing of those theories in the essays and speeches of T. H. Huxley.

Dickens, Charles *(1812–70)* British novelist who fought in many of his novels against the excesses of utilitarianism and advocated a more charitable, humanistic approach to social reform. *Hard Times* (1845) fought in particular against utilitarian-minded educators who sought to remove all moral feeling and imagination from the classroom (a kind of education similar to the one John Stuart Mill received).

Disraeli, Benjamin *(1804–91)* Tory Prime Minister whose political career tended to alternate with that of Gladstone. Disraeli was also a respected novelist.

Fourier, Charles *(1772–1837)* French utopian socialist whose ideas were put into practice at Brook Farm (a commune that was formed in 1841 in Massachusetts and that receives a strong critique in Nathaniel Hawthorne's novel *The Blithedale Romance*).

Freud, Sigmund *(1856–1939)* Austrian psychiatrist; founder of psychoanalysis. His studies of human development and the significance of dreams have had a profound influence on all areas of modern thought. In his systematic, materialist approach to human problems he is very much a Victorian; however, most of the Victorian sages would not have agreed with the deterministic aspects of his theories.

Froude, Richard Hurrell *(1803–36)* One of the leaders of the Oxford Movement.

Gladstone, William Ewart *(1809–98)* Whig Prime Minister whose political career tended to alternate with that of Disraeli. Like Tennyson, Gladstone was a great friend and admirer of Arthur Hallam.

Gordon, Charles George *(1833–85)* Victorian soldier who embodied the spirit of the British Empire. General Gordon died a famous, heroic death at the siege of Khartoum.

Hallam, Arthur Henry *(1811–33)* English poet and essayist whose death prompted Tennyson to write *In Memoriam*. At the time of his death, Hallam was engaged to one of Tennyson's sisters.

Huxley, Thomas Henry *(1825–95)* English scientist and researcher who popularized the theories of evolution (as formulated by Charles Darwin) through a long series of essays and lectures. Huxley, both an agnostic and a skeptic in the matter of religion, encouraged his age to throw off spiritual language and ideals and adopt a material, scientific view. Huxley is the grandfather of novelist **Aldous Huxley** *(1894–1963)* and biologist **Julian Sorell Huxley** *(1887–1975)*; both shared their grandfather's skepticism.

Keats, John *(1795–1821)* British Romantic poet; Tennyson began as a Romantic poet in the tradition of Keats before maturing into the central poetic voice of the Victorian Age.

Keble, John *(1792–1866)* Anglican divine who was a leader in the Oxford Movement and whose 1833 sermon "National Apostasy" is generally considered the birthday of the Movement.

Kingsley, Charles *(1819–75)* English clergyman, poet, and novelist (he wrote the beloved children's classic, *The Water-Babies*). When, in an

1863 review in *Macmillan's Magazine*, he attacked Newman and the Catholic Church, it sparked a year-long debate that led Newman to write his autobiography, *Apologia Pro Vita Sua*, as a way of defending his decision to convert to Catholicism.

Lyell, Sir Charles *(1797–1875)* English geologist whose *Principles of Geology* (1830–33) was avidly read by Tennyson and represents the chief source for the scientific speculations that underlie *In Memoriam*.

Malthus, Thomas *(1766–1834)* English economist who made a scientific, utilitarian, dispassionate study of population and argued that whenever population increases too much, such factors as disease, war, and crime naturally arise to check the increase. John Stuart Mill was strongly influenced by Malthus and himself advocated population control. Dickens is surely parodying Malthus when he has Scrooge tell the charity collectors that they had best let the poor get about their dying and decrease the surplus population.

Marx, Karl *(1818–83)* German philosopher, economist, and political activist whose theory of dialectical materialism (formulated with the help of Friedrich Engels) lies at the heart of much modernist theory and ideology. Marx wrote his major work, *Das Capital,* in the reading room of the British Museum; though the Victorian sages were sympathetic to Marx's socialist ideas, they tended to humanize them. Most of the key Victorians also rejected the deterministic aspects of Marx's theories.

Mill, James *(1773–1836)* Utilitarian philosopher and father of John Stuart Mill; he put his theories into practice in the education of his son.

Mill, John Stuart *(1806–73)* Utilitarian philosopher who, after a mental breakdown in 1826–27 that was caused in part by the passionless utilitarian education given him by his father, sought to humanize the cold theories of the utilitarians by factoring in a regard both for the aesthetic cultivation of feeling and the dignity of the individual. Mill, author of *On Liberty* and *The Subjection of Woman*, fought tirelessly for freedom as a member of Parliament; his *Autobiography* was published posthumously. In 1830, he fell in love with a married woman named **Harriet Taylor** *(1807–58)*; the two were constant companions but did not consummate their relationship until they were married in 1851, two years after the death of Harriet's husband.

Newman, John Henry Cardinal *(1801–90)* British clergyman who, after leading the Oxford Movement in its attempt to purify the Anglican Church, had a crisis of faith and joined the Roman Catholic Church in 1845. Newman was at first rejected and even scorned by his countrymen as a traitor; however, when (in 1864) he wrote an autobiography defending himself against the charge of being anti-British and explaining his reasons for joining the Catholic Church *(Apologia Pro Vita Sua)*, he was re-embraced and became something of a national institution.

Owen, Robert *(1771–1858)* Welsh-born utopian socialist who founded the New Harmony Community in Indiana in 1825.

Pusey, Edward *(1800–82)* One of the founders of the Oxford Movement, who, after Newman's "defection" to the Catholic Church, became the head spokesman for the Movement.

Ricardo, David *(1772–1823)* British economist of a utilitarian bent who shared Adam Smith's free-market concepts and who discerned "a guiding hand" not only in trade relations but in worker's wages. Ricardo formulated a theory of the "iron law of wages" that showed that when wages were high, the numbers of workers increased, which in turn led to a decrease in wages and a decrease in the worker population (that is, a vicious cycle). Along with Malthus, he thus saw a need for population control.

Ruskin, John *(1819–1900)* One of the most influential thinkers of his day, Ruskin wrote beautifully written and deeply insightful art criticism that not only set the aesthetic taste of his country but uncovered the relationship between art and society. Though he was never a Marxist, Ruskin's critiques of capitalist society warned against the alienation of the worker from his labor and the exploitation of the factory hand.

Saint-Simon, Comte de *(1760–1825)* French philosopher who, along with his followers (the Saint-Simonians), laid down the groundwork for utopian socialism and developed a scheme of history that influenced John Stuart Mill.

Shelley, Percy Bysshe *(1792–1822)* British romantic poet who shared Byron's emotional excesses and over-self-consciousness and who was, likewise, held at bay by many Victorians. Browning began as a disciple of Shelley before shifting to a more Victorian outlook.

Smith, Adam *(1723–90)* Scottish philosopher and economist whose *Wealth of Nations* (1776) called for a free-market, laissez-faire economy regulated not by government controls but by an invisible "guiding hand"; his theories were most fully realized in Victorian England.

Tennyson, Alfred, Lord *(1809–92)* The most representative poet of his age, Tennyson embodied to the full both the crisis of faith that befell so many thinkers in 19th-century England and the Victorian spirit of progress that eventually subsumed that crisis. After the publication of his monumental epic *In Memoriam* in 1850, Tennyson was dubbed poet laureate: a position he held with dignity until his death.

Tocqueville, Alexis de *(1805–59)* French historian who, in his *Democracy in America* (1835–39), argued that in a democracy there can sometimes arise a "tyranny of the majority." John Stuart Mill was strongly influenced by this notion and used it as a counter to some of the extreme theories of his day.

Ussher, James *(1581–1656)* Irish archbishop who worked out a complex biblical chronology that placed Creation at 4004 B.C. His notion of a young earth was exploded by the "new science" of the 19th century.

Victoria, Alexandrina *(1819–1901)* Queen of England 1837–1901; in her marriage to **Prince Albert** *(1840–61)*, she lived out the "family values" that were so central to the middle-class morality that dominated the age. When Albert died, she withdrew from the public for many years to mourn him; during this time, she told Tennyson that *In Memoriam* was, next to the Bible, her greatest comfort. Though, by this time in English history, real power was in the hands of Parliament and the prime minister, Victoria continued to be a powerful image to her age of the glories of the British Empire.

Wells, Herbert George *(1866–1946)* English novelist and advocate of social reform who embodied fully the Victorian spirit of progress and expressed that spirit in a series of utopian novels that bespoke a glorious future. Oddly, Wells (the father, along with Jules Verne, of science fiction), was also one of the first to write dystopic novels. Wells was widely read in Victorian England, and he even wrote a history of the world (that begins with the prehistoric cave man) on which a generation of students was reared.

Wordsworth, William *(1770–1850)* British romantic poet who co-authored *Lyrical Ballads* with his friend Samuel Taylor Coleridge and wrote an epic-length poetic autobiography *(The Prelude)*, in which he recounted a mental/spiritual crisis that befell him shortly after the French Revolution. It was through reading Wordsworth's poetry that John Stuart Mill was able to find resolution for his own mental crisis. Arnold was a great fan and advocate of Wordsworth's poetry. Wordsworth was poet laureate from 1843 to 1850; upon his death, the laureateship passed to Tennyson.

ANNOTATED BIBLIOGRAPHY

I HAVE CHOSEN in this bibliography to adopt a paragraph format that I think will be more helpful to the general reader; the titles of books will be printed in italicized bold face, and the authors or editors will be indicated in bold face. After a section on general works, I will devote a section to each of the major writers covered in the book. You will note that in my bibliography I will be strongly encouraging you to purchase books from a series known as *The Norton Critical Editions*. In these excellent editions, the editors devote the first half of the book to an authoritative, well-annotated edition of either a single classic work or a selection of poems from a single poet, and the second half to a dozen or so essays written by various critics from various time periods and various schools. Each book in the series also offers an extensive bibliography. These books are often the best single resource for a given book or author.

GENERAL WORKS *(Chapter 1)*

I strongly suggest that all readers of this book purchase *Victorian Poetry and Prose*,* edited by **Lionel Trilling** and **Harold Bloom** (Oxford Univeresity Press, 1973; ISBN 0-19-501616-5). This is

---

* Denotes essential reading

the textbook that I use when I teach the Victorian Age, and I have tried to chose my primary texts in such a way that anyone who has this book will have access to nearly all the necessary works. The textbook is well annotated with good introductions and is a good length (about 700 pages); it is also available in an inexpensive paperback. In the paragraphs below, I will counsel you as to when I think you might want to buy other primary materials to supplement the textbook.

Another excellent textbook is the standard, well-respected *Norton Anthology of English Literature,* **Volume 2** (available in a number of different editions, any of which is acceptable; the most recent edition is the 7th: ISBN 0-393-97490-1), which covers all English literature from 1800 to the present. Although the Victorian Age represents only a section of this book, it is a large and well-represented section that is prefaced by an excellent introduction. If you are serious about English literature (and especially if your interest in Victorian literature is accompanied by an interest in the Romantics), you should really own a copy of this book. It also includes bibliographical information in the back.

As far as historical overviews, my favorite is the still standard *England in the Nineteenth Century* by **David Thomson**, Volume 8 of The Pelican History of England (Penguin, 1950; ISBN 0-14-020197-1). It does a fine job filling in the historical, economical, and political background to the age. To get a good understanding of the negative view of Victorianism that still dominates some minds (for example, that the Victorians are all repressed prudes and maniacal, "type-A" workaholics), consult the classic and very enjoyable *Eminent Victorians* by **Lytton Strachey** (first published in 1918, a very anti-Victorian decade), which offers biographies of Cardinal Manning, General Gordon, Florence Nightingale, and Dr. Arnold (Matthew's father). Back in the late 1980s (by which time the reputation of the Victorians had risen again), **A. N. Wilson** published his own biographical sketches of six Victorians (Prince Albert, Charlotte Brontë, William Ewart Gladstone, Cardinal Newman, Josephine Butler, and Julia Margaret Cameron) under the same title, *Eminent Victorians** (Norton, 1990; ISBN 0-563-207191-3). Wilson's book is excellent, and his sketches of Newman and Albert are must reading. To read both Strachey's and Wilson's books is to get a good rounded view of the positive and negative sides of the Victorian age. For a more positive look at the people and lifestyles of high Victorian England, see **Asa Brigg**'s *Victorian People: A Reassessment of Persons and Themes: 1851–1867* (University of Chicago Press, 1955; ISBN 0-226-07488-9) and **Basil Willey**'s classic *More Nineteenth Century Studies: A Group of Honest Doubters* (1956), which includes a fine sketch of Tennyson (out of print, but available on the web through Amazon.com). For a standard collection of essays about various Victorian writers, see *Victorian Literature: Modern Essays in Criticism*, edited by **Austin Wright** (Oxford University Press, 1961; out of print but available through Amazon.com).

I should also note in passing that there are available Norton Critical Editions of **Darwin** (includes selections from his writings), of **Marx**'s *Communist Manifesto*, and of **Thomas Malthus**'s *An Essay on the Principle of Population.*

T. H. HUXLEY *(Chapters 2, 4)*

Trilling/Bloom contains the complete text of "On the Physical Basis of Life"; however, I would strongly suggest you supplement this selection by purchasing a small but useful book, *Selections from the Essays of Huxley,** edited by **Alburey Castell** for Crofts Classics (ISBN 0-88295-043-6). This edition contains substantial excerpts from a dozen of Huxley's major works on science, education, culture, and agnosticism. A standard secondary resource that discusses the impact of Darwin's theories and the propagation of those theories by Huxley on British thought in the 19th century is **William Irvine**'s *Apes, Angels, and Victorians: The Story of Darwin, Huxley, and Evolution* (McGraw-Hill, 1955; out of print but available through Amazon.com).

CARDINAL NEWMAN *(Chapters 3–4)*

Trilling/Bloom contains the seminal chapter of Newman's *Apologia Pro Vita Sua*, in which he reflects on his decision to join the Catholic Church; however, anyone who is serious about Newman must purchase **David J. DeLaura**'s* excellent edition of Newman's *Apologia*. This edition which is one of the finest additions to the Norton Critical Series (ISBN 0-393-09766-8), not only contains the usual biographical and critical material, but includes the texts of the debate between Newman and Kingsley that actually sparked Newman's writing of his autobiography. Those interested in Newman's views on education may want to purchase **Newman**'s *The Idea of a University*, which is available in many editions from Loyola Press, Yale University Press, and University of Notre Dame Press; take your choice. For an inexpensive paperback collection of Newman's various writings on the Church and on education, see *The Essential Newman*, edited by **Vincent Ferrer Blehl** (a Mentor-Omega Book from the New American Library, 1963); best to look for this one in a used bookstore.

JOHN STUART MILL *(Chapters 5–6)*

Trilling/Bloom contains (in addition to Mill's "What is Poetry" and brief selections from *On Liberty* and *The Subjection of Women*) the seminal chapter from **Mill**'s *Autobiography* in which he suffers his mental crisis; however, as with Newman, I would strongly suggest you purchase **Jack Stillinger**'s* seminal and authoritative edition of Mill's *Autobiography* (Riverside Edition: ISBN 0-395-05120-7), which includes a very helpful introduction and is well annotated and indexed. Of especial interest is the way Stillinger includes in his notes some of the passages that Mill deleted from his work on the advice of his wife (many of which deal with his relationship with his family). Almost all of Mill's work is available in numerous editions. Those interested in his work as a freedom fighter and political reformer will certainly want to consider a recent Norton Critical Edition that contains the complete texts of

Mill's *On Liberty, The Subjection of Women*, and "The Spirit of the Age" (edited by **Alan Ryan**; ISBN 0-393-97009-4). I would also strongly recommend an inexpensive paperback edition that I consult frequently: **Mill's *Essays on Literature and Society*,** edited by **J. B. Schneewind** (Collier, 1965). This book contains a dozen essays by Mill, including "The Spirit of the Age," his twin essays on Bentham and Coleridge, and his review of Carlyle's *French Revolution*. Best to look for this one in a used bookstore.

ALFRED, LORD TENNYSON *(Chapters 7–17, 20–22)*

Trilling/Bloom contains a pretty generous selection from Tennyson's poetry (including a fair amount of his *In Memoriam*); however, I would strongly suggest that you purchase one of my favorite Norton Critical Editions (I use it for my senior seminars on Tennyson): **Tennyson's Poetry,*** edited by **Robert W. Hill** (second edition: ISBN 0-393-97279-8). This edition contains the entire text of *In Memoriam* and *Maud* as well as generous selections from Tennyson's Arthurian epic, *Idylls of the King* (needless to say, all the poems discussed in this series are anthologized in full). It also contains several critical essays that merit reading: Hallam's review of Tennyson's *Poems, Chiefly Lyrical,* and John Stuart Mill's review of *Poems;* some of the adverse criticism of those same poems; a seminal essay on Tennyson by T. S. Eliot; and helpful essays on *In Memoriam, Maud, Idylls of the King,* and Tennyson's thoughts on evolution. (Hint: if you can find the first edition of this book in a used bookstore, go ahead and buy it!) You may also be interested to know that there is available a Norton Critical Edition of just **In Memoriam** (editor, **Robert H. Ross**; ISBN 0-393-09379-4); if you are a fan, you may want this edition since all the critical material in the back is devoted to this single poem. The standard biography of Tennyson is the excellent and highly-readable **Tennyson: The Unquiet Heart*** by **Robert Bernard Martin** (Oxford University Press, 1980; out of print but can be found in any good library and is available through Amazon.com for the great price of $15). This book will tell you everything you want to know about the life of Tennyson, with some good thoughts on the poetry as well; it perfectly balances criticism with adulation and allows Tennyson to emerge as a real man, with all his genius and his personal failings fresh and accessible to the reader. You might also consult a good collection of essays edited by **Harold Bloom** for Modern Critical Views: Victorian Renaissance, *Alfred, Lord Tennyson* (Chelsea House Publishing, 1985; available through Library Binding). Bloom also has a book devoted to Tennyson in his series, Bloom's Major Poets: Comprehensive Research and Study Guides. Unfortunately, most of the good critical books on Tennyson are out of print, though you should be able to find most of them in a good academic library. They include **A. Dwight Culler**'s *The Poetry of Tennyson* (1977), **Daniel Albright**'s *Tennyson: The Muses' Tug-of-War* (University Press of Virginia, 1986; considers the struggle in Tennyson between the sublime and the commonplace), and two book-length studies of *In Memoriam* and the *Idylls*, **Timothy Peltason**'s *Reading* In Memoriam (Princeton University Press, 1985) and **John D. Rosenberg**'s *The Fall of Camelot* (Belknap Press, 1973). Still, all in all, your best sources for criticism on Tennyson are the essays anthologized in the Norton Critical Edition of Tennyson's Poetry (see above).

THOMAS CARLYLE *(Chapter 18)*

Trilling/Bloom contains a good selection from *Sartor Resartus* (as well as selections from his *On Heroes, Hero-Worship*, and *The Heroic in History* and *Past and Present*). For most people this will be all they can take of Carlyle, with his contorted, Germanic syntax and his esoteric ideas and associations. However, if you are brave (or foolhardy), you may purchase the whole text of *Sartor Resartus* in an excellent, well-represented collection, *A Carlyle Reader*, edited by a fine Carlyle scholar, **G. B. Tennyson**, who has written his own (unfortunately out-of-print) book-length study of *Sartor Resartus* (the reader has been newly reprinted by Copley,

ISBN 1-583-90008-x and can be purchased through Amazon.com). A standard biography is **Fred Kaplan**'s ***Thomas Carlyle: A Biography*** (Cornell University Press, 1983).

JOHN RUSKIN *(Chapter 19)*

Trilling/Bloom offers selections from Ruskin's *Modern Painters, The Stones of Venice* ("The Nature of Gothic"), and *Unto this Last*; however, fans of Ruskin will want to supplement this selection. I would suggest a far more thorough compilation that well represents Ruskin's oeuvre, ***The Genius of John Ruskin: Selection from His Writings***, edited by **John D. Rosenberg**. This is one of the respected Riverside Editions (Houghton Mifflin, 1963; reprinted by University Press of Virginia, 1998); it contains a brief but very helpful annotated bibliography. Tim Hilton has recently completed the second installment in a fine two-volume biography, ***John Ruskin: The Later Years*** (Yale University Press); Volume 1 (***John Ruskin: The Early Years***) was published in 1984.

MATTHEW ARNOLD *(Chapters 23–24)*

Trilling/Bloom contains a selection of Arnold's poetry (most of the finest short lyrics are included: "Dover Beach," "The Scholar Gypsy," and "Stanzas from the Grand Chartreuse") as well as the preface to the first edition of his poems and three seminal essays: "The Function of Criticism at the Present Times," "The Study of Poetry," and "Literature and Science." I would, however, strongly suggest that you purchase an excellent Riverside Edition: ***Poetry and Criticism of Matthew Arnold***,* edited by **A. Dwight Culler** (ISBN 0-395-05152-5). This edition has good notes in the back and is notable for containing in its entirety Arnold's lengthy poem "Empedocles on Etna," as well as the complete text of *Culture and Anarchy*. A must buy for Arnold fans, or at least for those who wish to understand why Arnold was one of the most influential writers of his age. There are many biographies and studies available on Arnold (interest in his work and ideas continues to be on the rise), but I still think the most accessible biography is **Lionel Trilling**'s *Matthew Arnold* (first published in 1939, expanded in 1949; available from Harcourt Brace, ISBN 0-15-657734-8). I should also add two newer books: in 1996, **Nicholas Murray** published a fine, well-rounded biography, *A Life of Matthew Arnold* (St. Martin's Press); more recently, **Ian Hamilton** published an iconoclastic (but finally, I think, unsuccessful) book, arguing that Arnold was a better poet than sage: *A Gift Imprisoned: The Poetic Life of Matthew Arnold* (Basic Books).

VICTORIAN FILM FESTIVAL

IN THIS APPENDIX, I will offer a list of entertaining films in English (roughly 75 percent from America; 25 percent from Britain) that deal with the Victorian Era. Unless otherwise noted, all are appropriate for family viewing. These films are not, of course, documentaries, but they will help you to visualize the era and get a feel for its mood and spirit. Most are available at a good video store, and most can be purchased for about $15. The titles of films will be printed in italicized boldface, followed by parentheses that include the director's name, the date of release, and one or two of the key actors. So make some popcorn, curl up on the sofa, and enjoy!

Let's begin with film adaptations of Charles Dickens; the best were directed by David Lean: ***Great Expectations*** (1946: John Mills) and ***Oliver Twist*** (1948: Alec Guinness). Make sure you also see the musical version of *Oliver Twist* (which won the Academy Award and brings Victorian London to shimmering life): ***Oliver!*** (Carol Reed, 1968: Ron Moody). MGM/David O. Selznick also produced two fine adaptations: ***David Copperfield*** (George Cukor, 1934: Freddie Bartholomew) and ***Tale of Two Cities*** (Jack Conway, 1935: Ronald Colman; pre-Victorian setting, of course). There are numerous film versions of *A Christmas*

Carol; the best, made in England, remains *A Christmas Carol* (Brian Desmond, 1951: Alastair Sim), though TNT recently made a good made-for-TV version with Patrick Stewart as Scrooge.

If you're still in a literary mood after watching these splendid Dickens films, make sure to rent **The Barretts of Wimpole Street** (Sidney Franklin, 1934: Norma Shearer, Fredric March, Charles Laughton), a moving, well-played, and fairly accurate account of the elopement of Robert Browning and Elizabeth Barrett. Laughton is great as Elizabeth's domineering, psychotic father. Please make sure you do *not* rent the poor 1956 remake with Jennifer Jones. Also, you really must see a very Hollywoodized, very romanticized, yet nevertheless splendid and engrossing film about the life of the Brontë sisters and their brother: **Devotion** (Curtis Bernhardt, 1946: Ida Lupino as Emily, Olivia de Havilland as Charlotte). The film includes eerie, Freudian dreams from the psyche of the future author of *Wuthering Heights* and actually includes a morning greeting between Dickens and Thackeray! Speaking of **Wuthering Heights**, this film has been made many times, but never so romantically or so powerfully as by William Wyler (1939: Laurence Oliver, Merle Oberon; one of my four or five favorite films of all time). The best version of **Jane Eyre**, despite a competent adaptation by Franco Zeffirelli (1996), remains the 1943 version (Robert Stevenson: Orson Welles, Joan Fontaine). Wilkie Collins's Victorian thriller, **Woman in White**, was made into an atmospheric film in 1948 (Peter Godfrey: Gig Young, Sidney Greenstreet). There are two good adult adaptations of the novels of late Victorian author Thomas Hardy: **Far From the Madding Crowd** (John Schlesinger, 1967: Julie Christie), **Tess** (Roman Polanski, 1979: Nastassja Kinski).

Several of H. G. Wells's sci-fi/fantasy novels have been made into splendid films, most notably **Things to Come** (William Cameron Menzies, 1936: Raymond Massey), **The Man Who Could Work Miracles** (Lothar Mendes, 1936: Roland Young), **The Island of Lost Souls** (Erle C. Kenton, 1932: Charles Laughton; remade twice under the novel's original title: *The Island of Dr. Moreau*), and **The**

Invisible Man (James Whale, 1933: Claude Rains; the film that made him a star though his face only appears for a few seconds!). The family will also enjoy *The Time Machine* (George Pal, 1960: Rod Taylor) and *The War of the Worlds* (Byron Haskin, 1953: Gene Barry), both of which won Oscars for special effects. Two adaptations of George Bernard Shaw that catch elements of the late Victorian spirit are *Major Barbara* (Gabriel Pascal, 1941: Wendy Hiller, Rex Harrison; takes a swipe at the Salvation Army and captures the Victorian spirit of progress) and *Pygmalion* (Anthony Asquith, Wendy Hiller, Leslie Howard) which, of course, was turned into the splendid musical *My Fair Lady* (George Cukor, 1964: Rex Harrison, Audrey Hepburn; Academy Awards for best picture and best actor). For a film about those wonderful Victorian showmen, see *The Story of Gilbert and Sullivan* (Sidney Gilliat, 1953: Robert Morley); these masters of light opera have been taken up again in an excellent, recent film, *Topsy-Turvy* (Mike Leigh, 1999: Jim Broadbent) which adds a psychological dimension and is for adults only. For a splendid and elegant look at late Victorian decadence, see the excellent film version of Oscar Wilde's *Picture of Dorian Gray* (Albert Lewin, 1945: George Sanders, Hurd Hatfield). Speaking of Wilde, a good film version has been made of *The Importance of Being Earnest* (Anthony Asquith, 1952: Michael Redgrave; recently remade) that captures well the mood of England in the 1890s. Less adequate, but still entertaining are *An Ideal Husband* (Alexander Korda, 1947: Paulette Godard; recently remade with a good cast) and *Lady Windermere's Fan: The Fan* (Otto Preminger, 1949: George Sanders). Several films, not for kids, have been made about Wilde himself (and his sexual scandal trial), most notably *Oscar Wilde* (Gregory Ratoff, 1959: Robert Morley) and *The Trials of Oscar Wilde* (Ken Hughes, 1960: Peter Finch). The more recent *Wilde* (Brian Gilbert, 1997: Stephen Fry) is very well done but leaves nothing to the imagination (*not* for the squeamish!).

Then, of course, there is always Sherlock Holmes, that great Victorian detective. He appears in countless films. One of the best of the early films is *The Hound of the Baskervilles* (Sidney Lanfield, 1939: Basil Rathbone, Nigel Bruce). Holmes meets Sigmund Freud in the somewhat entertaining *The Seven Per Cent Solution* (Herbert Ross, 1976: Nicol Williamson, Robert Duvall), Jack the Ripper in the so-so *Murder by Decree* (Bob Clark, 1978: Christopher Plummer, James Mason), and Victoria herself in the splendid *Private Life of Sherlock Holmes* (Billy Wilder, 1970: Robert Stephens, Colin Blakely). *Young Sherlock Holmes* (Barry Levinson, 1985: Nicholas Rowe) offered a Spielberg-production look at the young detective as he encounters an Indiana Jones–like Egyptian cult. All four of these films capture different aspects of the Victorian Age. For a twist, see a film in which H. G. Wells chases Jack the Ripper, via a time machine, into modern San Francisco: *Time After Time* (Nicholas Meyer, 1980: Malcolm McDowell, David Warner; this one's too scary for kids). Continuing on the subject of London fog, make sure to see *Dr. Jeckyll and Mr. Hyde*, the best version of which was made by Rouben Mamoulian (1931: Fredric March in a brilliant Oscar performance). For more London fog make sure not to miss *Gaslight* (George Cukor, 1944: Charles Boyer, Ingrid Bergman in an Oscar performance), an eerie, atmospheric film about a man trying to drive his wife insane; this film is actually a remake of a British original (Thorold Dickinson, 1940: Anton Walbrook) that is even more atmospheric in its recreation of foggy Victorian London. An interesting, literary film from Hollywood, *Trouble for Two* (Walter Rubin, 1936: Robert Montgomery, Rosalind Russell), reworks some stories from Robert Louis Stevenson, including a London suicide club! Of course, if you want foggy England at its eeriest, there are the countless versions of *Dracula*; the most opulently produced is Francis Ford Coppola's richly detailed *Bram Stoker's Dracula* (1992: Anthony Hopkins, Gary Oldman; most definitely not for kids!). An entertaining look at mid-Victorian England is afforded in *The Great Train Robbery* (Michael Crichton, 1978: Sean Connery, Donald Sutherland; yes, that's the same Crichton who wrote *Jurassic Park*).

The glorious British Empire has always been a great subject for moviemakers. My favorite film in this category is Alexander Korda's rousing *The Four Feathers* (Zoltan Korda, 1939: John Clements, Ralph Richardson; in early Technicolor), a movie that captures better than any other the importance of honor and bravery in the Victorian Age (there are many other versions of this movie; make sure you get this one!). Another great film in this category is *Khartoum* (Basil Deardon, 1966: Charlton Heston, Laurence Olivier; with Ralph Richardson as Prime Minister Gladstone); the movie chronicles the tragic end of the great General Gordon (Heston) as he is defeated in a siege led by a crazed warrior-prophet hypnotically played by Olivier. Heston appeared in another British Empire siege film, *55 Days at Peking* (Nicholas Ray, 1963: Charlton Heston, David Niven, Ava Gardner), about the 1900 Boxer Rebellion in China. *Zulu* (Cy Endfield, 1964: Michael Caine) carries us to the African front. For adventurous fun mixed with high comedy and underdog heroism, you can't beat *Gunga Din* (George Stevens, 1939: Cary Grant; based on a Rudyard Kipling story). For more on the British in India, check out: *Flame over India* (J. Lee-Thompson, 1959: Kenneth More, Lauren Bacall; great adventure aboard a train), *The Drum* (Zoltan Korda, 1938: starring one of the greatest of all child actors, the Indian Sabu), *The Rains Came* (Clarence Brown, 1939: Myrna Loy, Tyrone Power; a "disaster movie" played out in India), *Charge of the Light Brigade* (Michael Curtiz, 1936: Errol Flynn, Olivia de Havilland; this spends more time in India than in the Crimea, and it's not too historical, but it captures what Americans like to think of as the British sense of heroism and the stiff-upper-lip that never says die), *Lives of a Bengal Lancer* (Henry Hathaway, 1934: Gary Cooper; more British heroism from the point-of-view of Hollywood anglophiles; very entertaining). Two other films that capture the India of Rudyard Kipling are *The Man Who Would Be King* (John Huston, 1975: Sean Connery, Michael Caine; Christopher Plummer as Kipling; be sure to rent this one) and *The Jungle Book* (many versions of this, but my favorite is the

1942 version directed by Zoltan Korda and starring the incomparable Sabu). Three English brothers join the French Foreign Legion in **Beau Geste** (many remakes; the best is by William Wellman, 1939: Gary Cooper).

For the slow decay and fall of the British Empire in India (which is really outside the Victorian Era), see **A Passage to India** (David Lean, 1984: Judy Davis, Alec Guinness; from the E. M. Forster novel; Lean's last film) and **Gandhi** (Richard Attenborough, 1982: Ben Kingsley; won Academy Award); you might also want to rent from your public library the highly praised Masterpiece Theatre miniseries **The Jewel in the Crown**. Another film that catches the British Empire just before its decline (WWI) is, of course, the epic **Lawrence of Arabia** (David Lean, 1962: Peter O'Toole, Omar Sharif; Academy Awards for best picture and best director). For a grand tour of the entire Victorian world undertaken by the most reserved of gentlemen, see Jules Verne's **Around the World in Eighty Days** (Michael Anderson, 1956: David Niven, Cantinflas, + 44 cameos; AA for best picture). Three other Verne novels have been turned into splendid family films of high adventure that comment nicely on the wonder and optimism of Victorian science: **Journey to the Center of the Earth** (Henry Levin, 1959: James Mason), **20,000 Leagues under the Sea** (Richard Fleischer, 1954: Kirk Douglas, James Mason; from Disney), **In Search of the Castaways** (Robert Stevenson, 1961: Hayley Mills, Maurice Chevalier; a Disney reworking of Verne's *Captain Grant's Children*).

The world of the Victorian missionary is best captured in two films: **Stanley and Livingstone** (Henry King, 1939: Spencer Tracey) and **The Inn of the Sixth Happiness** (Mark Robson, 1958: Ingrid Bergman). The Victorian explorer is the subject of numerous film versions of two of H. Rider Haggard's novels, *She* and *King Solomon's Mines*. Somehow none of these films really capture the magic and wonder of the novels, but the 1950 version of **King Solomon's Mines** (Compton Bennet: Stewart Granger, Deborah

Kerr) does at least offer a nice tour of the African frontier. The best film on this aspect of the Victorian Age relates the story of the famous explorer Richard Burton: *The Mountains of the Moon* (Bob Rafelson, 1989: Patrick Bergin; not for kids). Then, of course, there are countless versions of the Tarzan legend. The best are still *Tarzan the Ape Man* (W. S. Van Dyke, 1932: Johnny Weissmuller, Maureen O'Sullivan) and *Tarzan and His Mate* (Cedric Gibbons, 1934: Johnny Weissmuller, Maureen O'Sullivan, who is remarkably scantily clad!). The recent Disney animated version, *Tarzan* (1999) does have some fun with the Victorian Jane. Many attempts have been made to film Arthur Conan Doyle's *The Lost World*, but none have been successful.

There are three marvelous children's stories that gently evoke the Victorian Age, all of which are based on books by Frances Hodgson Burnett: David O. Selznick's *Little Lord Fauntleroy* (John Cromwell, 1936: Freddie Bartholomew), *The Little Princess* (Walter Lang, 1939: Shirley Temple; at the end of the film, Shirley actually meets both Queen Victoria and General Gordon; effectively remade in 1995 under the title *A Little Princess*), and *The Secret Garden* (Fred M. Wilcox, 1949: Margaret O'Brien; features three of the great child performances on film; a good remake was made in 1993, but I still prefer the original; make sure you see this one with your grandkids). And, of course, don't miss that most wonderful of all Victorian (actually, Edwardian) nannies: *Mary Poppins* (Robert Stevenson, 1964: Julie Andrews in her Oscar performance; the scene on the rooftops of London is sure to enchant even the most cynical of adults!). Speaking of English governesses, don't miss *Anna and the King of Siam* (John Cromwell, 1946: Irene Dunne, Rex Harrison; recently remade in a splendid production starring Jodie Foster) and, of course, its musical remake, *The King and I* (Walter Lang, 1956: Deborah Kerr, Yul Brynner in his Oscar performance). No adequate film version of *Alice in Wonderland* has yet been made; the Disney animated version (1951) does have some charm.

There is an old, creaky, yet still watchable movie about the great Tory Prime Minister *Disraeli* (Alfred E. Green, 1929: George Arliss, who won an Oscar for his role) as well as a film that, believe it or not, concerns itself with one of Disraeli's pet projects, the building of the Suez Canal, *Suez* (Allan Dwan, 1938: Tyrone Power). The great John Gielgud offers a fine portrait of Disraeli in *The Prime Minister* (Thorold Dickinson, 1941). Disraeli also appears in a recent film about the long period of grief that Victoria subjected herself to after the death of Prince Albert. This excellent film, which strikes to the very heart of the role of the monarchy during the Victorian Age, is called *Mrs Brown* (John Madden, 1997) and it is about how an earthy Scottish gardener (well played by Billy Connolly) helped pull Victoria (a memorable performance by Judi Dench; her Academy Award for playing Queen Elizabeth in *Shakespeare in Love* was, in part, a consolation prize for not winning a deserved Oscar for this performance) out of her isolation. Make sure you see this film. There is also a slightly faded, but fondly remembered film of the Queen: *Victoria the Great* (Herbert Wilcox, 1937: Anna Neagle). Victoria appears in a sentimental family film about a boy who breaks into Windsor Castle to meet the Queen: *The Mudlark* (Jean Negulesco, 1950: Alex Guinness).

INDEX